The Dark Social

This book explores how people interact online through anonymous communication in encrypted, hidden, or otherwise obscured online spaces. Beyond the Dark Web itself, this book examines how the concept of 'dark social' broadens the possibilities for examining notions of darkness and sociality in the age of digitality and datafied life. The authors take into account technical, moral, ethical, and pragmatic responses to ourselves and communities seeking to be/belong in/of/ the dark.

Scholarship on the Darknet and Dark Social Spaces tends to focus on the uses of encryption and other privacy-enhancing technologies to engender resistance acts. Such understandings of the dark social are naturally in tension with social and political theories which argue that for politics and 'acts' to matter they must appear in the public light. They are also in tension with popular narratives of the 'dark recesses of the web', which are disparaged by structural powers who seek to keep their subjects knowable and locatable on the clear web. The binary of dark versus light is challenged in this book. The authors' provocation is that practices of 'dark' resistance, motility, and power are enacted by emerging data cultures. This book draws together scholarship, activism, and creativity to push past conceptual binary positions and create new approaches to darknet and dark social studies.

The Dark Social: Online Practices of Resistance, Motility and Power will be a key resource for academics, researchers, and advanced students of media studies, cultural studies, communication studies, research methods, and sociology. This book was originally published as a special issue of *Continuum: Journal of Media & Cultural Studies*.

Toija Cinque is Associate Professor of Communications (Digital Media) at Deakin University, Melbourne, Australia.

Alexia Maddox is Senior Lecturer in Pedagogy and Education Futures at the School of Education at La Trobe University, Melbourne, Australia.

Robert W. Gehl is Ontario Research Chair of Digital Governance for Social Justice at York University, Toronto, Canada.

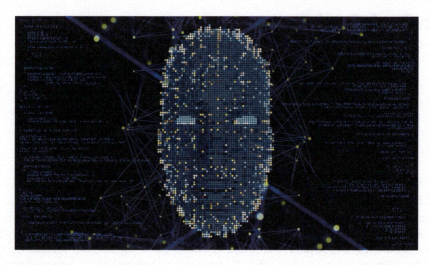

Artist credit: MF3d

The Dark Social
Online Practices of Resistance, Motility and Power

Edited by
Toija Cinque, Alexia Maddox and
Robert W. Gehl

LONDON AND NEW YORK

First published 2024
by Routledge
4 Park Square, Milton Park, Abingdon, Oxon, OX14 4RN

and by Routledge
605 Third Avenue, New York, NY 10158

Routledge is an imprint of the Taylor & Francis Group, an informa business

Introduction, Chapters 3–10 and Afterword © 2024 Taylor & Francis
Chapter 1 © 2021 Robert W. Gehl. Originally published as Open Access.
Chapter 2 © 2021 Toija Cinque. Originally published as Open Access.

With the exception of Chapters 1 and 2, no part of this book may be reprinted or reproduced or utilised in any form or by any electronic, mechanical, or other means, now known or hereafter invented, including photocopying and recording, or in any information storage or retrieval system, without permission in writing from the publishers. For details on the rights for Chapters 1 and 2, please see the chapters' Open Access footnotes.

Trademark notice: Product or corporate names may be trademarks or registered trademarks, and are used only for identification and explanation without intent to infringe.

British Library Cataloguing-in-Publication Data
A catalogue record for this book is available from the British Library

ISBN13: 978-1-032-59345-6 (hbk)
ISBN13: 978-1-032-59347-0 (pbk)
ISBN13: 978-1-003-45428-1 (ebk)

DOI: 10.4324/9781003454281

Typeset in Myriad Pro
by codeMantra

Publisher's Note
The creative works referred to in this book are for academic purposes only. The publisher, author(s), and editor(s) of this work recognise the right of the copyright holders on their creative works.

The publisher accepts responsibility for any inconsistencies that may have arisen during the conversion of this book from journal articles to book chapters, namely the inclusion of journal terminology.

Disclaimer
Every effort has been made to contact copyright holders for their permission to reprint material in this book. The publishers would be grateful to hear from any copyright holder who is not here acknowledged and will undertake to rectify any errors or omissions in future editions of this book.

Contents

Citation Information vii
Notes on Contributors ix

Introduction: Digital Cultures and Acts of Refusal, Secrecy and Power across Privacy Enhancing Technologies 1
Toija Cinque, Alexia Maddox and Robert W. Gehl

1 Dark Web Advertising: The Dark Magic System on Tor Hidden Service Search Engines 7
Robert W. Gehl

2 A Study of Mastodon, Galaxy3 and 8Kun as Post-social Media in Dark Webs: The Darker Turn of Our Intimate Machines 19
Toija Cinque

3 The Electrified Social and Its Dark Alternatives: Policing and Politics in the Computational Age 32
Alexia Maddox and Luke Heemsbergen

4 Bad Actors Never Sleep: Content Manipulation on Reddit 46
Martin Potter

5 Dark, Clear or Brackish? Using Reddit to Break Down the Binary of the Dark and Clear Web 59
Simon Copland

6 The Affective Pressures of WhatsApp: From Safe Spaces to Conspiratorial Publics 72
Amelia Johns and Niki Cheong

7 Great AI Divides? Automated Decision-Making Technologies and Dreams of Development 87
Jolynna Sinanan and Thomas McNamara

8 Shedding Light on "Dark" Ads 101
Verity Trott, Luzhou Li, Robbie Fordyce and Mark Andrejevic

9 Critical Data Provenance as a Methodology for Studying How Language Conceals Data Ethics 115
Robbie Fordyce and Suneel Jethani

10 Writing the Feminist Internet: A Chthonian Feminist Internet Theory for the Twenty First Century 128
Nancy Mauro-Flude

Afterword: Troubling the Dark Social 145
Melinda Hinkson, Roland Kapferer and P. David Marshall

Index 153

Citation Information

The chapters in this book were originally published in *Continuum: Journal of Media & Cultural Studies*, volume 35, issue 5 (2021). When citing this material, please use the original page numbering for each article, as follows:

Introduction
Introduction: digital cultures and acts of refusal, secrecy and power across privacy-enhancing technologies
Toija Cinque, Alexia Maddox and Robert W. Gehl
Continuum: Journal of Media & Cultural Studies, volume 35, issue 5 (2021) pp. 661–666

Chapter 1
Dark web advertising: the dark magic system on Tor hidden service search engines
Robert W. Gehl
Continuum: Journal of Media & Cultural Studies, volume 35, issue 5 (2021) pp. 667–678

Chapter 2
The darker turn of intimate machines: dark webs and (post) social media
Toija Cinque
Continuum: Journal of Media & Cultural Studies, volume 35, issue 5 (2021) pp. 679–691

Chapter 3
The electrified social and its dark alternatives: policing and politics in the computational age
Alexia Maddox and Luke Heemsbergen
Continuum: Journal of Media & Cultural Studies, volume 35, issue 5 (2021) pp. 692–705

Chapter 4
Bad actors never sleep: content manipulation on Reddit
Martin Potter
Continuum: Journal of Media & Cultural Studies, volume 35, issue 5 (2021) pp. 706–718

Chapter 5
Dark, clear or brackish? Using Reddit to break down the binary of the dark and clear web
Simon Copland
Continuum: Journal of Media & Cultural Studies, volume 35, issue 5 (2021) pp. 719–731

Chapter 6
The affective pressures of WhatsApp: from safe spaces to conspiratorial publics
Amelia Johns and Niki Cheong
Continuum: Journal of Media & Cultural Studies, volume 35, issue 5 (2021) pp. 732–746

Chapter 7
Great AI divides? Automated decision-making technologies and dreams of development
Jolynna Sinanan and Thomas McNamara
Journal of Media & Cultural Studies, volume 35, issue 5 (2021) pp. 747–760

Chapter 8
Shedding light on 'dark' ads
Verity Trott, Luzhou Li, Robbie Fordyce and Mark Andrejevic
Continuum: Journal of Media & Cultural Studies, volume 35, issue 5 (2021) pp. 761–774

Chapter 9
Critical data provenance as a methodology for studying how language conceals data ethics
Robbie Fordyce and Suneel Jethani
Continuum: Journal of Media & Cultural Studies, volume 35, issue 5 (2021) pp. 775–787

Chapter 10
Writing the Feminist Internet: a Chthonian Feminist Internet Theory for the twenty first century
Nancy Mauro-Flude
Continuum: Journal of Media & Cultural Studies, volume 35, issue 5 (2021) pp. 788–804

Afterword
Afterword: troubling the dark social
Melinda Hinkson, Roland Kapferer and P. David Marshall
Continuum: Journal of Media & Cultural Studies, volume 35, issue 5 (2021) pp. 805–811

For any permission-related enquiries please visit:
http://www.tandfonline.com/page/help/permissions

Notes on Contributors

Mark Andrejevic is Professor at the School of Media, Film and Journalism at Monash University, Melbourne, Australia.

Niki Cheong is Lecturer at the Department of Digital Humanities at King's College London, UK.

Toija Cinque is Associate Professor of Communications (Digital Media) at Deakin University, Melbourne, Australia.

Simon Copland is PhD Candidate in Sociology at Australian National University (ANU), studying online men's rights groups and communities 'manosphere'.

Robbie Fordyce is Lecturer in Big Data/Quantitative Analytics and Research Methods at the School of Media, Film and Journalism at Monash University, Melbourne, Australia.

Robert W. Gehl is Ontario Research Chair of Digital Governance for Social Justice at York University, Toronto, Canada.

Luke Heemsbergen is Senior Lecturer at the School of Communication and Creative Arts at Deakin University, Melbourne, Australia.

Melinda Hinkson is Director at The Institute of Postcolonial Studies, Victoria, Australia.

Suneel Jethani is Lecturer at the University of Technology Sydney, Australia.

Amelia Johns is Senior Lecturer at the School of Communication at the University of Technology Sydney, Australia.

Roland Kapferer is Lecturer in Anthropology and teaches Cyborg Anthropology: Human Possibilities in the Age of Digital Communication at Deakin University, Geelong, Australia.

Luzhou Li is Lecturer at the School of Media, Film and Journalism at Monash University, Melbourne, Australia.

Alexia Maddox is Senior Lecturer in Pedagogy and Education Futures at the School of Education at La Trobe University, Melbourne, Australia.

P. David Marshall is Professor of Communication at Charles Sturt University, Bathurst, New South Wales; and Emeritus Professor, Deakin University, Australia.

Nancy Mauro-Flude is Lecturer in Design and Social Context at the School of Design at RMIT University, Melbourne, Australia.

Thomas McNamara is Lecturer in Development Studies and Deputy Director of the Master of International Development at La Trobe University, Melbourne, Australia.

Martin Potter is Senior Lecturer and Researcher at Deakin University, Geelong, Australia, and Associate Investigator with the ARC Centre of Excellence for Australian Biodiversity and Heritage.

Jolynna Sinanan is Research Fellow in Automated Decision-Making and Global Contexts in the Australian Research Council's Centre of Excellence in Automated Decision-Making and Society and the Institute for Culture and Society at Western Sydney University, Australia.

Verity Trott is Lecturer in Digital Media Research in the School of Media, Film and Journalism at Monash University, Melbourne, Australia.

INTRODUCTION

Introduction: Digital Cultures and Acts of Refusal, Secrecy and Power across Privacy Enhancing Technologies

Toija Cinque ⓘ, Alexia Maddox and Robert W. Gehl

The Dark Social: Online Practices of Resistance, Motility and Power explores the way that users engage online by managing the capacity for anonymous communication in encrypted, hidden, or otherwise obscured online spaces. Scholarship on the Darknet and Dark Social Spaces tends to focus on the uses of encryption and other privacy enhancing technologies to engender resistance acts. Our provocation is that such practices are reflective of emerging data cultures. Here, the usual characterization of dark social spaces are by privacy enhancing technologies that facilitate oppositional acts, division and evasion. As a consequence, the actors using these technological affordances are commonly identified as subcultural groups, activists, marginalized cultures and communities, trolls and socially divisive. These are actors who seek to evade, refuse and/or disrupt institutional power. We want to suggest, however, that this approach creates an artificial binary positioning of a fringe of radical actors against institutions of governance, regulation and control. Similarly, approaches that distinguish between social agency and technological affordances protecting digital privacy, on the one hand, and institutional regulation and centralized surveillance on the other, do not acknowledge how powerful institutional actors use these decentralized technologies to reinforce their authority and control.

This special edition emerges from a selection of papers presented at the *Dark Social Spaces* symposium which was held during 2019 at Deakin University in Melbourne, Australia. The intention of the event was to provoke critical examination of dark social spaces. Our purpose during the symposium was to grapple with Darkness for how it might work as the nomenclature for the theoretical, empirical, creative methodological approaches to better understand engagement in dark social spaces. We questioned Darkness as a category, a space, a socio-historical moment, an ontological structure to make sense of what users do in encrypted places online. Workshop participants mapped communicative actions and the users themselves within liminal, interstitial spaces. We were moved to give critical consideration to the complex notional layers of *visibility* – versus invisibility – and the associated assumption that being visible usually equates with being seen. By extension being invisible or unseen requires vigilance. In doing so, we drew upon issues of contemporary surveillance and the typical language of the governers towards a deeper understanding of *how* one is watched, and the reflexive subject might watch-back. It is reasonable to argue that the result is creating active regimes of vigilance as they do so and affords a counter-mechanism to surveillance (see Cinque in this edition). Virtual displacement, constant movement and assumed identities might act collectively as a distinctive way of being social by distance(ing).

Such understandings of the dark social are naturally in tension with social and political theories which argue that for politics and 'acts' to matter they must appear in the public light. They are also in tension with popular narratives of the 'dark recesses of the web' which are leveraged by structural powers to keep their subjects knowable and locatable on the clear web. We argue that the binary of dark versus light is challenged by the swirling, brackish existence of identity, politics, and everyday communication practices that modulate between online and offline and being open and obfuscating. This special edition focuses on the tensions present in what is dark and social online, while also considering how practices do not neatly fit in a dark/light binary. Past the Dark Web itself, we suggest that the concept of 'dark social' expands opportunities for exploring notions of darkness and sociality in the age of digitality/datafied life to consider moral, ethical, and pragmatic responses to ourselves and communities seeking to be/belong in/of/the dark. The articles herein offer nuanced theoretical, empirical, creative, methodological, and ethical approaches to 'dark social' digital place[s], power, and practices whether technical, moral, or otherwise. We suggest that the overarching framing for such surpasses previous literature to consider the practices that exist outside the clear web in ways other than those conceived as 'moral darkness'. Humans and their communications – digital or otherwise – do not exist in solely transparent space and practice. Recognition of these complexities of being 'online' is a crucial step to explore and critique an age concerned with post-privacy, ubiquitous surveillance and authenticity of the message and messenger.

The threads of this thinking are woven throughout this special edition. The researchers' different academic backgrounds have meant that the topic has been approached through different critical entrance points, recognizing and embracing these differences to foster a critical examination of the nuances of dark social communication. What the edition does not do, however, is fall into false bifurcations in regard to the logics of power as we move away from structure and anti-structure and moral assumptions of 'good' and 'bad' practices. As such, digital camouflage might become the changeable aesthetic of contemporary socio-political and communicative action.

This guest-edited issue for *Continuum* presents ten new essays that consequently set the intellectual parameters of the topic in question and story the edition so that a clear thematic narrative emerges by its end. This special edition draws together scholars, activists, and artists who are pushing past conceptual binary positions to create new approaches to darknet and dark social studies. What is dark online often connotes moral registers towards what society hides or fears. Yet social spaces that are 'dark' offer autonomy and relief from the ever-lasting digital light in current iterations of capitalisms, authoritarianisms and surveillance cultures. A technical rather than moral definition of darkness (Gehl 2018) critiques moral determinism and opens for exploration those dark social spaces that seek legitimacy by offering linked anonymities for reader and publisher, against structural surveillance.

The special issue begins by navigating the maze of the Dark Web with Robert Gehl's ethnographically informed exploration of Dark Web advertising in 'Dark Web Advertising: The Dark Magic System on Tor Hidden Service Search Engines'. Gehl argues that through the ubiquitous online surveillance conducted across the Clear Web, where corporate social media track our consumption practices, our belief in the magical associations of advertising – from product to fantasy – can be mapped and our experience of this surveillant-driven magic becomes more real as its practitioners learn more about us. He signposts these characteristics of Clear Web advertising in order to juxtapose the peculiar practices of Dark Web advertising in which the production and circulation of advertisements occur on encrypted, anonymizing networks. Gehl highlights the distinction that the technical structure of systems like Tor bring to advertising, in that they cannot use cookies, logins, or IP address tracking. Thus, when advertisements appear on general-purpose search engines, they are not personalized. Through the categorization and tracing associations of over 300 banner advertisements appearing on Tor onion service search engines, Gehl illuminates the dominant values this dark magic system sprukes; an incantation of navigation, OPSEC, and the exploitation of oversharing. Through the analysis Gehl raises the critical question of this dark magic system: Can we reliably exploit the fruits of surveillance capitalism while still escaping its ever-watchful eye?

In a continued contemplation of the desire for escape from surveillance capitalism, *Toija Cinque* proposes A Study of Mastodon, Galaxy3 and 8Kun as Post-social Media in Dark Webs: The Darker Turn of Our Intimate Machines. Within this article, Cinque draws on auto-ethnographic methods to explore three distinct dark social spaces: the decentralized microblog platform Mastodon; Galaxy3, a social networking site only accessible via the Tor browser; and the infamous 8Kun image board. These spaces are part of a centrifugal flight away from their more visible counterparts (e.g. Facebook or Twitter). Despite being non-mainstream systems, Mastodon and Galaxy3, Cinque finds, are heavily moderated, with members consenting to moderation in order to improve civility. Even in the case of 8Kun, which is notorious as a free speech absolutist site, Cinque finds members who are dedicated to building a sense of community within a dark social space. Overall, Cinque argues that we need to examine 'emerging alternate systems for communication and social connection' to have a better grip on online cultures.

In their article, 'The Electrified Social and its Dark Alternatives: Policing and Politics in the Computational Age', **Alexia Maddox** and **Luke Heemsbergen** introduce the impetus for exploration of emerging alternate systems for communication and connection described by Cinque through the notion of an Electrified Social. They describe online social interaction that is 'in the electric light' of data surveillance whereby user data is relationalized and their relations are datafied. They contend that Facebook's understanding of the social graph and subsequent commercial 'federationalization' of such represents a pertinent and evolving example of electrified policing. Away from such 'electric light', the authors assert that darkness encourages exploratory forms of engagement, intercourse and exchange, that 'electrified light' forbids. Maddox and Heemsbergen adeptly provoke discussion on how we might imagine forms of sociality that operate in the dark as well as imagining past them. As a counterpoint for critical elaboration, Maddox and Heemsbergen present alternative techniques of social darkness including e2e (end-to-end encryption), cryptomarkets used by various communities, and the venerable craigslist to show how equals negotiate their equality in darkness. In this article, they argue that it is only in places of darkness, outside the electronic and photonic light, that experimentation and anomaly occur. Out of sight of what is anticipated they claim – including what is compiled on subjects, traded and accounted for as objects- – is the dark social.

Where Maddox and Heemsbergen' place 'electrified' transparency as antithetical to creative experimentation, **Martin Potter** explores the processes and actions for making the invisible visible within the Reddit environment. In 'Bad Actors Never Sleep: Content

Manipulation on Reddit' Potter considers the outcomes arising from Reddit seeking to identify and mitigate bad actor behaviour, address content manipulation and maintain the site's authenticity. Potter critically considers the dark social spaces through a historical synthesis of Reddit's approach to moderation, shifting rules and regulations in relation to security, and for addressing misinformation. Potter lucidly argues that recent developments around perceived political manipulation of and on Reddit and accusations of content manipulation and censorship have raised questions of trust in the Reddit platform. However, Potter observes that it is by understanding how community-driven platforms such as Reddit promote user agency, even acts of negative resistance, that a crucial step is taken in enabling digital imagination.

Continuing the interrogation of Reddit as a case study of the dark social, **Simon Copland's** article, 'Dark, clear or brackish? Using Reddit to break down the binary of the Dark and Clear Web' introduces the Brackish Web as a murky space between the Dark and the Clear Web. Using the case study of Reddit, a social news site that exists within the infrastructure of digital platforms on the Clear Web, Copland argues that sites and platforms can be brackish in two ways – through their technological affordances, and their politics, each of which is underpinned by a technological rationality. Within the article, Reddit is positioned historically to align with dark web technologies through the technological rationality of creating a platform designed to hand over control to users through its focus on pseudonymity and an ethos of free speech. The detailed analysis of the platform's historical formation then shifts to its current iteration where Copland points to the blurred distinction that has emerged as Reddit turned its attention towards advertising in order to increase profit, subsequently becoming more enmeshed in the structures of surveillance that underpin Clear Web platforms.

In 'The affective pressures of WhatsApp: from safe spaces to conspiratorial publics', **Amelia Johns** and **Niki Cheong** combine multiple approaches to study the flows of conspiracy theories through the encrypted message system WhatsApp. Their study is based on interviews with political activists in Malaysia. Drawing on media logics, affordance theory, and affect theory, Johns and Cheong find that these activists are able to organize outside of state surveillance. However, rather than simply suggest that organizing in the dark is an unadulterated good, they argue that the 'affective atmospheres' of WhatsApp groups can easily lead to sharing misinformation and conspiracy theories, even among activists. As they write, 'the insularity of members within a closed "socio-technical system" also *structures* practices that can lead users to only trust insiders and believe mainstream news and "official" accounts to be inauthentic and fake. This allows problematic information that contradicts official information, including rumour and conspiracy, to flow more freely through WhatsApp groups.'

Following on from the above case study of the dark social in the global south, in their article 'Great AI Divides? Automated Decision-Making Technologies and Dreams of Development' **Jolynna Sinanan** and **Thomas McNamara** interrogate three broad development imaginaries of (1) alleviating poverty and the creation of wealth; (2) good governance, and; (3) social inclusion. Theirs is a contribution to the ongoing conversations about de-westernizing digital research and their critical insights work to expand the concept scope of the political economy of AI, algorithms related research. The authors foreground the ongoing inequities that pervade both technological access and North-South global relations with an examination of how populations in locally bound contexts counter, reinforce or navigate experiences of information and communication technology (ICT) for Development. With their spotlight on the interplay between international narratives about the emancipatory potential of AI on the one hand with linked co-created moral discourses around the responsibility over the provision, use and consequences of automated decision-making technologies on the other the authors assert that themes of intentionality and uptake of AI technologies are more contentious in the Global South. They contend that the reasons for such are because populations in the Global South have arguably been subject to consecutive projects described as 'development' which have resulted in further entrenchment of systemic inequalities.

We now turn to the question of surveillant targeting that interloops the visible with the invisible but continues to highlight the issue of inequitable bias raised above. Whereas Gehl's analysis focused on advertising on Dark Web search engines, **Verity Trott, Luzhou Li, Robbie Fordyce** and **Mark Andrejevic** focus on 'dark ads' on Facebook. Dark ads are ads that are so highly targeted that they are invisible to most people – only the specific targets of the ads see them. As Trott et al. argue, since advertising is a cultural messaging system that generates and reinforces social stereotypes, we need more analysis of dark ads as powerful, hidden generators of biases. In 'Shedding Light on "Dark" Ads', Trott et al. propose a browser extension that can crowdsource Facebook ads in order to build a publicly accessible database of dark ads. The prototype database would allow us to make visible dark ads and see how they are targeted to specific demographic groups. While Gehl's analysis ends by discussing all the problems Dark Web advertisers face, Trott et al.'s work helps reveal the extremely sophisticated system of dark advertising in social media.

In the context of issues related to contemporary data provenance, **Robbie Fordyce** and **Suneel Jethani** engage with this concept long embedded in computer science. The idea of data provenance is unpacked in 'Critical data provenance as a methodology for studying how language conceals data ethics' as one to describe the way that the history of sets of data is allowed to be traced for the purposes of determining the accuracy and validity of a database. Using their qualitative data research, the authors transform this action into a critical concept by arguing that data provenance can be used to trace the acts of governance and rhetoric. Here, Fordyce and Jethani critically analyse the forms of discursive power that shape transactions in data. They find that their approach can create a history of the governance and justifications that are used to build and assemble datasets from multiple sources. They present the considered view that presently, data often lacks this information about its own discursive origins, unlike other forms of data provenance. Critical data provenance thus facilitates a model for thinking about how governance could be mapped onto data. What is being underscored is that *critical* data provenance is also a framework for critiquing the justifications used when dataset owners acquire data. The authors demonstrate their model of thinking and provide the analytical tools necessary to redeploy these ideas into new contexts. Particular examples include whether data stewards or users are themselves encouraged to be 'open', to 'share', or be 'transparent'. Moreover, innocuous phrases like 'safe' and 'data sharing' sound like communitarian concepts while potentially being restricted to transactions in user data between private organizations or when the data is being shared. They conclude that for their part the HASS disciplines can contribute to conversations in regard to data ethics by interrogating how certain terms are used to conceal behaviour that would otherwise go unnoticed.

Moving from tracing acts of governance and rhetoric to discursive resistance on the internet, **Nancy Mauro-Flude** takes us into an activist incursion through her article 'Writing the Feminist Internet: A Chthonian Feminist Internet Theory for the Twenty First Century'. The article responds to a collaborative performance work, *Writing the Feminist Internet*, and poetically engages the reader in the valences and anarchy of technopolitics. Mauro-Flude situates feminist webserver communities as chthonic dark social spaces through which new meanings and enunciations can 'brew'. Through her examination of feminist webserver peer production practices, Mauro-Flude poses broader questions about the convergence of theory, art practice and feminist waves. In this way, she envisions dark social spaces as a place where culture and speculative realism, fiction and imagining invoke a conception of a chthonic feminist critical theory. This article's inclusion evidences the capacity of the dark social to move across the spectrum from media scholarship on the technological infrastructures and data flows through to creative practice.

This Special Issue closes with a concluding essay capturing the freewheeling conversation that marked the coalescence of the dark social studies, at turns referencing current moments (ugh, Zoom) and at turns gesturing to the history of modern philosophy. Melinda Hinkson, Roland Kapferer and P. David Marshall respond to the collection of articles with their 'Afterward: Troubling the dark social'. In this 'troubling' they seek to foreshadow, from their juxtaposing points of view, what the dark social might mean for future studies.

Disclosure statement

No potential conflict of interest was reported by the author(s).

ORCID

Toija Cinque http://orcid.org/0000-0001-9845-3953

OPEN ACCESS

Dark Web Advertising: The Dark Magic System on Tor Hidden Service Search Engines

Robert W. Gehl

ABSTRACT
Drawing on Raymond William's concept of the 'magic system,' this article argues that advertising on the Dark Web is a 'dark magic system'. The article first defines 'Dark Web' and then analyzes over 300 banner advertisements appearing on Tor onion service search engines. The advertisements are categorized into navigation, individual vendors, services, and markets. Next, the article traces the associations the advertisements make between advertised objects and values. The predominant values the advertisements invoke include navigation, OPSEC politics, and a justification to exploit the openness of others. The article then traces the limits of the dark magic system, including the system's inability to offer metrics, the problems of 'onion cloners,' and the constant threat of scams. The article concludes with an argument that the dark magic system is incapable of addressing the sort of anonymized political communication the Dark Web might afford.

Introduction

Raymond Williams's essay 'Advertising: The Magic System' initially appeared in *The New Left Review* in 1960 and has since been heavily anthologized as a cultural studies classic (Williams 1960, 1993, 2000). Drawing on Marx's provocative concept of the commodity fetish, Williams argued that advertising's function is to create associations between the objects being sold and subjective values. Williams's commitment to socialism (Williams 1993, 410) prompted him to argue that the promised associations of the 'magic system' always fall short of social needs:

> If the consumption of individual goods leaves that whole area of human need unsatisfied, the attempt is made, by magic, to associate this consumption with human desires to which it has no real reference. You do not only buy an object: you buy social respect, discrimination, health, beauty, success, and power to control your environment (Williams 2000).

Despite appearing over 60 years ago, Williams's condemnation of the emptiness of the magic system seems more relevant today than ever. This is because the magical associations Williams mapped in his essay – beer with manliness, a washing machine with social

---

This is an Open Access article distributed under the terms of the Creative Commons Attribution-NonCommercial-NoDerivatives License (http://creativecommons.org/licenses/by-nc-nd/4.0/), which permits non-commercial re-use, distribution, and reproduction in any medium, provided the original work is properly cited, and is not altered, transformed, or built upon in any way.

proof of status – are only intensified and reified in contemporary online advertising, particularly within corporate social media, such as the properties owned by Facebook (Facebook, WhatsApp, Instagram)or Alphabet (the whole Google suite).

While we're on what I will call in this essay the 'Clear Web,' we are subject to monitoring by corporations (Fuchs 2012). We are constantly profiled, our tastes mapped, our desires fitted into psychographic categorization systems (Stark 2018). These elements of our online activities are filtered, sorted, and fed back to us. Lest each of us think that we are alone, corporate social media assures us we're not: our friends like this product, too. Our families love visiting this tourist spot. The influencers we follow recommend this shampoo. We can join in the magic, too, liking, sharing, and posting about our own transfigurations and transmutations through consumption. Thanks to ubiquitous online surveillance, our *belief* in the magic can be mapped. As we search for, purchase, rate, and talk about products through social media, advertisers and marketers gain a deeper understanding about which magical associations work for whom and how well. All the while, the surveillance-driven magic appears to get more and more fantastical, more *real*, as its practitioners learn more and more about us.

Dark web advertising's dark magic

I want to keep this discussion of the magic system of Clear Web advertising in mind as I turn to the object of this paper: the peculiar practices of *Dark Web* advertising, specifically on general purpose search engines that index Tor hidden services. I am interested in the production and circulation of advertisements happening on encrypted, anonymizing networks, which are very different contexts than the corporate-dominated Clear Web. Riffing off of Williams, I suggest that Dark Web advertising is a 'dark magic system.' Thinking of it this way requires me to trace the implied associations that Dark Web advertising is making. But my extensive, ethnographic experience studying both Dark Web and Clear Web advertising practices (Gehl 2016, 2018) also allows for me to conceptualize the particular relationship Dark Web advertising has with Clear Web practices.

First, however, I should clarify some terms. I define the 'Dark Web' as comprised of:

> websites built with standard web technologies (HTML, CSS, server-side scripting languages, hosting software) that can be viewed with a standard web browser, such as Firefox or Chrome, which is routed through special routing software packages .... The major differentiating factor between the Dark Web and the Clear Web is that these special routing systems are designed to provide anonymity for both visitors to websites and publishers of these sites (Gehl 2018, 8).

Tor, the most popular Dark Web system, features *onion sites*, websites which a) are only accessible via Tor and b) anonymize *both* the reader of the website *as well as* the publisher of the site.[1] Tor onion sites largely look like the regular web: we see them through a web browser, they are built with HTML and other web languages. They have text, images, links, and URLs. However, unlike the Clear Web, they are 'dark' in the sense that they anonymize both readers and producers of content.

Note that this is not a moral definition. I am not using the term 'dark' to describe the *content* of Dark Web sites – I'm focusing on the technical structure of systems like Tor. Certainly, there are unethical, exploitative, prurient, and vicious sites on the Dark Web, but there are such sites across the entire Internet.

As a system using standard web technologies, the Dark Web includes familiar types of websites: search engines, blogs, forums, and wikis. Within many of these there are Web-style advertisements, predominantly banner advertisements appearing on search engines and to a lesser extent on social media. Such advertisements are my focus.

Approach to studying advertising on tor search engines

Here, I draw on several years of ethnographic observation of Dark Web advertising practices, particularly on Tor onion sites (Gehl 2016, 2018), and couple that experience with a systematic review of 320 banner advertisements posted across 24 general-purpose search engines (i.e. search engines claiming to both have crawled all Tor hidden services and be able return accurate search results). I analyse a snapshot of current Tor search engine advertising through the conceptual lenses I developed during my ethnographic analysis of the Dark Web.

Many Tor users have established search engines which offer search results based on their indexes of onion sites. I have been observing these search engines since 2014, and focused a chapter of my book on them (Gehl 2018, chap. 5). The search engines appropriate much of the look and feel of Google – search bar, text results, and very often, advertisements paid for by third parties. While I have observed Dark Web-based advertising in multiple places, one consistent location for such advertisements is on general-purpose search engines, such as Torch, TorDex, or Submarine. Not all search engines sell advertising space – notable here are Ahmia and Not Evil.

Because the Dark Web anonymizes readers and creators of content, when advertisements appear on general-purpose search engines, they are not personalized. They can't use cookies, logins, or IP address tracking. In fact, if the search engines used these tactics, they would likely be shunned by users – the Dark Web is designed to mitigate these tracking technologies. Thus, the advertisements I see will be the same as what you see if you were to look at the precise same time as me. Moreover, Dark Web search engine advertising has been stable over the past few years: I have not observed much churn in the advertisements over the years, especially in terms of the categories I will discuss below. Advertisements for directories and single vendors appear today much as they did during the early days of my research. The advertisements I collected in March of 2021 are comparable to the screenshots of the search engines I have collected over the past half decade.

The 320 advertisements were collected over a period of several consecutive days as a snapshot of search engine advertising. I did not examine speciality search engines, such as ones that focus on drug markets (e.g. Recon). Search engines – general or otherwise – are not the only places where Dark Web advertisements can be found. I should also note that some of the search engines I looked at are likely 'clones,' meaning that they are essentially fraudulent versions of an original search engine – I will discuss this issue below. Rather than remove them from the collection as duplicates, I think it's important to trace the relationships between possibly cloned engines and advertisements and the original engines and advertisements.

Williams (1960) used a variety of approaches to study the magic system, including historical analysis, political economic analysis, categorization of advertisements into types, and above all, tracing the associations the advertisements create between product and fantasy. In the interest of space, I will emulate the latter two, categorization and tracing associations. For both purposes, I visited the sites being advertised (although I have not bought anything on the Dark Web).

Because the users of the Dark Web are anonymized, we have little insight into their identities. The Dark Web is not amenable to gathering any sort of demographic information. However, Williams's orientation to the associational, semiotic nature of advertising helps us here – we can consider the magical associations that Dark Web advertisements are making and infer the values of the audience the advertisers are imagining. Moreover, because the Dark Web has been developed in part as a reaction to the surveillance practices of the Clear Web, we can also conceptualize the dark magic system's product offerings as part of that reaction.

Categories of dark web advertisements

A large proportion of the advertisements are for *navigational sites*: lists of links, directories, and even other search engines. One third of the advertisements I collected fall into this category. They reflect the fact that Tor onions are hard to navigate, even with a search engine. There are many advertisements for sites such as the 'Hidden Wiki,' 'Tor Links,' or 'Onion Links | Verified & Safe.' Clicking through, we see collections of ostensibly vetted links of onion sites the user can visit, in categories such as blogs, forums, image boards, markets, and porn sites. Twenty of these navigational sites explicitly advertise themselves as anti-scam lists, offering lists of identified scam sites or verified, trusted sites.

These somewhat dull advertisements for navigational sites compete with more exciting offers, including advertisements for *individual vendors*, small shops selling products. A third of the advertisements I collected fall into this category. A common advertisement is 'BUY REAL MONEY' on a garish yellow background with stacks of green money on either side. Clicking through, we're invited to 'Change your Life NOW!!!'. This Dark Web site offers to sell real money, including Euros, GBP, USD, Swiss Francs. The vendor claims they have access to actual currency marked for destruction at various central banks. Other vendors offer stolen credit card information, prescription drugs, or hard narcotics. No matter the product, nearly every individual vendor claims to be the most trusted, most reliable purveyor of the goods – or your money back.

A related category is for *services*, people who are selling their skills rather than a product. One eye-catching advertisement asks: 'your wife are cheating you?' [sic]. If so, the advertisement suggests that '[you] Get in control. Hire a hacker.' Indeed, many hacker services are advertised across the Dark Web, claiming to be able to hack into social media accounts, recover lost passwords, exfiltrate corporate or government secrets, or, as this particular advertisement promises, monitor one's wife. Another advertisement, the 'Porn Hacker,' offers to hack into paid porn accounts. This advertisement features animated GIFs of actual pornography – predominantly nude women – and promises access to premium pornography sites like Brazzers, LiveJasmin, Pornhub, and Chaturbate. Several advertisements offer an escrow service to aid in commerce. And perhaps the most infamous service advertised on the Dark Web is the 'hitman for hire' service – there are several banner advertisements offering that service.

But individual vendors and service providers often gather at *multi-vendor markets*, another common advertisement category. There's a lot of competition between markets, and so there's a lot of attention-seeking in their advertisements. One advertisement I've seen many times during my years exploring the Dark Web is an animated gif of a pair of jiggling breasts in a tank top, alternating with the phrase 'HIDDEN MARKETPLACE' and images of USD and Euro signs. Clicking through, we find the Hidden Marketplace has vendors offering credit cards, fake money, money transfers, gift cards, gadgets, and 'Porn and Erotic' products. The bulk of their products, it appears, are monetary: presumably stolen credit information or counterfeit monies. Other markets specialize in drugs, and some claim to sell weapons.

The remaining advertisements in the collection fall outside these broad categories. There are advertisements for stolen bitcoin wallets, cryptocurrency multipliers that promise to double your Bitcoins, gold bullion, hidden social media and forums, fixed football matches, and, interestingly enough, advertisements selling advertising space on other sites. They often use flashing gifs, nude women, and close-up shots of money to catch the eye.

Dark magic associations

Based on my categorization and analysis of search engine-based advertisements, I argue that there are three key associations happening between the advertisements and larger, networked practices, forming a dark magic incantation:

navigation, OPSEC, and the exploitation of oversharing.

One relatively banal – yet important – association many advertisements make is between their services and the ability to navigate the Dark Web. This ability to navigate is informed by what I call 'OPSEC politics,' a social structure beyond the gaze of the surveillance-plagued Clear Web, where the advertisements promise to keep their patrons safe from corporations or law enforcement. In turn, OPSEC politics provides a justification for the exploitation of others – specifically, the exploitation other people's personal information. The fruits of this exploitation make up the bulk of the advertised products.

In sum, the dark magic system promises control over one's environment by exploiting the 'Clear Web' magic system. These features almost tell us more about surveillance capitalism than they do about the Dark Web. So, for good measure, we can also consider how the dark magic system itself collapses under the weight of its own absurdities: like the magic system Williams critiqued, the many of the associations and promises of Dark Web advertising dissipate under the most cursory of examinations. In this sense, like William's magic system, Dark Web advertising shows us the limits of imagination about how an anonymizing system might actually serve social needs.

Navigating the dark

A major association made by the advertisements served on search engine sites is the ability to find new onions, to trace the Dark Web, and to recognize 'legit' sites from scam sites. This can be readily seen in the advertisements for directories – collections of links –

and the surprising number of search engines advertising their services, even on other search engine sites. In many ways, this is redolent of the early 2000s, when Google's search competed with Yahoo's directory as key entry points into the Clear Web. Likewise, would-be Dark Web users might turn to the search engines to find things, or to directories, which collect and categorize links. (In fact, they're likely doing both, as well are relying on resources on the Clear Web, such as Reddit).

Many of the link directories or search engines present themselves as revealing scams or providing vetted links. One advertisement that I've seen over the years is the Tor Scam List, which claims to name and shame Tor vendors and sites that are fraudulent. Conversely, advertisements for single vendors or multi-vendor markets associate themselves with trustworthiness, using 'trusted' or 'verified' in their advertisements, or put various logos of ostensibly legitimate authorities (Reddit, DeepDotWeb, or a search engine logo) on their sites to present themselves as legit.

The dark magic association here is clear: perhaps the Dark Web is a terrifying place for outsiders, but, armed with the advertised services and links, we can conquer the dark, easily tell friend from fraudster, and find the products we need.

OPSEC politics

Mere navigation is not enough, however. The dark magic system also promises operational security (OPSEC). Originally developed by the U.S. military during the Vietnam War (Redacted 1993), OPSEC has become a term of art, particularly among users of the Dark Web. Perhaps the clearest definition of OPSEC comes from security researcher The Grugq, who says that OPSEC simply means:

> keep your mouth shut. Don't say it. The less you say, the harder it is for people to figure out what you're doing ... In short, shut the fuck up (The Grugq 2012).

Essentially, having good OPSEC means not revealing personal information – name, age, gender, location. The central values are secrecy and distrust. Encryption of connections and messages, mixing of currencies and network traffic are among the techniques of choice. This privacy mentality has become an underlying ethos for many on the Dark Web, becoming what I call OPSEC politics, 'a rational means to structure relationships and, from there, conceive of a social order' (Gehl 2018, 112).

Adhering to this disposition, the dark magic system promises to maintain anonymity, even as we buy from vendors. The Hidden Marketplace promises, 'You can be assured of your safety and anonymity. We mix your bitcoin and encrypt messages and personal information.' Another common advertiser, easyCards, uses what Rachel-Heath Ferguson (2017, 694) calls 'OpSec Linguistics':

> Why do you write messages using so weird language/making mistakes?

> That's important rule we also would recommend you to follow. First of all - we don't want to let anybody know our location. Speaking English using some words more frequently than the others may expose our native language. Thanks to writing in weird but understable style, we are sure about impossibility to track our roots using that way.

The occasional advertisements for Dark Web social media also adhere to OPSEC politics. A Dark Web social networking site advertises itself: 'tired of surveillance? Enjoy freedom of speech and privacy.' After joining the social network, a user can enjoy the same affordances of Facebook: sharing media, liking posts, and making (pseudonymous) friends, but with no oversight from a centralized corporation. In this case, one of the promises of the dark magic system is an escape from surveillance capitalism.

Exploitation of personal information

To those invested in Dark Web OPSEC politics, Clear Web practices are derided as 'oversharing.' Oversharing is seen as a loss of control, a naive and foolish giving away of personal information. In contrast, the hardcore OPSEC of the Dark Web is heralded as a rational response to the surveillance society. As one Dark Web search engine site (which sells advertising space) puts it, 'In a world where everyone is over exposed, the coolest thing you can do is maintain your mystery!' And the dark magic system promises the ability to exploit the information of those who overshare.

Take, for example, influencer cultures. These are micro-celebrities who build followings in corporate social media, particularly Instagram (Abidin 2015). They share their lives and engage in interactions with their loyal followers. Influencers seek to develop relationships with audiences by being 'authentic,' performing a reality that is accessible and yet entertaining for their followers (Duffy and Hund 2019). Influencers win at the logics of corporate social media – they gain likes, followers, comments. They produce themselves through corporate social media, which means they produce a great deal of data about themselves. Not all social media users are influencers, of course, but the logic of influencing reflects the general logic of corporate social media: share. Be open. Connect with others.

What the dark magic system reveals is that those who adhere to the logics of corporate social media may see their openness exploited. The ill-gotten fruits of oversharing are offered for sale in the dark magic system. One market advertising itself offers hacked Facebook accounts. Another market features vendors selling 'fullz,' or 'complete identities, which include name, address, email address, phone number, date of birth and Social Security number' (O'Rourke 2016). Many vendors and markets offer carding services – that is, stolen gift cards or credit card information.

The advertisements for these stolen data promise access to corporate social media accounts or easy money based in part on information that others – predominantly social media users – have shared. As security researchers have shown, the data that inform credit card fraud and identity theft are often gathered via Clear Web social media. The information people share on social media allow illicit data brokers to 'to put the pieces of someone's identity together' and thus gain access to their financial accounts ('Criminals Target UK Youth as Identity Fraud Rises 2016). As cybersecurity researcher Jason Nurse argues, identity theft is often achieved through 'the monitoring of individuals on social media as they post and interact online' (Nurse 2019, 10). Nurse argues that data thieves exploit 'the nature to overshare [and] the poor management of security and privacy online' (Nurse 2019, 10).[2]

The exploitation of 'oversharing' is the same logic that drives so-called 'revenge pornography,' a form of 'non-consensual pornography, sexually explicit photographs that were exchanged in a trustful communicative space are made public or are shared without the permission of the depicted individual; with harmful consequences' (Venema and Lobinger 2017).[3] Some of the marketplaces advertising on Dark Web search engines include vendors selling 'Nude sex pictures from many ex girlfriends.' Such sites have appeared on the Dark Web for years. In these instances, those who upload, sell, or consume the images justify doing so by arguing that the 'girlfriends' should not have shared their nude photos online, implicitly faulting the women for having bad OPSEC. Like any justification of the exploitation of personal information, this is another instance of victim blaming.

Don't believe in dark magic

Can we use this dark magic? Can we buy something more than counterfeit money, hacking services, or gold bullion? Will the dark magic incantation – navigation, OPSEC, and the ability to exploit the Clear Web users – lead to Dark Web success? Can we reliably exploit the fruits of surveillance capitalism while still escaping its ever-watchful eye?

Perhaps. I cannot truly say – I have not used a methodology that can reveal any truths in Dark Web advertising. I haven't bought or sold any products or placed any advertisements on any search engines – nor do I see an Institutional Review Board allowing for such activities! But, given the sheer number of advertisements, vendors, and markets I've observed, I will say it's entirely possible that stolen personal information, credit card data, drugs, guns, and bitcoins are changing hands on the sites and services advertised on general-purpose, Dark Web search engines.

Even still, I don't recommend we believe in dark magic. A range of problems haunt the dark magic system. And the vast majority of them involve the desire to scam other Dark Web users, rather than offer legit services to them.

First, the most notorious problem of Tor onion services is 'cloning,' where 'legit' sites are duplicated by scam sites (Steinebach et al. 2019, 9). Given that Tor URLs are alphanumeric strings (for example, a1b2c3d4e5f6g7h8.onion, or even 52 alphanumeric characters) that are not easily memorized by humans, it's easy to establish a site with nearly the same information but at a different URL – a 'cloned' onion. What's the difference between a clone and an original? Beside the operator, the clone often uses a different Bitcoin address.

Cloning affected my collection of advertisements. While I was examining search engines and gathering banner advertisements for this study, I found multiple instances of the Torch search engine, a popular search service. I initially thought they were mirrors, or redundant servers. Closer examination revealed subtle differences that indicate that Torch is aggressively being cloned. I found over two dozen Torch URLs. I gathered the advertisements on six of them and started comparing the advertisements' URLs. I found that each of the Torch clones pointed to more clones, this time of the Tor Scam List, which offers 'verified sites'. Each of the Tor Scam List clones, in turn, pointed to more clones, this time of sites such as easyCards and the HD Wiki, with more URLs and, tellingly, different Bitcoin addresses (in case anyone wanted to donate money to support the site). And, in a dark magic circle of cloning, these clones pointed to more clones of Torch. Clearly, someone is trying to intercept bitcoins, advertisement revenues, logins, or network traffic – likely for defrauding Dark Web consumers.

Similarly, another problem is the fact that there is no intellectual property protections on the Dark Web. An egregious example is a site claiming to be a 'Partner Company' of the search engine DuckDuckGo. This site offers a search bar labelled as 'DuckDuckGo' but is selling banner advertisements around that search box. It even has a DuckDuckGo favicon. But it's clearly not DuckDuckGo; it's just an attempt to capture some of that popular site's traffic. Moreover, this site's sole purpose seems to be to direct users to a 'Lucifer Market' – many of the advertisements it runs are for this market (though they appear to be for other things, including hitmen for hire).

And none of this is to speak of the fact that buying on the Dark Web is riddled with fraud, ranging from products not being delivered to large-scale exit scams perpetrated by market operators.

These problems are faced by would-be buyers perusing the dark magic system. But perhaps the biggest flaw in the dark magic system is the burden that would-be *advertisers* face. Cloning, phishing, and other deceptions indicate that the search engine sites one might want to place an advertisement on may not be the actual search engine site one is trying to advertise on. Thus, even buying advertisements in the dark magic system is problematic: how do you know that the advertisement space vendor you're working with is legit? How do you know you're exchanging bitcoins for advertising space? On TorDex, a search engine, the operator put up a warning: 'tordex@elude.in is the only email, do not send payments to anyone else for advertisements!' That sounds legit. Unless it's not.

And even if we manage to advertise on a 'legit' site, how do we know how our advertisement is performing? Recall that Tor is an anonymizing network. The standard advertising metrics, such as counting clicks, unique visitors, or impressions, are deeply problematic because Tor onions do not log traffic like standard websites. Thus, any claims based on unique visitors can be gamed. And yet, the sites selling advertising space brag about their metrics. As one Dark Web search engine boasts, 'Advertise with us! ... Our search engine recives [sic] millions of unique views a month and your advertisement will be shown to real users of the dark net looking to buy.' A Dark Web advertisement network says 'transparency matters' and boasts that it has served over 9 million 'total unique impressions.' Perhaps the best clue as to how well these numbers can be gamed comes from Daniel's Hosting, a respected hosting service on Tor. Daniel's Hosting includes code to embed an old-school, 1990s-style hitcounter on your onion site. But, in a tip of the hat to the unreliability of these statistics, his hitcounter allows you to 'preload' it with as many hits as you like, which he notes is useful for, as Daniel's admits, 'faking' your numbers.

Again, to be fair, there's clearly commerce happening on the Dark Web, and moreover, enterprising entities are trying to clean up the Dark Web magic system with advertisement brokerage networks, brokering deals between advertisers and search engines, among other sites. But even this approach is subject to the same uncertainties – cloning, obscure URLs, and bogus metrification.

Ultimately, the dark magic system – particularly advertisements appearing around the general-purpose search engines that I have discussed in this paper – collapses under the weight of its own absurdities. This might be best illustrated by who's *not* advertising. When it comes to the dark magic system, it is rare for a reputable market – the kind of market subject to serious research (e.g. Espinosa 2019; Pace 2017; Bancroft and Peter 2016; Barratt and Maddox 2016) – to advertise their presence via the general purpose search engine banner advertisements I've encountered. As of this writing, legit markets – which is to say, markets where one can more reliably buy the product one is trying to buy – tend not to advertise on these search engines. One exception may be for the White House Market, but there was only one advertisement for White House in my collection, and I have rarely seen other 'legit' markets advertise in this manner.[4]

The dark magic system falls apart under the most cursory of examinations. The sheer number of clearly scam sites (Bitcoin doublers being the most common example), the anxious uncertainty that the advertisement even links to a legit site, the laughable gestures towards Clear Web metrics like 'impressions,' and the high likelihood that the sites advertised are short-term grifts, all demonstrate the illusory nature of this system.

Conclusion

All of the factors that reveal dark magic advertising for the illusion that it is beg the question: what is the Dark Web for? Is it an unethical reflection of the Clear Web? Is it a haven for exploitation, cruelty, and con artistry? Is it the highest expression of libertarian economics?

Raymond Williams's core argument about the 'magic system' of advertising points to another answer. His central criticism is not that advertising is crude, but that 'advertising is the consequence of a social failure to find means of public information and decision over a wide range of everyday economic life' (Williams 2000). For Williams, advertising is a symptom of the failure of capitalism to fulfill human needs. When a product or practice is associated with something more – something that we cannot clearly say the product provides – 'we have a cultural pattern in which the objects are not enough but must be validated, if only in fantasy, by association with social and personal meanings which in a different cultural pattern might be more directly available' (Williams 2000). Being anonymous and connecting with one another, the dark magic system tells us, is not enough: one must have more, one must become a master of OPSEC and an exploiter of anyone who is not as skilled in staying anonymous.

This is made all the more tragic when we consider how the Dark Web's magic is built in part on the exploitation of Clear Web surveillance. Trevor Smith sums up the contradiction quite well:

> From Edward Snowden's revelations about extensive government spying, we know that there is a possibility that all of our online actions, no matter how private we hope them to be, are being watched. At the same time, we are constantly warned of the dangers of online anonymity which can facilitate everything from illegal criminal activity to abusive trolling. Both of these contradictory aspects of the how online space operate point to it being characteristic of the social realm (Smith 2017, 36).

In the dark magic system, the most common social relations imagined for the anonymizing Dark Web are those of exploitative commerce – at best, scams, and at worst, the illegitimate exploitation of how we're legitimately exploited in corporate social media. This is in stark contrast to many of the creative aspects of anonymity (Beyer 2014, 6–7), as well as the long tradition of anonymity in service to political debate.

As Smith argues:

> Political speech and action are risky and require courage. The shield of anonymity has been, and continues to be, essential to the expression of dissenting points of view. If politics is to maintain its agonistic edge and not devolve into anti-political consensus, then making it easier to take part by shielding one's private life from one's public statements is necessary (Smith 2017, 111).

The Dark Web can indeed make it easier for such a shield to exist. The problem is that this affordance is largely ignored in the dark magic system of search engine advertising in favour of a rapacious individualism. Like the magic system in general, the dark magic system purports to be a way to fulfill social relations through consumerism, but it can never do so. The deeper social needs we have – solidarity, the end of exploitation, including the end of our being exploited by corporate social media – will never be filled by magic, dark or otherwise. Rather than presenting the Dark Web as an antidote to the rampant consumerism of the Clear Web, an alternative to surveillance capitalism where social relations beyond the gaze can bloom, the dark magic system presents itself solely as a dark and cloudy mirror to surveillance capitalism.

Notes

1. Unless either party reveals their identity. For an example, see Facebook's onion service, facebookcorewwwi.onion.
2. In addition to gathering information via social media, carders and fullz vendors also glean information from data breaches. While this is not necessarily tied to what the OPSEC-minded might call 'oversharing,' a data breach is also indicative of the excesses of personal information gathering happening in surveillence capitalism.
3. As I discuss in *Weaving the Dark Web*, I would avoid labelling the non-consensual sharing of someone's images as 'pornography.' I draw on Barbara DeGenevieve's definition of pornography as 'consensual acts being depicted … for the sexual arousal and masturbatory entertainment of the viewer.' Thus, for DeGenevieve, rape scenes, snuff, abuse, and child sex images are not pornography: they are non-consensual, and thus 'prosecutable crimes' (DeGenevieve 2007, 235). By that definition, so-called 'revenge porn' images are evidence of a crime, not pornography.
4. The only locations serving banner advertisements that likely lead to the market or product advertised are specialized sites like Recon, a site that is attempting to inherit the legitimacy of Grams. Recon is a specialized search engine, focusing predominantly on drug vendors, rather than a general-purpose search engine promising an index of all Tor onion sites.

Disclosure statement

No potential conflict of interest was reported by the author(s).

References

Abidin, C. 2015. "Communicative ♥ Intimacies: Influencers and Perceived Interconnectedness." *Ada New Media* (blog). 1 November 2015. https://adanewmedia.org/2015/11/issue8-abidin/

Bancroft, A., and S. R. Peter. 2016. "Concepts of Illicit Drug Quality among Darknet Market Users: Purity, Embodied Experience, Craft and Chemical Knowledge." *International Journal of Drug Policy* 35 (September): 42–49. doi:10.1016/j.drugpo.2015.11.008.

Barratt, M. J., and A. Maddox. 2016. "Active Engagement with Stigmatised Communities through Digital Ethnography." *Qualitative Research* 16 (6) (May): 701–719. doi:10.1177/1468794116648766.

Beyer, Jessica L. 2014. *Expect Us: Online Communities and Political Mobilization*. Oxford; New York: Oxford University Press.

'Criminals Target UK Youth as Identity Fraud Rises.' 2016. "CIFAS." 5 July 2016. https://www.cifas.org.uk/newsroom/criminals-target-uk-youth-as-identity-fraud-rises

DeGenevieve, B. 2007. "Ssspread.Com: The Hot Bods of Queer Porn.'." In *C'lickme: A Netporn Studies Reader*, edited by Katrien Jacobs, Marije Janssen, and Matteo Pasquinelli, 233–236. Amsterdam: Institute of Network Cultures.

Duffy, B, and E. Hund. 2019. "Gendered Visibility on Social Media: Navigating Instagram's Authenticity Bind." *International Journal of Communication* 13: 20.

Espinosa, R. 2019. "Scamming and the Reputation of Drug Dealers on Darknet Markets." *International Journal of Industrial Organization* 67 (December): 102523. doi:10.1016/j.ijindorg.2019.102523.

Ferguson, R. 2017. "Offline 'Stranger' and Online Lurker: Methods for an Ethnography of Illicit Transactions on the Darknet." *Qualitative Research* 17 (6): 683–698. doi:10.1177/1468794117718894.

Fuchs, C. 2012. "The Political Economy of Privacy on Facebook." *Television & New Media* 13 (2): 139–159. doi:10.1177/1527476411415699.

Gehl, R.W. 2016. "The Politics of Punctualization and Depunctualization in the Digital Advertising Alliance." *The Communication Review* 19 (1): 35–54. doi:10.1080/10714421.2016.1128187.

Gehl, R.W. 2018. *Weaving the Dark Web: Legitimacy on Freenet, Tor, and I2P*. Cambridge, MA: MIT Press.

The Grugq. 2012. "OPSEC: Because Jail Is for Wuftpd." 21 May 2012. https://www.youtube.com/watch?v=9XaYdCdwiWU

Nurse, J. R. C. 2019. "Cybercrime and You: How Criminals Attack and the Human Factors that They Seek to Exploit." *ArXiv:1811.06624 [Cs]*, May. 662–690. doi:10.1093/oxfordhb/9780198812746.013.35.

O'Rourke, M. 2016. "The Costs of Low-Tech Hacking." *Risk Management* 63 (7): 40.

Pace, J. 2017. "Exchange Relations on the Dark Web." *Critical Studies in Media Communication* 34 (1): 1–13. doi:10.1080/15295036.2016.1243249.

Redacted. 1993. "Purple Dragon: The Origin and Development of the United States Opsec Program." Series VI, Vol. 2, No. 609. United States Crytologic History. Fort Meade, MD: National Security Agency. Accessed 2017-02-09. https://www.nsa.gov/news-features/declassified-documents/cryptologic-histories/assets/files/purple_dragon.pdf

Smith, T.G. 2017. *Politicizing Digital Space*. University of Westminster Press: London. Accessed 2017-06-26. https://doi.org/10.16997/book5

Stark, Luke. 2018. "Algorithmic Psychometrics and the Scalable Subject." *Social Studies of Science* 48 (2): 204–231. doi:10.1177/0306312718772094.

Steinebach, M., M. Schäfer, A. Karakuz, K. Brandl, and Y. Yannikos. 2019. "Detection and Analysis of Tor Onion Services." In *Proceedings of the 14th International Conference on Availability, Reliability and Security*, 1–10. ARES '19. New York, NY, USA: Association for Computing Machinery. 10.1145/3339252.3341486.

Venema, R., and K. Lobinger. 2017."And Somehow It Ends up on the Internet.' Agency, Trust and Risks in Photo-Sharing among Friends and Romantic Partners." *First Monday*, July. doi:10.5210/fm.v22i7.7860.

Williams, R. 1960. "The Magic System." *New Left Review*, June 1960. Accessed 2020-11-09. https://newleftreview.org/issues/I4/articles/raymond-williams-the-magic-system

Williams, R. 1993. "Advertising: The Magic System." In *The Cultural Studies Reader* edited by Simon During, 410–423. London and New York: Routledge.

Williams, R. 2000. "Advertising: The Magic System." *Advertising & Society Review* 1 (1). doi:10.1353/asr.2000.0016.

🔓 OPEN ACCESS

A Study of Mastodon, Galaxy3 and 8Kun as Post-social Media in Dark Webs: The Darker Turn of Our Intimate Machines

Toija Cinque

ABSTRACT
Newly emerging technologies for digital communication facilitate rapid data collection, storage and processing whereby subsequent interactions can be unpredictable. This creates a 'darker turn' in *neo*-communicative practices. That which is 'dark' is understood as communication that has either limited distribution, is not open to all users – closed groups by way of example – or is veiled. Dark social spaces are, however, indistinct requiring further study. This is giving rise to new work in what I call 'dark social studies'. To further explore the nature and use of dark social spaces, a digital (auto) ethnographic study of 'dark' social connection was undertaken. The analysis specifically focused on Mastodon, Galaxy3 and 8Kun's '. onion' available over Tor (The Onion Router). This article concludes that for a number, virtual 'dark' spaces provide affirmative, intimate and vital zones of connection to others and peer collaboration. Further, the interconnected and interactive capacity of dark social spaces facilitates user expectations for dark connection while exposing simultaneously the limitations of our intimate machines.

The promise of great acceleration

This article develops a conceptual framing of 'dark' through an interpretation of intimacy for the ways emerging *dark social spaces* might clarify especial communication that would otherwise be inaccessible online. A definition of dark can first be underpinned by following a technical description that relates to access whereby information is: (a) hidden by facilitating encryption; (b) hidden through regulatory constrains for select access; (c) hidden because information is closed off to select groups accessible to individuals by invitation only, and; (d) 'dark' through access to required telecommunications services themselves. The provocation herein is that there are four broad socio-technological concerns connected to the big social media services that have helped increase the tendency for users to actively seek alternative spaces to *social-network*. These are digital privacy and (perceived loss of) agency; platforms monetizing user data by selling this to advertizers; the negative effects (and affects) associated with mainstream social media engagement, and; the increasing integration of IoT devices in everyday life. The surrounding concerns can be found and underscored in popular media.

This is an Open Access article distributed under the terms of the Creative Commons Attribution-NonCommercial-NoDerivatives License (http://creativecommons.org/licenses/by-nc-nd/4.0/), which permits non-commercial re-use, distribution, and reproduction in any medium, provided the original work is properly cited, and is not altered, transformed, or built upon in any way.

Ahead of launching their fictional book *Attack Surface*, the latest in a three-book cyberpunk series, science-fiction writer Cory Doctorow (2020) declared to audiences:

> If you found yourself in tech because you were excited by how much self-determination and power and pleasure you got from mastering technology, and then found your entire professional life devoted to ensuring that no one else ever felt that, this is the time for your moral reckoning.

(Greenberg 2020, np)

The term *Attack Surface* is also used to describe the range of points or vectors through which an attacker could infiltrate a network or virtually enter an environment (usually uninvited), but this essay is not intended as a 'moral reckoning'. Nor is it intended as a discussion of binary oppositions[1] applied to the web using cinematic tropes of good (clear/white) versus evil (dark/black), but a consideration of the contribution to social, affirmative communication that dark social spaces might afford. Emphatically for some, the communicative future is at a crossroads now, being controlled and constrained by a 'new frontier of power' that extends beyond the conventional terrains of public and private institutions. In their study of 'the age of *surveillance capitalism*' Zuboff critically examined the impact of data 'management' in that not only are surveillance assets (data and information) and capital being accumulated, but also individual rights and many operations function without meaningful mechanisms of consent (Zuboff 2019; see also Mosco 2015; Fuchs 2014). Increasingly in the West, the balance of power is transitioning from nation-states to private mega-corporations that feature the sensibilities of surveillance capitalism. Zuboff's consequent claim is that it is arguably 'up to us to use our knowledge, to regain our bearings, to stir others to do the same, and to found a new beginning' (Zuboff 2019, 524). This is a useful assertion that prepares readers for what follows. That is, the reasons for such a position reasonably stems from four broad themes that frame core issues for why dark social spaces have emerged.

As I have elsewhere summarized (Cinque 2021) the first is in regard to the obvious privacy-invasive social media giants Facebook, Twitter, Instagram, Tik Tok, Snap Chat and so forth. Second, are platforms, advertising technology companies,[2] surveillance contractors and intelligence agencies that collect and monetize our actions and related data about such; as well as the increased ease of use and interoperability brought about by Web 2.0. The third factor is in regard to the negative individual and societal affects associated with depressed mental health and wellbeing cause by 'psychologically damaging social networks' such as from sleep loss, anxiety, poor body image, real world relationships, and the fear of missing out (FOMO) (Royal Society for Public Health (UK) and the Young Health Movement 2021). Fourth is acceleration towards post-quantum IoT. While quantum computing is "still in its nascent age, its evolution threatens the most popular public-key encryption systems (Fernández-Caramés 2020, 6457). Fernández-Caramés (2020, 6457) undertook a detailed examination of what they called 'post-quantum IoT systems (IoT systems protected from the currently known quantum computing attacks)' that has 'researchers currently developing solutions to mitigate such a threat' into the future (Fernández-Caramés 2020, 6457). The provocation is that as quantum computing's digital components are: (1) further miniaturized; (2) coupled with advances in electrical battery capacity, and; (3) interconnected across telecommunications infrastructures – the ontogenetic capacity of the advanced network/s affords *supralevel surveillance*.

IoT systems from the micro-level (embedded within the body or worn on the skin) to the mid-level of society and environment (found in so-called SMART devices from phones to domestic appliances to street sensors and connected homes/government/health services, and natural environments), and further entangled at the macro-level (geo-satellites orbiting the globe) are 'watching' but exposed to differing levels of security protections. Predictions are that there will be 75 billion IoT devices used in homes and workplaces in 2025 (Statista 2016). While this relates to 'things' in the home and in many aspects of daily life, new communication spaces might be a space away from such; even a place to gain better understanding about the implications.

Returning to *supralevel surveillance*, individuals' data is commodified through their devices and the services that they provide (Gillespie 2018; Neff and Nafus 2016; Nissenbaum and Patterson 2016). Increasingly, data and personal information are retrievable, sharable and potentially exposed across a variety of now 'intimate' machines. I use 'intimacy' in this context in regard to: (a) connection with likeminded others for the flourishing of the self through issues of identity and gender; (b) the personal nature of content shared in micro-communities across devices from topics across personalized medicine, fertility tracking, reproductive health, menstrual cycles, individuals' biometric information including heart rate, body temperature and so on, to naked images; (c) that data can be collected from devices on and in the body itself. An intimate step further is that multiple sites 'implicitly contain a rich array of personal information, including cues to a speaker's biometric identity, personality, physical traits, geographical origin, emotions, level of intoxication and sleepiness, age, gender, and health condition' (Kröger, Lutz, and Raschke 2020, 242). Real-time global digital markets, indeed.

A further point for this article pulls on a thread from the work of Baruch Spinoza (1632–1677), philosopher and maker of telescopic lenses, that we need to move away from thinking primarily about technological artefacts and their origins (a material totality of things or objects) because they are just a vector of forces, whereas the better considerations are around what they are capable of doing, for whom and how. For its part, the dark net is composed of sites that are hidden on the internet using encryption to facilitate anonymous 'peer-to-peer' sharing of data but affording a cultural and legislative 'darker turn'. Certainly, much discussion about 'dark' cultures on the internet is with regard to its use for committing crimes and/or to evading authorities. With anonymization software such as Tor and a Virtual Private Network (VPN), transactions can be processed anonymously without revealing a user's location (Ghappour 2017), but a VPN for its part alone cannot guarantee anonymity to the server or the internet service provider (ISP). Together, – this is what make aspects of the web hidden or 'dark'. Another description and related to the first is that because of the capacity for anonymization, the dark web has been used for such nefarious purposes as selling illegal drugs, firearms and services (border crossings, Doxing, Phishing, iCloud activation) – a famous example are actions of Dread Pirate Roberts (DPR), founder in 2011 of the Silk Road – or circulating child pornography (Caldwell 2016).

Detailed work by Faizan and Khan (2019) that manually categorized 6,000 html files for hidden services on the dark web found that bitcoin doubling, adult content, drugs, ethical hacking and uncensored journalism made up sizable parts of the hidden services in the study's dataset. These categories bear witness to the formation of dark micropublics. A crowning argument is, however, that not all users of dark websites and anonymization tools (Tor, Freenet, I2P etc) are engaged in criminal behaviours. Eric Jardine, Andrew Lindner and Gareth Owenson's 2020 empirical study found that 'only a small fraction of users globally (~6.7%) likely use Tor for malicious purposes on an average day' (31,716). Crucially, many seek (and find) a different social belonging (Drake 2020; Gehl 2018). There is also an intimacy of being alone together. Others are needing anonymity online such as journalists, people talking to journalists, activists to parents wishing to avoid their baby monitors being hacked (and hijacked by marketers) and their infant children harassed. There are also active movements specifically formed to 'fight repressive censorship' and control of the internet (www.internetfreedom.org). Freenet Project for its part in the mesh of connections is a distributed peer-to-peer network 'for censorship-resistant communication and publishing' (https://freenetproject.mk16.de). Now our communications and household items can be cloaked from tracking for commercial gain and spying (Greenberg 2016) and in the process many advertizers are deprived of controlled and quantifiable audiences from which to harvest data.

For the willing then, is the Fediverse. This is a decentralized communication system made up of groups of interconnected, or federated, servers used for web publishing. Specific examples from the Fediverse are capacities for social networking, microblogging, blogging, and file hosting. Each server is a node that is independently and voluntarily hosted, and which is able communicate with each other server using FLOSS-licence protocols (Free/Libre and Open-Source Software) for any and all purposes. This is analogous to the early days of the internet (mostly populated by white, educated men in the first instances) and an additional conceptual sedimentary layer to the notion of 'homesteading' on the virtual frontier (Rheingold 1993).

That is, once users contributed message postings on the virtual frontier in Usenet newsgroups, Internet Relay Chat (IRC), bulletin board services (BBS) – the strata now are more inclusive of women, people from LGBTQI communities and of colour. Long ago, the early adaptors recognized that (then) existing mainstream media dominantly catered for a mass market whereas technologies of the 'electronic age' had little necessity to require an audience. Yet the early socially interactive internet activities have in fact been some of the most successful vehicles for the promotion of the internet. As indicated above, recent and emerging scholarship examines how social media have been used by activists in a neoliberal setting as tools of resistance (Fenton 2016; Poell and van Dijck 2018), with others now accounting for encryption-led dark nets.

By way of example, common now are decentralized CryptoParties.[3] These are globally hosted gatherings created in the context of the Australian Cybercrime Legislation Amendment Bill (2011) and assented to on 12 September 2012 as an Act to implement the Council of Europe Convention on Cybercrime, with the sober reasoning that these sorts of laws hold no water when everybody encrypts their communication. In CryptoParties, people meet virtually to pass on their knowledge or to learn about encrypting their online communications and digital media technologies for safer

Internet browsing, and '[w]hile some people offer help in realizing these practices, others attend with their laptops, tablets and smartphones to learn how to encrypt' (Kannengießer 2019, 1060). While the English language is currently predominant on this site, there is a wiki in development in which registered users can create pages and upload files. Ultimately, these sorts of practices in the dark structures of social spaces unearths a new identification of the dark in that there is resistance through ritual. The nature of what is afforded because of what is taken away is being reflected in everyday 'real' lives.

Outside the walled garden: digital method

What follows is a critical review of engagement in interconnected, smaller networked systems of servers that exist to receive public content and to distribute it to places it would not otherwise reach.[4] The starting point for critical elaboration is the respected and respectful culture one (mostly) experiences and starts the conversation about dark social studies as a field. The broad swathe of personal and social intimacies draws a picture of how various forms of closeness, whether desired or not, are informed by regimes of soft power (and intended enlightenment), which can in the broader context, impact on lived experiences. From both a scholarly distance and intimately shared, we see that cultural norms are framed by the principle of anonymity and diligence in maintaining such in the face of the powerful mainstream social offerings. An argument could be made that finding a large tranche of curious 'new' users poking around and subsequently 'mainstreaming' the '.onion' and others is not desirable for a number. While that might be the case in some instances, albeit largely hidden from view, there are numerous sites that are welcoming and predominantly easy to navigate. Those that are not are likely intended that way such that an 'error 503' message might also mean that one is being blocked. In the context of dark online interactions and not ignorant to what's posted there that might be 'inappropriate', illegal and/or offensive, this present work seeks to understand the extent to which users experience social connection.

I use a digital (auto)ethnographic approach (Pink et al. 2015; Finnegan 1997) for three brief case studies. Taking the key methodological principle of 'multiplicity' that stresses the importance of customizing digital ethnography to the research (Pink et al. 2015, 8–9), I explore the recent additions to the list of alternate social-networking spaces. Further, I draw on personal narratives (understood as how identity might be constructed/created – not simply communicated – through the stories someone tells about themselves) where acknowledgement of socio-cultural story-telling conventions that have impacted the frameworks someone uses to tell their life story allows for a deeper connection between reader and story (Finnegan 1997). The combined approach is built on critical questions of data access and control through the promotion of open-source software, its development and use. I specifically focus on Mastodon (see recent work by Zulli, Liu, and Gehl 2020), Galaxy3 and 8Kun's '.onion' via Tor. The aim here is to gauge the nature of public/social commentary, reaction and creative expression within the digital social spaces of the dark web.

Be it 'lurking' or actively posting comments, photographs, re-posting, creating personal sites or social pages, or uploading fan-fiction/art/vids among other subgenres, my prediction was that I would find the valuable opportunities taken by users for shaping and engaging with public opinion. With reference to Kozinets (2020), a netnographic method (online ethnography) and immersion in the users' world through online spaces was drawn upon to specifically ask questions of: (1) how the selected dark social spaces have been engaged with by users; (2) how users share their experiences, and; (3) the nature of the creative practices or shared stories that might emerge as a result. In a focused cultural analysis of dark social spaces that brings to the surface identity politics and the wider social struggles in which a number might feel themselves to have a stake, this article explores the contested interpretations of 'dark' which are made salient. This 'dark social' study involved experiencing through observing, reading, viewing content and relevant posts (including the original and those re-posted) (ethics approval HAE-16-001). The focus was predominantly on the text as well as the many cases of emotive imagery that users felt connected to including photographic, audio and video material.

A limitation associated with the dataset is that of the hundreds of pages checked and analysed manually only 40 were used in detail because a number were in languages other than English and consequently removed. This is a cultural bias to be addressed in future studies for greater representation from international users and their communities.

A study in dark social practices via Mastodon, Galaxy3 and 8Kun

Mastodon

Located in the Fediverse is Mastodon, which is a German-born microblogging social network launched in October 2016 whereupon users 'toot' (and a step further is the 'sticky toot' or pinned post), as opposed to 'tweet'. The layout is akin to Twitter (in late 2020). Each user has a count of Followers and the number they themselves are Following. While the site activates anonymous communications there might still linger some anxiety that size does matter. Site statistics or 'server stats' are detailed for account holders as are 'Trending Now' topics using hashtags, for example #fediverse or #books. Members can 'Explore Radical Town' based on their interests or sign up to join independent groups or 'instances' featuring representational images of each and filtered by topics from food, music, gaming, fandom, adult content and others. In one fan site, a user asserted that they were there because they were curious about how others were responding to an alternative-music star's recent death and had the platform recommended to them by other fans. For another user they had moved on from Tumblr since the 2018 restriction of 'explicit' images – seen by a number as crucial aspects of community building and self-expression – with an ensuing loss of their freedom of expression on that site. However, the darkly posted digital paratexts from visual image forms and accompanying creative writing that featured within the communications technologies interrupted the present and fertilized the immediate contemporary experience of dark social uses and practices for these fans while acting as a 'counterpolitics of visibility' (Mondin 2017, 288). What these examples do is present characterizations of the site that are indicative of user motives for engaging therein.

Users can sort their choices by language, which is practical because not all groups use English. Not everyone has the same interests or share the same opinions. Because users are diverse there have been calls to 'defederate' some servers' content from reaching the network. Such calls to sanction some users raises interesting rhetorical questions about 'what is reasonable content'. The conversation here is balanced between a voluntary loss of *negative liberty* or freedom from (freedom from unwanted information or influence) and an increase in *positive liberty* or freedom to (to read or say anything). Freedom from surveillance and interference can be read as a form of negative liberty in this example. What became apparent through this research of the dark discussions that accompany an image around a particular topic is that while users see the same text/footage/image each reads them in slightly different ways. For some, an image brought up long forgotten memories that they then shared, while the same image was a cause of frustration for others. By way of creative extension, the digital space was conferring the means for many to re-create the 'conversation' – be it with regard to politics, art to technology. In sum, the characterization of Mastodon brings into relief important insights for the way new spaces for connection and communications are being used.

Galaxy3

Devoid of slick visual communication is the functional Galaxy3[5] over Tor that pitched itself as 'a social media platform for free speech' but with fairly heavy content moderation including offending links being removed and the right to 'delete any account at anytime'. Specific examples of rules include no pornography or gore being permitted; no images of children of any form; no commercial trade (including markets or services especially activities that might be illegal and users are warned not to solicit other members into doing anything criminal), and; there is no cyber-begging allowed. This does not stop some trying with one user seeking the drug Teva-Fentanyl (opioids used to treat severe pain) to which another user overtly replies with a reminder that members are not allowed to make such requests for banned substances nor draw others to engage in illegal behaviour on the site.

Users can read from 'the wire', a thread of conversations or choose from open groups (click a link to join) and closed groups (click to 'request membership'). Galaxy3 groups are listed either alphabetically, by popularity or by Featured Groups including 'Food and Drinks' with 83 active members that seemingly compete for the best recipes, without images, but assurances that each was delicious upon making and nutritious (reading the ingredients I had no reason to doubt them and was pleasantly surprised when inspired to try to recreate some when flat out of new meal ideas). At the time of writing the theme seemed to be chilli ('Competition Chilli', 'Chile Colorado') with chicken featuring predominantly. Without doubt there might be covert code words used that act to alert site moderators to inappropriate content that would lead them to block an offender. This could be read as a means to moderate the site by stealth. But, posts can still be read and appreciated at face value affording conversations in this virtual environment. One member's share of a proposed KFC secret herbs recipe became a learned discussion, without flaming or negative comments, about whether one can actually be 'allergic' to MSG (monosodium glutamate). The representative conversation by way of example acting here to demonstrate how individuals converge and form communities but are equally free to diverge.

Other groups in Galaxy3 include Heavy Metal fans (<\m/METAL FANS\m/> (18 members at the time of writing) whose own rules include: '1. Be nice to people 2. Code good dude: P and 3. Use good encryption and privacy services and tell others to do the same'–to which one user commented 'does "hello world" count as good code?'. For its part, Raven's Room

(179 active members at the time of writing) was 'opened for people who have just started wandering around Darknet to find and chat with each other and find solutions quickly if they have any problems'. Some questions, along the lines of 'is it true that you can buy all sorts of illegal goods on the darkweb' seemed likely to lead to such posters being flamed, or simply being excluded from the group and its forum. Instead, a number have been sent links that once clicked included the picture of a gorilla rudely giving 'the finger' and the like. This act can be read as a rhetorical device of meme culture being morphed into refusal and social regulation. Other questions/requests were related to trouble shooting advice for navigation in the space that were mostly responded to in a speedy manner in useful ways (with instructions or links). In brief, my time spent in this space unearthed actions similarly read and felt in Mastodon and Galaxy3 as being by and for communities of like-minded others that are finding (and making) a 'home' in this alternate space.

8Kun

Recently relaunched in November 2019 is 8Kun[6] (previously 8Chan which went offline in August the same year) where visitors are invited to 'Speak freely–legally' with the caveat (in red text in the banner) that 'On 8Kun, boards and posts are user-created and do not necessarily represent the opinions of the 8kun Administration', but content in violation of US laws will be removed and the poster banned. At the time of writing, the site reported that there were some 54, 612, 960 posts made on active boards since 15, October 2019. Indeed, many sites market themselves by flagging the number of users they have (albeit that it is not possible to get completely accurate user numbers on hidden sites given that people split identities and usually hold more than one as an Operational Security practice). The more users there are, the more effective the system overall and thus worth promoting for their integral purpose. And, despite dark social spaces seemingly being minority players for now in comparison to the large number of subscribers for the mainstream sites, there is a sense that change is taking place as others become dissatisfied with the unhidden/exposed nature of 'clear' web of commercial, accessible but surveilled options. One user that identified as an international researcher living abroad stated that they had 'stopped posting on [another social media site] for fear of how their political views on Covid19 management would be perceived and acted upon by authorities in their home country' (the statement is paraphrased here from the original to maintain the anonymity of the user). They stated that they found the forum to facilitate their open communication thus affording civic participation otherwise truncated. Others offered the same user technical support and guidance for up-to-date data sources on their research topic. Away from imperatives of surveillance capitalism described by Zuboff and others, one finds the tone of interactions adding to the sense that these are overarchingly compassionate users that care about their communities. At the same time, user engagement in dark social spaces is increasingly becoming normalized. In these places beyond 'social media' (Boccia Artieri, Brilli, and Zurovac 2021), exist *communities of care*. Here, each might exist even for the briefest moment in time or be ongoing for years. The shared purposes, interests and goals are constitutive of what is distinctive about them such that they afford flourishing as individuals therein find much needed advice, support or just a place to 'be' (themselves).

Summary and discussion of the dark

Despite everything seemingly set to the contrary in terms of standard remunerative business models, the emergence of dark social sites would seem to cater to, or leverage off, users' perceived need to move away from established, techno-driven cognitive capitalism. In recognition of consumer sentiments around digital privacy, Apple for its part, offers users App Tracking Transparency in its latest update of its operating system (iOS 14.5) meaning that other companies' apps and websites such as Facebook will also need to ask permission to collect personal data first. Rising from consumer sentiment and expectations is the apparent emphasis on communications models that emphasize the convergence between compassion, identity and technology.

Trust is still an issue on sites such as 8Kun, however, for the number that have gone dark in their social networking. For sites that have a reputation in the popular press for remaining 'hidden' there is increasing promotion of their own popularity to potential members as well as functionality that would allow for users speaking different languages to join. For other content from social/interest groups to markets, keen users would be guided to dark.fail[7] with its overarching philosophy of providing users with embedded URLs that are verified by PGP (a random symmetric-key cryptography each browsing session).

Reflectively navigating through the sites noted above my personal memories were revived of days taking a statistics course over summer; a time when my then home institution first went 'online'. I opened Netscape browser and had a private moment thinking 'okay, what do I look for'. I was a 'noob' just as I read now that others are shining brightly and seeking shortcuts or 'sauce' (a term used for information and/or help navigating the dark web and deep web). A leap forward in time finds a new generation feeling the same keen interest in what's next. Indicative comments from users:

A: I really like the vibe of Tor web, but like I did when I used the internet for the first time. I really don't know what to do.

B: I did try it for a while to actually find out what's happening there, but I found it too confusing and I don't I didn't really know at what point it was it was very it was very intimidating for me when I first joined and I didn't know what's out there, so I kind of stopped.

C: Thanks for your help 'X' to solve that problem; worked a treat!

My sense of the socially dark spaces is that what is required for navigation and participation is time. One needs to be patient because pages requested from Tor take longer to load or just time-out. In addition is the need to read for information and upskill where necessary.

Dark social spaces for resistance, emancipation and individual becoming

A cross sectional view of the sedimentary layers of knowledge about online communications finds parallels in relation to the contemporary desire for social-networking options now in the face of current criticism over the commercial sites harvesting data and limiting functionality within walled gardens. Intimacy is used here to locate it at the intersection of techno-social and institutional relations. The dark web might not seem the most obvious site for consideration of the intimate where many ethnographic approaches speak to larger structural conditions and focus on dark practices from the perspective of being illegal and/or immoral. The aim here is to showcase dark sites (variously interpreted) of social connection that speaks, on the one hand, to the intimate worlds of subjects located in the virtual spaces while remaining attuned, on the other, to other regulatory frames that undergird these worlds. As demonstrated, the sites viewed (and used) do have 'rules' 'and norms that shine a light on goals that might be related more to liberty as opposed to complete anarchy.

During my own hidden years exploring in these spaces, I have felt keenly that there is a gazing elite. In this context the notion relates to the techno-related narratives (usually in regard to hacking and content creation/sharing) that require a level of skill of a complexity (a particular language) that might act to exclude a number. Moreover, as the examples above underscore, while it is possible to create an online community that can interface with the rest of the Fediverse and other networks–one/s that operates according to particular local rules, guidelines, modes of organization, and ideology – problematic is that as each community has its own set of rules, federated/virtual Feudalism can result. This is where each is a kind of dictatorship unto itself. A call is raised then for more liberal democratic systems. As this happens, each virtual community is able to define itself not only through its own memetic language, interests, and scope, but also in relation to the other, via difference. Moreover, there is an algorithmic language in this mediating culture that sits between technology and users. In other words, digital communities each have their own set of [ab]norms, goals, regulations and controls that not all have the time, willingness or the capacity to learn and follow.

Conclusion

This article grew out of four broad socio-technical concerns connected to the big social media services that have helped increase the tendency for users to actively seek alternative spaces: (1) digital privacy and agency; (2) monetarization of user data; (3) negative effects and affects associated with social media engagement, and; (4) increased integration of data-gathering devices in everyday life. In parallel with Zuboff (2019), Braidotti (2019) insists with reference to the practices of cognitive capitalism within the knowledge economies of First and Second World developing nations that the corporate social media companies operate within, that 'if we are all part of a system that capitalizes on all that lives, we (remember to position "we" differently in different perspectives) need to work from within to make differences that actually matter'. This lucid statement is passionate without being untenable and speaks truth to power that many are dissatisfied with being quantified, studied, capitalized upon and farmed. In the context of communications be it hidden or otherwise remains the challenges for protecting people who are vulnerable, those unable to give *informed* consent online for a range of reason from literacy levels to being underage, people with a cognitive impairment, or mental illness, and the care for whom is magnified in this era of the 'datalogical turn' (Clough 2018). Putting users at the centre of the thinking for how and why the dark social cultures are working requires more attention to be directed towards social issues such as of specific cultural groups.

There are also affirmative opportunities to go beyond one's echo chamber and there is plurality and difference that can only grow. Additionally, in the process of decentralizing content, advertisers are deprived of a controlled and quantifiable audience. But John Perry Barlow (n.d., np) once predicted:

> ... really it doesn't matter. We are going there whether we want to or not. In five years, everyone who is reading these words will have an email address, other than the determined Luddites who also eschew the telephone and electricity.

While far beyond email now, these words have held true and there is now a new social re-engineering underway presently in emerging alternate systems for communication and social connection.

Notes

1. For a nuanced evaluation see Coëgnarts, M and Kravanja, P. (2014). 'On the Embodiment of Binary Oppositions in Cinema: The containment Schema in John Ford's Westerns', *Image [&] Narrative*, Vol. 15, No. 1, pp 30-43.
2. For an alphabetical list and links <https://www.wikiwand.com/en/List_of_advertising_technology_companies>
3. For definitions, to find and/or host a CryptoParty see: https://www.cryptoparty.in
4. https://socialhome.readthedocs.io/en/latest/running.html#running
5. galaxy3bhpzxecbywoa2j4tg4muepnhfalars4cce3fcx46qlc6t3id.onion [Tor]
6. jthnx5wyvjvzsxtu.onion [Tor]
7. Darkfailllnkf4vf.onion

Disclosure statement

No potential conflict of interest was reported by the author(s).

ORCID

Toija Cinque http://orcid.org/0000-0001-9845-3953

References

Australian Cybercrime Legislation Amendment Bill. 2011. Cth.
Barlow, J. P. n.d. "Is There a There in Cyberspace?" UTNE. Accessed 8 April 2014 and 2021. <http://www.utne.com/community/isthereathereincyberspace.aspx?PageId=2#ArticleContent>

Boccia Artieri, G., S. Brilli, and E. Zurovac. 2021. "Below the Radar: Private Groups, Locked Platforms, and Ephemeral Content." *Social Media+ Society* 7 (1). doi:10.1177/2056305121988930.

Braidotti, R. 2019. "Posthuman Knowledge." Lecture delivered at Graduate School of Design, Harvard University, March 12. Youtube (30: 04) <https://www.youtube.com/watch?v=0CewnVzOg5w>

Caldwell, L. R. 2016. "Ensuring Tech-Savvy Criminals Do Not Have Immunity from Investigation", U.S. Department of Justice. BLOGS, November 21. ≤https://www.justice.gov/opa/blog/ensuring-tech-savvy-criminals-do-not-have-immunity-investigation>

Cinque, T. 2021. "A Study in Anxiety of the Dark: What It There to Be Afraid of in Social Online Spaces?" *M/C Journal* 24 (2). 'Dark' Special Issue. Luke J. Heemsbergen, Alexia Maddox, Amelia Johns, Toija Cinque and Robert W. Gehl (eds). doi:10.5204/mcj.2759.

Clough, P.T. 2018. *The User Unconscious: On Affect, Media, and Measure*. Minneapolis: University of Minnesota Press.

Coëgnarts, M and Kravanja, P. (2014). "On the Embodiment of Binary Oppositions in Cinema: The containment Schema in John Ford's Westerns", *Image [&] Narrative* 15 (1): 30-43.

Doctorow, C. 2020. *Attack Surface*. London: Head of Zeus.

Drake, V. 2020. "Why Pixelfed Won't Save Us from Instagram", *The Start Up*, February 17. <https://medium.com/swlh/why-pixelfed-wont-save-us-from-instagram-4c991557d5cf>

Faizan, M., and R. A. Khan. 2019. "Exploring and Analyzing the Dark Web: A New Alchemy." *First Monday* Accessed 22 December 2020. <https://journals.uic.edu/ojs/index.php/fm/article/download/9473/7794≥

Fenton, N. 2016. *Digital, Political, Radical*. Cambridge: Polity Press.

Fernández-Caramés, T. M. 2020 July. "From Pre-Quantum to Post-Quantum IoT Security: A Survey on Quantum-Resistant Cryptosystems for the Internet of Things." *IEEE Internet of Things Journal* 7 (7): 6457–6480. doi:10.1109/JIOT.2019.2958788.

Finnegan, R. 1997. "Storying the Self: Personal Narratives and Identity." In *Consumption and Everyday Life*, edited by H. Mackay, 65–112. London: Sage.

Fuchs, C. 2014. *Social Media: A Critical Introduction*. London: Sage.

Gehl, R.W. 2018. *Weaving the Dark Web: Legitimacy on Freenet, Tor, and I2P*. Cambridge, MA: MIT Press.

Gehl, R.W., and F. McKelvey. 2019. "Bugging Out: Darknets as Parasites of Large-scale Media Objects." *Media, Culture & Society* 41 (2): 219–235. doi:10.1177/0163443718818379.

Ghappour, A. 2017. "Searching Places Unknown: Law Enforcement Jurisdiction on the Dark Web." *Stan L. Rev* 69 (2017): 1075. Accessed 22 December 2020. <https://repository.uchastings.edu/faculty_scholarship/1583>

Gillespie, T. 2018. *Custodians of the Internet: Platforms, Content Moderation, and the Hidden Decisions that Shape Social Media*. New Haven: Yale University Press.

Greenberg, A. 2016. "Now You Can Hide Your Smart Home on the Darknet." *Wired*, July. Accessed 26 February 2017. <https://www.wired.com/2016/07/now-can-hide-smart-home-darknet/≥

Greenberg, A. 2020. "His Writing Radicalized Young Hackers. Now He Wants to Redeem Them." *Wired*, October 12. Accessed 12 November 2020. <https://www.wired.com/story/his-writing-radicalized-young-hackers-now-he-wants-to-redeem-them/>

Heemsbergen, L. J., A. Maddox, T. Cinque, A. Johns, and R. W. Gehl. 2021. "Dark." In *M/C Journal*, edited by Luke J. Heemsbergen, Alexia Maddox, Amelia Johns, Toija Cinque, and Robert W. Gehl, Vol. 24. (Original work published April 26, 2021). https://doi.org/10.5204/mcj.2791

Jardine, E., A. M. Lindner, and G. Owenson. 2020 December 15. "The Potential Harms of the Tor Anonymity Network Cluster Disproportionately in Free Countries." In *Proceedings of the National Academy of Sciences of the United States*, edited by Douglas S. Massey, Vol. 117, 31716–31721. doi:10.1073/pnas.2011893117. (First published November 30, 2020). Accessed January 12 2021.

Kannengießer, S. 2019. "Reflecting and Acting on Datafication – CryptoParties as an Example of Re-active Data Activism." *Convergence* 26 (5-6): 1060–1073. doi:10.1177/1354856519893357.

Kavallieros, D., D. Myttas, E. Kermitsis, E. Lissaris, G. Giataganas, and E. Darra. 2021. "Understanding the Dark Web." In *Dark Web Investigation. Security Informatics and Law Enforcement.*, edited by B. Akhgar, M. Gercke, S. Vrochidis, and H. Gibson., 3-26. New York: Springer. doi:10.1007/978-3-030-55343-2_1.

Kozinets, R.V. 2020. *Netnography: The Essential Guide to Qualitative Social Media Research*. Third ed. London: Sage.

Kröger, J. L., O. HM. Lutz, and P. Raschke. 2020. "Privacy Implications of Voice and Speech Analysis – Information Disclosure by Inference." In *Privacy and Identity Management. Data for Better Living: AI and Privacy. Privacy and Identity 2019*, edited by M. Friedewald, M. Önen, E. Lievens, S. Krenn, and S. Fricker. IFIP Advances in Information and Communication Technology, Vol. 576, New York. Springer. 242-258. doi:10.1007/978-3-030-42504-3_16.

Mosco, V. 2015. "The political economy of communication: A living tradition." In Power, Media, CultureL A Critical View from the Political Economy of Communication, edited by Luis A. Albornoz, pp. 35–57. Palgrave Macmillan: London.

Mondin, A. 2017. "'Tumblr Mostly, Great Empowering Images: 'Blogging, Reblogging and Scrolling Feminist, Queer and BDSM Desires." *Journal of Gender Studies* 26 (3): 282–292. doi:10.1080/09589236.2017.1287684.

Neff, G., and D. Nafus. 2016. *Self-tracking*. Cambridge, MA: MIT Press.

Nissenbaum, H., and H. Patterson. 2016. "Biosensing in Context: Health Privacy in a Connected World." In *Quantified: Biosensing Technologies in Everyday Life*, edited by D. Nafus, 79–100. Cambridge, MA: MIT Press.

Pink, S., H. Horst, J. Postill, L. Hjorth, T. Lewis, and J. Tacchi. 2015. *Digital Ethnography: Principles and Practice*. London: Sage.

Poell, T., and J. van Dijck. 2018. "Social Media and New Protest Movements." In *The SAGE Handbook of Social Media*, edited by Jean Burgess, A. Alison Marwick, and T Poell, 546–561. London: Sage.

Quandt, T, ed. 2021. "Dark Participation in Online Communication: The World of the Wicked Web." *Media and Communication* 9 (1). Accessed 3 March 2021. <https://www.cogitatiopress.com/mediaandcommunication/issue/view/207>

Rheingold, H. 1993. *The Virtual Community: Homesteading on the Electronic Frontier*. Vol. 32. Reading, MA: Addison-Wesley.

Royal Society for Public Health (UK) and the Young Health Movement. 2 April 2021. ""#statusofmind". A 2017 Report Examining the Positive and Negative Effects of Social Media on Young People's Health." <https://www.rsph.org.uk/our-work/campaigns/status-of-mind.html≥

Spinoza, B. 1985. *The Collected Writings of Spinoza (Vol. 1: 1985; Vol. 2: 2016)*. Edwin Curley, translator. Princeton: Princeton University Press. ©1985-2016.

Statista. 2016. "Number of IoT Devices 2015-2025." November 27. Accessed 18 March 2021. https://www.statista.com/statistics/471264/iot-number-of-connected-devices-worldwide/

Zuboff, S. 2019. *The Age of Surveillance Capitalism: The Fight for a Human Future at the New Frontier of Power*. New York: Public Affairs.

Zulli, D., M. Liu, and R. Gehl. 2020. "Rethinking the 'Social' in 'Social Media': Insights into Topology, Abstraction, and Scale on the Mastodon Social Network." *New Media & Society* 22 (7): 1188–1205. doi:10.1177/1461444820912533.

The Electrified Social and Its Dark Alternatives: Policing and Politics in the Computational Age

Alexia Maddox and Luke Heemsbergen

ABSTRACT
This article contrasts the dark with the electrified light of datafied life to bring into relief the impact of data surveillance upon social transformation. Our argument is that darkness remains fundamental to creative social experimentation and thus to a society's capacity for change and sustained transformation. This argument might seem antithetical to the age of information. Yet, we find darkness encourages exploratory forms of engagement, intercourse and exchange, that electrified light forbids. We draw on Rancière's considerations of politics and the police to suggest that the policing by digitally-electrified light extinguishes the politics of experimentation that test the make-up and limits of social interaction. Our work is structured by first explaining the baseline of the digital electric policing through the conceptualization of Facebook's social graph, then switches to antithetical examples of politics enabled in the dark. We use the examples of the Dark Web, end to end encryption, and trustless infrastructures like Craigslist to illustrate generative tensions that are the signatures of what we understand as the dark social. We conclude that the dark social involves a decentralized capacity to experiment and transform what is social.

Introduction

Two strangers meet in a parking lot to exchange a bag of hammers, never to meet again. A Chinese national in Australia thumb-swipes cryptocurrency to her friend in exchange for $AUD. An anonymous user buys $C_9H_{13}N$ from an anonymous seller. Two lovers exchange secrets across the world, which they know will never be read again. These strange assortments of acts all exist as decentralized experimentations we term dark sociality that escape the otherwise ubiquitous computational gaze the current age holds in the light. That is to say, in an age of ubiquitous surveillance, computation and prediction, only those interactions left in the dark can create what is social. Darkness is the place we can explore in solitude (who we want to be, who we are); it is the relations we have with other individuals away from what is seen by most (how we are with those we know, or might want to). And, we argue, darkness is antithetical to the electrified light that polices and extinguishes any politics and experimentations that test the make-up and limits of social interaction.

The article explores these themes through first considering society's relation to light in terms of knowledge and control. Specifically, it builds its enquiries from Schivelbusch's (1988) insights around how the industrialization of light decreased autonomy of households and increased control of what had previously been dark streets, and reimagines these forms of control and its resistance in the computational age. By engaging with critical theory and enquiry to interrogate the master category (Sassen 2005) of computational light, this article calls forth discussion on how we might imagine forms of sociality that operate in the dark as well as imagining past them. As such, this article provides provocation around what we term 'the electrified social' through empirical cultural critique of socio-technical examples of the Social Graph, and as its antithesis dark spaces such as the Dark Web, end-to-end encryption, and craigslist. It is an important endeavour to do so as computational light, to us, evokes the motif of politics and the police introduced by Rancière (1999) to describe policing as the organization and legitimizing of power, with politics being antagonistic to policing, breaking tangible configurations to test the assumptions of equality in society. These politics usher in hope for what Barratt, Aldridge, and Maddox (2018) has deemed a new dark age – meaning not a lack of knowledge, but a lack of certainty, predictions and methods of control.

Subsequently, we theoretically explore how darkness accompanies electrical light as a condition of experimentation in data societies of surveillance. This critique articulates how the malleable and porous architectures of uncertainty, through which social experimentation (and politics) emerges, position these liminal acts of becoming in generative tension with the fictive certainties of computational light. From this position, we see how computational certainties are built on brittle categories that fracture and break under social pressures (and therefore break the social) and how experimentation in the dark adapts through ambiguities, divergence and contradictory processes. We then argue that dark social experimentation occurs through paradoxical processes, which produce a liminal space of generative tensions that become potential levers for social change and transformation.

In this article, we argue that it is the electrified light of ubiquitous surveillance that polices the organization/legitimizing of power and seeks to extinguish (dark social) mechanisms of experimentation and socio-cultural change through the desire for static, predictable and accountable socio-technical configurations. This argument is then grounded within socio-technical acts by firstly illustrating the electric social that polices our lives through its exemplar: The Social Graph. The paper then defines the antithesis of the electrified social through presenting exemplars of dark social spaces that sustain decentralized experimentation of culture, relations, ideas, practices and politics, and more generally a sociality that emerges through residing outside computational logic. The following exemplars illustrate the dark social contexts through which our aforementioned hammer-strangers in a parking lot (craigslist), new arrivals exploring fungibility and anonymous drug users (Dark Web), and distant lovers (e2e encryption) harness liminal spaces to further push their lived experience in contradiction to the inescapable computational light.

The electrified social

The promise of data and algorithms offers a computational certainty (Barratt, Aldridge, and Maddox 2018) on the logics of how humans should live. The promise of these logics electrifies the social into a dataset of certainties that offer a lack of human becoming and regulates us to only what is widely known of us. We define the electrified social through anticipated, compiled and accounted for subjects and relations. Being known in an electric social is to be stratified. There, our data are relationalized while our relations are datafied. This intense visibility translates into bounded architectures of power and control that inhibit emergent social transformation and experimentation: there is nothing left to do in the dark.

That data and the algorithm fulfil the organization and legitimizing of power in the current networked society is not a new claim, nor one that is transfixed on light and dark. Danaher et al. (2017) argue that in this algorithmic age, proliferating forms of computational governance increasingly influence, shape and guide our behaviours. For example, Henman (2020) discusses how governments use artificial intelligence to detect patterns, sort populations according to different outcomes scores or risks, and make predictions. Henman also identifies challenges of deploying artificial intelligence in public administration via accuracy of data collected, bias and discrimination alongside expectations surrounding control and compliance (symbolic power). These computational logics are also often imbued with biases that explicitly stratify societies' extant cleavages like race or gender (Noble 2018; Costanza-Chock 2020) and make clearer still the delineations of power, control, and autonomy. Henman (2020) illustrates these AI biases using a media report on Amazon discovering its AI to sort through and select job applications was biased against women (Dastin 2018), and scholarly works discussing how the use of COMPAS in American sentencing and parole decision-making was reproducing systemic biases against Afro-Americans (Allen 2019; Benjamin 2019). Leveraging these examples, we argue such computational governance creates new forms of visibility that actively organize and legitimize allowed limits of sociality while discouraging those who exist or seek to exist outside the lowest common computable correlation that structural biases and statuses allow. We conceptualize the power of electric light as the photonic measurement and electronic computation of what used to be social, as it polices through both constructive organization and the threat of (legitimate) violence. This is the policing that amounts to an electrified social.

To better contextualize the idea of electrified social, we can consider social shifts in society attuned to electrical and industrial light. In an opus of science sociology concerned with the industrialization of light, Schivelbusch (1988) observes how previously autonomous household units were integrated into larger systems by gas and then electricity lines, which literally and figuratively lit up larger systems of control. The state put many more social interactions into view. Schivelbusch traces how the state used the visibility electric light afforded to extend its appendages of control into the otherwise dark streets. Years later, these patterns of governmental control were reflected in turn-of-the-century political administration discourse when, for example, US Supreme Court Associate Justice Louis Brandeis penned his oft quoted phrase 'Sunlight is said to be the best of disinfectants; electric light the most efficient policeman' (Brandeis 1913). The context of this claim was within a Harper's article rallying against the growing power of investment banks, but Brandeis opens his essay with the claim that 'Publicity is justly commended as a remedy for social and industrial diseases'. While the industrial disease he speaks to is explicated as hidden financials and excessive commissions, social disease is left undefined – and is apparently running rampant in what people do in the dark.

Moving history forward once again, consider the logic of Brandeis' liberal practices of society for the social, nearly 75 years later. Here, the idea of a social society was transforming into a neoliberalist society – or lack thereof – via Margaret Thatcher scoring political points through their infamous claim that there was no such thing as society. Thatcher was right, insofar as the neoliberal project measured 'society' away bit by bit, dis-integrating community by each measured metric on metric. In Zuboff's (2019) more recent framing, groups and individuals are dis-integrating byte by byte, until all that is left is digitally ascertainable commodity streams, accounted for, traded, compiled and risk-assessed. In the space that used to be amorphous and social, digital (binary) relations between individuals are scaled to the level of big data. This definition of an electrified social bathed in light shows a most efficient form of policing, but in ways past what Schivelbusch or Brandeis imagined. The control of what is lit up – streets, homes or otherwise dark corners – extinguishes potentials outside of those casting the light. The undying light makes visible those actions that are measurable as acceptable (or not!), while the receding dark extinguishes any chance for new experiments in sociality.

To clarify what is at stake, we turn to a definition of policing as distinguished from politics. At risk of oversimplifying Rancière (1999), we introduce the claim that policing is the organization and legitimizing of power, while politics is antagonistic to policing, breaking tangible configurations to test the assumptions of equality in society. Data and the algorithm fulfil legitimizing power and the organizing powers of the networked society as they coalesce into platforms of control. They do so at scales of efficiency that have, as of the time of writing, created a tetrad of trillion-dollar ($US) companies measured by market capitalization: Alphabet, Apple, Amazon, Microsoft, with Facebook close behind at $760 billion. Apple by itself is as of 2021 measured at $2 trillion, or 10% of the yearly GDP of the entire US economy.

These quantifications of economic success are in some ways a symptom of an idea that Chris Anderson (2008) infamously put to *Wired* as 'The end of theory'. His claim was that with enough data, we don't need explanatory stories anymore: 'There is now a better way. Petabytes allow us to say: "Correlation is enough."' (Anderson 2008, np). This type of organizing is enunciated through anticipatory governance of both personal (Helles and Flyverbom 2019) and international concerns (Madsen et al. 2016). The end of theory and anticipatory governance both show the ways that electric digital measurement and computation of what used to be society and individuals indeed polices through constructive power relations that organize. Or as Rancière explains, the police is 'the set of procedures whereby the aggregation and consent of collectivities is achieved, the organization of powers, the distribution of places and roles, and the systems for legitimizing this distribution.' (Rancière 1999, 28). Here, algorithms are creating new forms of visibility that actively organize and legitimize 'positive' sociality as well as discourage 'negative' social actions that ostensibly existed outside of the reaches of electric light. Making subjects and objects visible, knowable, and thus governable through electric light differs from making subjects and objects knowable through narratives or other ways employed prior to the ubiquity of digital networks and nanometre silicon. Managing visibility through datafication produces specific 'techniques of intervention' (Flyverbom 2019, 45) that organize society, and police its limits. This is the policing that enacts what is an electrified social.

Yet legitimization/organizing through electrified policing does not equal justice. Strong scholarship of critical data studies show that electric policing has indeed exasperated inequalities measured in societies (Hoffmann 2019) and across them (Milan and Treré 2019). The considerations of policed-in disparity reflect a call for design justice (Costanza-Chock 2020) to dismantle structural inequality and advance collective liberation through critiquing the aura of truth surrounding computational powers of analysis (Boyd and Crawford 2012).

And it is here where we can more precisely consider Rancière's (1999) politics, as antagonistic to policing, breaking tangible configurations to test the assumptions of equality in society;

> [The] break is manifest in a series of actions that reconfigure the space where things have been defined ... spectacular or otherwise, political expression is always a mode that *undoes the perceivable divisions of the police order*: an open set of practices driven by the assumption of equality between any and every speaking being and by the concern to test this equality. (Rancière 1999, 30, emphasis added)

We argue that in an electrified social, the only way to encounter equality, and proceed to test the ways to undo the perceivable divisions of the police order is in the darkness. Breaking the light is to come alive in the dark.

The social graph

The acuity of our claim to darkness can be measured by how corporate infrastructures such as Facebook use the light in what they described as 'the social' and the 'social graph' specifically. As a general arbitrator of internet history and knowledge, Wikipedia at least suggests the term 'Social Graph' was popularized by Facebook, and via Wikipedia's Neutral Point of View (NPV) vernacular (see Tkacz 2014) offers that 'The social graph has been referred to as "the global mapping of everybody and how they're related"' (Wikipedia 2020). Outside the common NPV 'view', Mark Zuckerberg understood capturing individuals' relational connections in the social graph as something powerful. In 2007 at Facebook's F8 developer conference, Zuckerberg directly correlated Facebook's power – measured through engagement, reach, and capacity to grow and retain users – to the social graph: 'It's the reason Facebook works. It's changing the way the world works,' (Zuckerberg in Farber 2007, np). At the time Facebook had 20 million active users; as of 2021 they claim 2.8 billion.

The plan at the Facebook F8 conference on 24 May 2007 was to federalize the mapping and mining of these relations to 3rd-party developers: 'Today social networks are completely closed nets ... today we are going to end that.' (Zuckerberg in Farber 2007, np). The graph was operationalized for developers in Facebook's Developer Guidelines (Facebook 2021) through the scientific language of Social Network Analysis (SNA): nodes – basically individual objects, such as a User, a Photo, a Page, or a Comment; edges – connections between objects or a collection of objects; fields – data about an object, such as a User's birthday, or a Page's name. The guide goes on to forecast use via policing the organization of this specific platform epistemology/ontology:

> Typically, you use nodes to get data about a specific object, use edges to get collections of objects on a single object, and use fields to get data about a single object or each object in a collection. (Facebook 2021, np)

Here the social becomes discrete visible ties of objects and calculable inferences therein.

Consider four years after F8, Alexis Madrigal, an American journalist, defined dark social as 'means like email and IM [Instant messaging] that are difficult to measure', that were key to sharing information online. He claimed that most referrals to his magazine's (*The Atlantic*) pages were 'dark' anyway, as opposed to trackable via SNS like Facebook. Madrigal went on to point out that 'the social sites that arrived in the 2000s did not create the social web, but they did structure it', continuing, 'In large part, they made sharing on the Internet an act of publishing (!), with all the attendant changes that come with that switch.' (Madrigal 2012, np). Publishing the social managed its visibility in a radical new way, leading to new formations of police and forms of policing at the expense of the dark and its socializing opportunities for testing equity.

In the light of the electrified social, our relations are datafied, and our data is made relational. The act of reading, leveraging, or even contributing to this graph is not a socializing project, it is an observational-surveillant one. It is a product of making efficient both the mapping and enactment of organization, and through allowing others to leverage 'the social graph' to spread information, making efficient the power of the police. Facebook's real-name policy shows an example of the power of policing here. Constructing and enforcing 'authentic' identity online through real names disposes the performativity that might otherwise create actually authentic social interactions in that space (Haimson and Hoffmann 2016). The result is an organization and legitimizing of power for some individuals and some identities, with refutation of others. Visibility is managed in the electric social so to create knowable, governable, and marketable objects and subjects.

Apart from Facebook's governing powers of how things are organized, user-generated activities further police an electrified social. Reading the graphs of others is not socializing. It is instead a practice that always others, delineates and dis-integrates an experiential social community of practice into discrete sets of edges, nodes, and objects. We note that this management is not the study of relationships, but of communicative regimes (Schrock 2015) that regiment – police – the capacity for enacting these relations, and afford their dissection, byte by byte. The numerous experimental results of Facebook use correlating with negative shifts in mental health (see Frost and Rickwood 2017) provides data here – and we are told that the correlation alone is enough! – to show the effects of attempting to define the social in this way. It is anything but. Measuring and laying bare the relationship between humans is not the same as having relationships with humans. While relationships can prosper via Facebook, they occur within the electrified social. This electrified social's effects on capacities to police relations, and discourage politics, are interpreted in psychological terms as Frost and Rickwood's meta-analysis suggests (e.g. addiction, anxiety, depression, body image, alcohol use). The personal terms of relation are met via disinfecting whatever personal and private textures could other-wise be felt in the dark. The summary of an electrified social is being both the vehicle and result of electrified light designed to dis-integrate the social and disinfect what might have been. So, let us turn to the dark.

Dark social spaces

Dark social spaces are the liminal spaces (of land, of time, of code, of imagination) through which emergent socio-technical forms articulate experiments in alternative social futures and hidden presents. Their spaces subvert the electric gaze through their interstitial properties. The exemplars explored in this section highlight the crystalline fragility of policing in electric light, and the assumption of the durability of static, predictable and accountable nature of socio-technical configurations. We begin from the position that the cohesive structures of globally distributed digital communities are enabled through system retention rather than lower order homogeneity and stasis in social relations (Maddox 2016). This paradox of continuity through dynamism is fundamental to the ways digital communities accommodate social change. Following on from this work, we argue digital community needs a dark heart, a space open to generative tensions, in order to achieve continuity through constant transformation. Just as computational sentiment analysis has difficulty identifying irony, it is the generative tensions threading through dark social spaces that defy electrification.

The first attribute of these spaces we identify are the radical shifts between the private nature of the platforms and the publicness of infrastructure found in the Dark Web. The second attribute we encounter builds from a specific application of the Dark Web through cryptomarkets, where the stability of dynamic spaces is maintained by constant transformation. This process illustrates how disrupted spaces articulate continuity through redirection, replication and proliferation. This ungovernable growth of cryptomarkets was coined the hydra effect by media commentators (Ormsby 2013). The first two attributes point to contradictory structural characteristics of dark social spaces that find new ways to test both policing and politics. The remaining three attributes occur at the level of intimate socialities, that show where and how politics has potential outside of the otherwise policed light. VPN technologies exemplify the ways that anonymity creates visible power symmetries, which in turn support the potential of an egalitarian politics. End-to-end encryption (e2e) demonstrates a form of dark connections that in turn illustrates how externally ascribed legitimacy seeks to regulate and control whilst internally ascribed legitimacy seeks to acknowledge and validate. The final exemplar of the dark social this article explores is a consideration of craigslist as trustless infrastructure: here what is social is inverted, hidden and relational, articulating through submerged social networks.

Dark web

The Dark Web has acted as a visceral space combining anonymity and radical transparency within which social experimentation may occur beyond the electrified light. The actor in the Dark Web is technically defined as unseen: anonymity for both publisher and user (Gehl 2018). We build on Gehl here by recognizing Gehl's focus on legitimacy – whether pertaining to violence in society, propriety with regards to resource claims, or notions of authenticity. We argue that the double-blind nature of the Dark Web allows such a search for legitimacy among equals – or what Rancière would call 'politics'. The reconfigurations of sociality here have no purchase to the hierarchies thought to organize the structure of society, they are instead de-structuring and freeing experiences – continual testing of limits.

In the Dark Web context, unregulated drug markets have been developed through privacy and encryption technologies, referred to as cryptomarkets. The communities surrounding cryptomarkets draw together cypherpunks, cyberlibertarians, hackers, online dealers and drug users in what may be referred to as a temporary autonomous zone (TAZ). The TAZ is postmodern anarchistic space, a liberated area (of land, of time, of imagination) that can be thought of as a guerrilla operation which dissolves itself to re-form elsewhere/elsewhen before the state has built the capacity to 'crush it' (Truscello 2003). However, these zones are highly visible rather than hidden and mix platforms with infrastructure. Gehl and McKelvey (2019, 10) argue that darknets are media systems, of which the Dark Web is one, that impose a 'radical making public of our private platforms' and exist in between the platform and the infrastructure. The paradigmatic yet partial inversions of platform and infrastructure, public and private, point to the liminal and unpredictable nature of this space. Consequently, the question becomes, how do people navigate such a partially resolved space? Drawing on and deriving from the work of Smith and Walters (2017) on agential and subversive pathways forged within built environments, here we highlight the role of desire or 'desire lines' to navigate this emergent environment that is constantly rebuilt through code. Desire lines, Smith and Walters (2017) argue, are resistant, complex and contingent navigational practices that are constructed through a logic of efficiency or discovery and in solidarity with other users to take this space beyond its intended use. Through this conceptualization, we can understand the subject can navigate an imposed spatial order through creating unsanctioned lines of use. Consequently, these dark spaces that are both locational and imagined suggest a visible autonomy that is linked to the darkness and escapes from policing. They are careful, deliberate and at times subversive pathways navigated through shifting platforms and infrastructures to redraw relationships of power and articulate politics of resistance. The desire lines of the Dark Web demonstrate that built environments, from physical place to code, are not static but bend and change in response to human agencies and act as the formative pathways through which solidarities and politics occurs.

Focusing on the technology that constitutes this space, Barratt, Aldridge, and Maddox (2018) identify that the Dark Web goes by many names, including the darknet, the hidden web, or the hidden Internet. They outline that websites on the dark or hidden web can only be accessed via anonymity tools such as Tor and I2P. Tor-hidden services, they explain, have URLs ending in .onion, referencing the routing technique that – with multiple layers of encryption resembling an onion – enables anonymous communication over computer networks. This layer of redirection acts to hide the IP (Internet Protocol) addresses of their servers so that their physical location cannot be determined. A persistent URL for a location in the Dark Web occurs, but may disappear overnight. For example, in the cryptomarket environment, marketplaces tend to change their IP address or can themselves disappear overnight through law enforcement activities or an exit scam. Users are then redirected to either the new market .onion URL or migrate to another marketplace (see Maddox 2020 for a further discussion of this). This digital redirection and migration reveals a paradox of dark social spaces, through their continuity from expendable URLs and Marketplaces that proliferate through decentralized replication.

The constant instability and redirection within dark social spaces forms their dynamic foundation and is also the mechanism for their continuity. The paradox of continuity through decentralized redirection is linked to practices of replication and proliferation (Maddox 2020) that are in generative tension with the static categorizations and constrained structures of computational light. When accessing a .onion website for a cryptomarket in the Dark Web that has been taken down, people perceive that the link doesn't work, have an unresolved desire, and ask, where to next? This seeking and demand drives innovation and iteration from what was to what is next. Given that many of the cryptomarkets are based upon open-source software principles or an available template for a P2P e-commerce platform, it is possible for community members to replicate and iterate marketplaces. The ability for people to hack, tinker and replicate the code base of a cryptomarket means that new environments can be constructed that draw on elements from old code and iterate the latest versions based upon security and usability improvements. The politics of doing so, always evolving away from staid police norms, is understood in both metaphorical and literal terms as users attempt to escape the grasp of police action, either normatively or kinetically, that makes the darknet visible.

In the Dark Web, experimentation is not afforded by a single technology but is instead a recombinant of technological affordances and their social appropriation based upon a hacktivist ethic. From (unpublished) fieldwork experience it appears that some hackers consider penetration testing of darknets a community service, with these publicized flaws then becoming visible and addressed in later versions. McKelvey (2015, 736) argues that hacktivism has evolved into a diverse movement to protect an Open Internet against its commodification and securitization. Therefore, we can conceptualize the Dark Web as being constituted through occasionally illegal, but commonly socially licit publishing, sharing and anonymizing practices that utilize decentralizing technologies to circumvent the electrified light.

We have seen these values expressed through other technological formats with The Pirate Bay, a P2P file-sharing platform, enacting the hacker ethic dedicated to sharing, openness and decentralization (McKelvey 2015). In a similar manner to The Pirate Bay, the first widely known cryptomarket, Silk Road, acted as a decentralized platform, harnessing P2P technologies and practices to circumvent the controlled distribution of digital artefacts. In the cryptomarket context, these values and practices have been extrapolated to drugs. The constantly evolving combination of technologies being appropriated for social experimentation in the cryptomarket environment allowed for unregulated replication, code tinkering, and version iteration which Maddox et al. (2016) have previously referred to as constructive activism. Unlike other forms of online activism, commonly defined by connective action (Bennett and Segerberg 2012), constructive activism involves collaborations in code to build a new world in the shell of the old. The activist sentiment here is to disengage with the political system rather than to change it. In this section, we consider how this paradox of collective continuity can be articulated through the 'hydra effect' commonly associated with the cryptomarket space. The term was coined by media commentators (Greenberg 2013; Ormsby 2013) who observed the digital replication and proliferation of new cryptomarkets to fill the vacuum after the closure of Silk Road, with Martin (2014, 64) extrapolating this out as a structural characteristic of the cryptomarket ecosystem. This structural characteristic, that was generated in the dark, further illustrates how collective continuity occurs through decentralized replication and proliferation.

VPNs and end-to-end encryption

There are other examples of being dark and digital outside the web, such as VPNs and end-to-end encryption (e2e). VPNs ostensibly (Heemsbergen and Molnar 2020) provide that same promise of double-blind anonymity for reader, publisher, and here the internet service provider through terms and conditions that make (somewhat fraught expectations of anonymity via) promises to wipe logs, tunnel traffic, and take anonymous payment. VPNs claim to ensure that exploration of what is social, and what might be political, is enacted by equals: you are not a geoblocked citizen of one nation or another. You are not geolocated or tracked by IP so that any hierarchies of who should have or not have data are masked. Instead, VPNs work outside the light of the police and engage in experiences that enable shifts in what was knowable or doable in the light. VPNs make the hierarchies in the web visible, stripping away the policed light of ostensible 'equality' in user-generated content, by enabling equality in access. They also portend the need to snuff out more overt forms of state-based censorship. In this way, VPNs demonstrate how double-blind anonymity creates power symmetries.

E2e differs in that it allows spaces where users know with whom they're communicating, but offers a communal space of socializing that has 'gone dark' from the police in all the tropes we're familiar with. Politicians and police forces tell us terrorists have gone dark, with examples of child pornography always following closely by way of justification for 'backdoors' and other schemes to electrify the social unknown. Yet e2e does not only allow its users to evade legitimized violence, but legitimate their own social configurations with each other outside the shadow the light of structural power produces. This highlights the generative tension of internalized versus externalized legitimacy. The shadow of hierarchy is not formed from some obelisk, but from the spotlight of the police that defines and develops the point of reference for policing; light makes its carrier uniquely visible too. Encrypted group chats shun the hierarchy of those with the light. Within the spaces created, new hierarchies can of course be enacted, or old ones carried out. However, the point is that the space created affords a sociality that is based on equality in who chooses to participate.

Trustless infrastructures

As a final exemplar of dark spaces online, we come to the banal and old-fashioned set of web pages found through craigslist.org. Craigslist has been described by Jessa Lingel (2020) as an optimistic artefact of what the people's internet once was, and still could be. It serves as the last bastion of the internet before the commodification of the social graph in electrified light. In discussion with Lingel around the issue of trust at AOIR 2019, the authors suggested that trust on craigslist had no infrastructure. Craigslist is basically an online classified advertisement service, where both service/product poster and buyer remain largely in the dark about everything other than what they share as part of the ad and reply. Craigslist adverts, and users, don't have much metadata. This did not sit well with the police – interpreted according to Rancière as well as the police forces that viewed craigslist as a cesspool of vice. The moral panic that every possible thing that could happen on craigslist was happening on craigslist was a well mediated trope. Popular media accounts ran 'craigslist killer' stories – including a 320-page 'full account of the shocking crime spree of the infamous Craigslist Killer' by a producer of a TV news programme and a *Boston Globe* journalist.

Yet a more nuanced look at what was at play shows the story of politics and the police. The lack of infrastructure can be read as a lack of electric public: what was social was hidden and relational for those involved. Contrast this with the prodigiously developed infrastructures of trust in Web 2.0 formulations of internet commerce and community. Seller ratings, real-name policies, enforceable terms of service, refunds. Consider the infrastructure of 'trust' from a service like Airbnb, which has a very deep and electrically policed series of fallbacks that stratify the policing of vendors and users; you get a refund regardless of whether your counterpart in the exchange disappears. This is enabled by models and aggregates of risk that allow the firms to write off the individual bad actor via making their aggregates and correlations visible, knowable and thus governable. On offer through Airbnb is not rentals but an electrified social trust seen in other 'social' web services via a specific type of policing dependent on tracking histories of interaction and organizing layers of society. Thinking back to Craigslist, our experiences in the dark are the instances of socializing 'reciprocity' themselves.

These dark social spaces that occur in the Dark Web, or arise through VPNs and e2e technologies and express across trustless infrastructures are where what was once understood as 'social' can thrive and transform. This is not a new argument in many ways. A lack of electric/institutional gaze is needed to explore our individual cares and secrets and slowly integrate them into ourselves and each other. Similarly, 'offline' histories and case studies of perceived social deviance have slowly documented their movement from marginalization and social exclusion to mainstream incorporation (for example, gender and sexuality). The role of the frayed fringes of the 'demimonde' therefore allows us to experiment and fulfil both potential individual identities and communal ones (Maddox et al. 2016), whether that be performed through, for instance, sharing exploration of taking a psychedelic drug in the bath (Gómez Emilsson 2020) or creating safe spaces for diverse and divergent identities. These spaces dark to the police enable a double-blind encounter where politics are sought to be expressed through power symmetries and desire lines.

Conclusion

To see in the dark is to understand not only how technology works to make social connection, interaction, and exchange difficult to intercept, track and trace, but to understand why these unseen spaces function to support emergent socio-technical experimentation. This idea of emergent experimentation allows us to see how the dynamic nature of change, and its discontinuities, is fundamental to the ability for politics to flourish outside of the electrified social.

We have contrasted emergent experimentation to the electric light in which any hopes to test equality are obviated by being known in an electric social that stratifies – as our data is relationalized and our relations are datafied. Facebook's understanding of and commercial 'federationalisation' of the social graph showed a pertinent and evolving example of electrified policing. On the other hand, we offered techniques of social darkness that ranged from e2e, to cryptomarket communities, and the venerable craigslist to show how equals negotiate their equality in darkness. In this article we have argued that it is only in places of darkness, outside the electronic and photonic light, that experimentation and anomaly occur. Out of sight of what is anticipated, what is compiled and definitional on subjects, and traded and accounted for as objects, is the dark social.

Disclosure statement

No potential conflict of interest was reported by the author(s).

ORCID

Alexia Maddox http://orcid.org/0000-0002-5618-5476
Luke Heemsbergen http://orcid.org/0000-0001-8600-5280

References

Allen, J. A. 2019. "The Color of Algorithms: An Analysis and Proposed Research Agenda for Deterring Algorithmic Redlining Artificial Intelligence and Predictive Algorithms: Why Big Data Can Lead to Big Problems." *Fordham Urban Law Journal* 46 (2): 219–270.

Anderson, C. 2008. "The End of Theory: The Data Deluge Makes the Scientific Method Obsolete." *Wired Magazine*, June 23. Accessed September 21, 2021. https://www.wired.com/2008/06/pb-theory/

Barratt, M. J., J. Aldridge, and A. Maddox. 2018. "Dark Web." In *SAGE Encyclopedia of the Internet*, edited by Barney Warf, 185–188. Thousand Oaks: SAGE Publications, .

Benjamin, R. 2019. *Race after Technology: Abolitionist Tools for the New Jim Code*. Medford, MA: Polity.

Bennett, W. L., and A. Segerberg. 2012. "The Logic of Connective Action." *Information, Communication & Society* 15 (5): 739–768. doi:10.1080/1369118x.2012.670661.

Boyd, d., and K. Crawford. 2012. "Critical Questions for Big Data; Provocations for a Cultural, Technological, and Scholarly Phenomenon." *Information, Communication & Society* 15 (5): 662–679. doi:10.1080/1369118x.2012.678878.

Brandeis, L. D. 1913. "What Publicity Can Do." *Harper's Weekly*. December 20, 10-13. New York City, New York: Harper & Brother.

Costanza-Chock, S. 2020. *Design Justice: Community-led Practices to Build the Worlds We Need*. Cambridge, Massachusetts: MIT Press.

Danaher, J., M. J. Hogan, C. Noone, R. Kennedy, A. Behan, A. De Paor, H. Felzmann, et al. 2017. "Algorithmic Governance: Developing a Research Agenda through the Power of Collective Intelligence." *Big Data & Society* 4 (2): 1–21. doi:10.1177/2053951717726554.

Dastin, J. 2018. "Amazon Scraps Secret AI Recruiting Tool that Showed Bias against Women." *Reuters*, October 11. Accessed September 21, 2021. https://www.reuters.com/article/us-amazon-com-jobs-automation-insight-idUSKCN1MK08G

Facebook. 2021. "Graph API." Accessed 30 June 2021. https://developers.facebook.com/docs/graph-api

Farber, D. 2007. "Facebook's Zuckerberg Uncorks the Social Graph." *ZDNet*, May 24. Accessed September 21, 2021. https://www.zdnet.com/article/facebooks-zuckerberg-uncorks-the-social-graph/

Flyverbom, M. 2019. *The Digital Prism: Transparency and Managed Visibilities in a Datafied World*. Cambridge: Cambridge University Press.

Frost, R. L., and D. J. Rickwood. 2017. "A Systematic Review of the Mental Health Uutcomes Associated with Facebook Use." *Computers in Human Behavior* 76: 576–600. doi:10.1016/j.chb.2017.08.001.

Gehl, R., and F. McKelvey. 2019. "Bugging Out: Darknets as Parasites of Large-Scale Media Objects." *Media, Culture & Society* 41 (2): 219–235. doi:10.1177/0163443718818379.

Gehl, R. W. 2018. *Weaving the Dark Web: Legitimacy on Freenet, Tor, and I2P*. Cambridge, MA: MIT Press.

Gómez Emilsson, A. 2020. "5-MeO-DMT Awakenings: From Naïve Realism to Symmetrical Enlightenment." *Qualia Computing: revealing the computational properties of consciousness*. Accessed September 21, 2021. https://qualiacomputing.com/2020/05/19/5-meo-dmt-awakenings-from-naive-realism-to-symmetrical-enlightenment/

Greenberg, A. 2013. "Meet the Dread Pirate Roberts, the Man behind Booming Black Market Drug Website Silk Road." *Forbes*, September 1. Accessed September 21, 2021. https://www.forbes.com/sites/andygreenberg/2013/08/14/meet-the-dread-pirate-roberts-the-man-behind-booming-black-market-drug-website-silk-road

Haimson, O. L., and A. L. Hoffmann. 2016. "Constructing and Enforcing" Authentic" Identity Online: Facebook, Real Names, and Non-normative Identities." *First Monday* 21: 6. doi:10.5210/fm.v21i6.6791.

Heemsbergen, L., and A. Molnar. 2020. "VPNs as Boundary Objects of the internet:(Mis) Trust in the Translation(s)." *Internet Policy Review* 9 (4): 1–19. doi:10.14763/2020.4.1513.

Helles, R., and M. Flyverbom. 2019. "Meshes of Surveillance, Prediction, and Infrastructure: On the Cultural and Commercial Consequences of Digital Platforms." *Surveillance & Society* 17 (1/2): 34–39. doi:10.24908/ss.v17i1/2.13120.

Henman, P. 2020. "Improving Public Services Using Artificial Intelligence: Possibilities, Pitfalls, Governance." *Asia Pacific Journal of Public Administration* 42 (4): 209–221. doi:10.1080/23276665.2020.1816188.

Hoffmann, A. L. 2019. "Where Fairness Fails: Data, Algorithms, and the Limits of Antidiscrimination Discourse." *Information, Communication & Society* 22 (7): 900–915. doi:10.1080/1369118X.2019.1573912.

Lingel, J. 2020. *An Internet for the People: The Politics and Promise of Craigslist*. Princeton: Princeton University Press.

Maddox, A. 2016. *Research Methods and Global Online Communities: A Case Study*. London, UK: Routledge.

Maddox, A. 2020. "Disrupting the Ethnographic Imaginarium: Challenges of Immersion in the Silk Road Cryptomarket Community." *Journal of Digital Social Research* 2 (1): 31–51. doi:10.33621/jdsr.v2i1.23.

Maddox, A., M. J. Barratt, S. Lenton, and M. Allen. 2016. "Constructive Activism in the Dark Web: Cryptomarkets and Illicit Drugs in the Digital 'Semimonde'." *Information Communication and Society* 19 (1): 111–126. doi:10.1080/1369118X.2015.1093531.

Madrigal, A. 2012. "Dark Social: We Have the Whole History of the Web Wrong." *The Atlantic*, October 12. Accessed September 21, 2021. https://www.theatlantic.com/technology/archive/2012/10/dark-social-we-have-the-whole-history-of-the-web-wrong/263523/

Madsen, A. K., M. Flyverbom, M. Hilbert, and E. Ruppert. 2016. "Big Data: Issues for an International Political Sociology of Data Practices." *International Political Sociology* 10 (3): 275–296. doi:10.1093/ips/olw010.

Martin, J. 2014. *Drugs on the Dark Net: How Cryptomarkets are Transforming the Global Trade in Illicit Drugs*. Basingstoke: Palgrave Macmillan.

McKelvey, F. 2015. "We like Copies, Just Don't Let the Others Fool You: The Paradox of the Pirate Bay." *Television & New Media* 16 (8): 734–750. doi:10.1177/1527476414542880.

Milan, S., and E. Treré. 2019. "Big Data from the South(s): Beyond Data Universalism." *Television & New Media* 20 (4): 319–335. doi:10.1177/1527476419837739.

Noble, S. U. 2018. *Algorithms of Oppression: How Search Engines Reinforce Racism*. New York: New York University Press.

Ormsby, E. 2013. "Remember, Remember . . . Silk Road Redux." *All Things Vice*. November 7. Accessed September 21, 2021. https://allthingsvice.com/2013/11/07/remember-remember-silk-road-redux/

Rancière, J. 1999. *Disagreement: Politics and Philosophy*. Minneapolis: University of Minnesota Press.

Sassen, S. 2005. "Digging in the Penumbra of Master Categories." *British Journal of Sociology* 56 (3): 401–403. doi:10.1111/j.1468-4446.2005.00072.x.

Schivelbusch, W. 1988. *Disenchanted Night: The Industrialisation of Light in the Nineteenth Century*. Oxford: Berg Publishers.

Schrock, A. R. 2015. "Communicative Affordances of Mobile Media: Portability, Availability, Locatability, and Multimediality." *International Journal of Communication* 9 (1): 1229–1246. Accessed September 21, 2021. https://ijoc.org/index.php/ijoc/article/view/3288

Smith, N., and P. Walters. 2017. "Desire Lines and Defensive Architecture in Modern Urban Environments." *Urban Studies* 55 (13): 2980–2995. doi:10.1177/0042098017732690.

Tkacz, N. 2014. *Wikipedia and the Politics of Openness*. Chicago: University of Chicago Press.

Truscello, M. 2003. "The Architecture of Information: Open Source Software and Tactical Poststructuralist Anarchism." *Postmodern Culture* 13 (3): 3. doi:10.1353/pmc.2003.0026.

Wikipedia. 2020. "Social Graph." Wikipedia, Accessed 18 November 2020. https://en.wikipedia.org/wiki/Social_graph

Zuboff, S. 2019. *The Age of Surveillance Capitalism: The Fight for a Human Future at the New Frontier of Power*. New York: Public Affairs - Hachette Book Group.

Bad Actors Never Sleep: Content Manipulation on Reddit

Martin Potter

ABSTRACT
The self-proclaimed front page of the internet, Reddit is a many faceted site, described variously as an assemblage of online communities, a social news aggregation website and a social media site. Reddit is one of the most popular sites online both in terms of visitation and interaction. Central to Reddit's popularity is its active community of users who contribute posts, comments and votes to subreddits resulting in a series of constantly changing bulletin boards comprised of over 3 billion submissions annually. Since its inception in 2005, Reddit has generated polarized engagement and responses to this community activity from wildly positive to highly toxic. Recent developments around perceived political manipulation of and on Reddit and accusations of content manipulation and censorship have raised questions of trust in the Reddit platform. Since 2019 Reddit has sought to identify and mitigate bad actor behaviour, address content manipulation and maintain the site's authenticity and the historical context of Reddit's attempts to address each is of central concern to this article. How this history then intersects with contemporary ideas of digital resignation and commons-based models of management informs analysis in the article on moderation practices, opens up new possibilities for future research into concepts of platform literacy and structural (digital) imagination.

Introduction

The self-proclaimed front page of the internet, Reddit, is a many faceted site described variously as an assemblage of online communities (Chandrasekharan et al. 2018, 2), a social news aggregation website (Armstrong 2018) and a social media site (Carman et al. 2018, 185). Reddit is one of the most popular sites online (eighteenth most popular site internationally and the seventh most popular in the USA (Alexa.com 2020)) and has approximately 430 million users (Perez 2019), 50+ million daily users (Sen, Venkat, and Singh 2021), 50 billion monthly views (Redditinc.com 2020a) and almost 2.5 million subreddits as of October 2020, with over 130,000 active subreddits (Frontpagemetrics 2020). Central to Reddit's popularity is its active community of users who contribute posts, comments and votes to subreddits resulting in a series of constantly changing bulletin boards comprized of over 3 billion submissions annually (Redditinc.com 2020b). Since its inception in 2005, Reddit has generated polarized engagement and responses to this community activity from wildly positive to highly toxic.

Recent developments around perceived political manipulation of and on Reddit and accusations of content manipulation and censorship have raised questions of trust in the Reddit platform (Freedom House 2019). Since 2019 Reddit has sought to identify and mitigate bad actor behaviour, address content manipulation and maintain the site's authenticity and the historical context of Reddit's attempts to address is of central concern to this article. This article commences with an exploration of how Reddit communities formed around 'subreddits' have been regulated over time. The article then unpicks a range of contrary testimony, interviews and literature to present a review of key moments in Reddit's censorship positions since its inception. The exploration of subreddit machinations and regulatory practices provides a context for recent disinformation campaigns run through 'toxic' subreddits which (although not part of the dark web *per se*) embody a negative perception of 'dark social' behaviour online. This history creates a context for the emergence of and response to 'bad actor' disinformation campaigns. The key case study is centred on Reddit's management of disinformation during the US election campaign. A key outcome is development of Reddit's annual security report is presented. How this history intersects with contemporary ideas around open source and commons-based models of management inform analysis in the article on moderation practices, platform literacy and structural (digital) imagination. Discussions of platform literacy and structural imagination open up new possibilities for future research.

Sub-Reddits on Reddit: toxic conviviality

The heart of the Reddit community is the provision for users to post content to individual forums called subreddits. Subreddits are created and moderated by Reddit users. Across all subreddits Reddit registered users and 'lurkers' (unregistered viewers of Reddit) can view posts and comments by the community. Registered users can upvote, comment, share, save, hide, report and give awards to posts and comments. Votes determine which posts are visible on the front page of the subreddit and even the front-page of Reddit. A key part of Reddit's model of keeping users on, and returning to, the site is geared towards user discovery of a daily deluge of new content (Massanari 2015, 27). As Carman et al. (2018, 185) highlight 'on Reddit, visibility is all-important.' Even the Reddit home page (subreddit 'r/popular') is constructed on this premise of visibility and is comprised of threads from high-profile posts across subreddits to create a global top list, with registered users seeing top threads from their subscribed subreddits and a filtering mechanism automatically applied to sort by 'Hot' and IP geographic location for logged out or unregistered users (u/simbawulf 2017).

As visibility is the main 'game' on Reddit, it is unsurprising there is manipulation of approval systems by a range of parties touting commercial, political and other positions (Carman et al. 2018, 186; McGregor 2016; Weninger, Johnston, and Glenski 2015; Horne and Adali 2017). Much of this manipulation has sought to exploit the importance of visibility on Reddit through manipulation of user and crowd behaviours via techniques such as vote brigading,[1] astroturfing,[2] shill posting,[3] and karma-whoring[4] and the use of software programmes, known as 'bots' that automatically perform tasks such as commenting, posting and voting to facilitate some of this activity rapidly and at large scale. Such manipulation of information on Reddit is increasingly resembling other, historical modes of disinformation and propaganda. The tendency of the Reddit crowd is shown to seek out news that is more negative, more certain, more emotional, more popular and focussed on the present (Horne and Adali 2017, np). Negative influence campaigns on Reddit represent an evolution in content manipulation but are not something fundamentally new. These campaigns are built on the same tactics as historical manipulations on Reddit such as compromised accounts, vote manipulation, and inauthentic community engagement targeted at key 'toxic' subreddits (u/worstnerd 2019a). Activity on these 'toxic' subreddits focus on spreading hate-speech, misinformation and exploiting or exposing people online, for example, through doxxing or leaking of personal information (Nithyanand, Schaffner and Gill 2017; Farrell et al. 2019). Aspects of this toxicity were, for a time, enabled by Reddit's 'stand for free speech' and refusal to ban 'distasteful subreddits' (Kulwin 2015, np).

When and how to censor: key moments highlighting Reddit's evolving practices and policies

Reddit's shifting positions around how and when to moderate, ban and censor have been an ongoing issue on the platform. Historically, the platform has been held up as a bastion of free speech (Copland and Davis 2020). In reality this has not been the case. In 2011 Begstrom highlighted that 'Reddit itself is struggling with its own community's expectations. Somewhere between anonymous and accountable, Reddit wrestles with itself' (Bergstrom 2011, np). Reddit straddled a contrarian position of purporting to not remove content in their early days, and moderating, banning and editing posts and comments deemed inappropriate 'based on our beliefs.' (Steve Huffman posting as u/spez: Reddit 2020; Ohanian in Hill 2012). Following the departure of co-founders Huffman and Ohanian (u/kn0thing) the 'no removal' position ossified to a position embodied by ex-Reddit CEO Yishan Wong's 2015 comment that 'every man is responsible for his own soul' (in Kulwin 2015). After Wong left Reddit as CEO in November 2014 and was replaced by Ellen Pao, a number of controversies drove further shifts in Reddit's rules and policies. In February 2015 Reddit banned involuntary pornography, in June 2015, five subreddits were banned for co-ordinated off-site harassment (i.e. harassment planned on the Reddit that was to occur in the physical world). These bans resulted in a slew of hate directed at Pao (Kienzle 2016, 30) amplified by the (Ohanian initiated) firing of Reddit's Ask Me Anything co-ordinator Victoria Taylor. Many popular subreddits were disabled by Reddit moderators as part of a collective 'blackout' protesting the firing of Taylor; however, there was little in the way of protest against the abuse of Pao (Matias 2016, 1138–1139). The blackout strategy was a powerful act of resistance by the volunteer moderators an indicates the space for resistance (even if this might be framed as negative resistance) for members of the Reddit community and was a key moment in forcing Pao's resignation.

Following Pao's resignation Huffman, Ohanian and Chris Slowe (u/KeyserSosa), the company's first employee, rejoined Reddit. Huffman subsequently reinforced that Reddit was not created to be 'a bastion of free speech' and had no obligation to communities whose purpose was 'reprehensible' (u/spez 2015). Ex-CEO Yishan Wong (u/yishan) commented on this post, noting Huffman had reinforced to Wong that censorship was always a part of Reddit, despite their early posturing of a no-censorship zone. Significantly, Wong claimed the hateful attacks on Ellen Pao by Reddit members gave the new management 'moral authority' to purge problematic subreddits and users, as well as enabling the founders to regain financial control of the company (u/yishan 2015a, 2015b). This purge and control were quickly actioned. The following year Huffman gestured towards increased commercial intent and the unique value of Reddit user data:

> We know all of your interests. Not only just your interests you are willing to declare publicly on Facebook – we know your dark secrets, we know everything …
>
> TNW Conference (2016) [14m20 – 14m32].

This comment, alongside increased moderation, the move from open-source code to a closed model (u/KeyserSosa: Reddit 2017), substantial and contentious investment from Chinese technology company Tencent (Freedom House 2019; Constine 2019; Liao 2019), and a suspected campaign of leaking and vote manipulation from Russia (u/worstnerd 2019b) triggered numerous critical articles of the platform (Hautala 2017; Breland 2018; Marsh 2019). In 2019 and 2020 Reddit sought to further mitigate content manipulation on the platform which further amplified critiques that Reddit was bowing to a range of advertiser and political pressure to clean up the site. Reddit's approach to mitigating content manipulation was re-imagined in the run-up to 2020 elections in the light of 'bad actor' disinformation campaigns run during the 2016 US election. The following section of this article explores how and why this re-imagining happened, synthesizing a range of data, reportage and analysis including analysis of the first Reddit security reports of 2019 and 2020.

Bad actors never sleep

The term, 'bad actor' can suggest an individual that is easily identifiable by their offensive or antisocial behaviour – perhaps as suggested by the growing focus on online harassment. It can refer to disinformation actors, trolls, bots, and everything in between. Bad actors do not necessarily engage in vulgarity or abuse, but rather purposeful, targeted, and systematic manipulation. A definition of bad actors has to consider not just behaviours, but intent. (Stewart, Arif, and Starbird 2018)

Disinformation on social media is a normative and practical problem for electoral democracies. Disinformation is no longer about completely false news, but rather a constant drip, drip, drip of 'misleading content designed to deepen divisions in society' (Newman 2019, 13). Boyd (2018) details a journey of the development, co-ordination, and socializing of misleading content through dark websites like 4chan and Discord, then to closed or semi-closed networks such as WhatsApp groups, and then on to communities of interest (Reddit forums, YouTube channels). From this point, the misleading content is then seeded in a co-ordinated way on public social networks like Facebook, Twitter and Instagram before being spread widely and sometimes picked up by broadcast media. Boyd warns that the media are being 'played' and need to be more aware of the role they play in giving credence to unfounded claims. Russian interference in the 2016 U.S. presidential election often used this model of development, co-ordination, socializing and seeding misleading content. Russian interference centred on a disinformation campaign drive by thousands of Twitter, Facebook, and Reddit accounts pretending to be ordinary U.S. citizens. Such coordinated and sustained disinformation campaigns in which participants pretend to be ordinary citizens acting independently, can influence electoral outcomes and other forms of political behaviour (Keller et al. 2020). For example, Reddit was highlighted as a key site for disinformation in the 2016 US election (Nithyanand, Schaffner, and Gill 2017; Breland 2017; Hautala 2017). In the leadup to the 2016 US elections political subreddits on Reddit saw a massive leap in links to sites categorized as 'controversial sources' (Nithyanand, Schaffner, and Gill 2017, 9). Visitors to Republican-affiliated subreddits were 600% more likely to see links to controversial sources after the start of the Republican primaries, and 1,600% more likely after the Republican National Convention in July 2016, than they were before the campaigns started (Nithyanand, Schaffner, and Gill 2017, 11).

There was a strong correlation between Donald Trump's rise in popularity and increasing incivility observed in Republican or Trump supporting subreddits such as r/The_Donald and a substantial increase in volume of posts on Republican subreddits as opposed to Democratic party subreddits. Between December 2015 and Election Day on 8 November 2016 there was a 200% increase of Democratic party affiliated posts and 6,600% on Republican subreddits (Nithyanand, Schaffner, and Gill 2017, 14). Nithyanand et. al. (2017, 11) also note political discussion on Reddit became substantially more offensive following the launch of the campaign for US president in July 2016, with Republicans exhibiting more extremity than Democrats. An additional factor, according to both Breland (2017), is the use of Reddit to test and socialize disinformation campaigns. Due to a range of affordances of Reddit such as open access to content, subreddit structure allowing for targeted access to specific communities, decentralized, volunteer moderation and the (comparatively) relaxed rules around information Reddit was seen as an excellent testing ground for disinformation campaigns. The scale of Reddit as a staging platform is highlighted by the scope of analysis undertaken by Nithyanand et al. on every comment and post made in a set of political subreddits during this period; some 130 million comments in 3 million posts, contrasted with a random (10%) sample of non-political comments made during the same period. This is a total of 332 million comments across 12 million posts (Nithyanand, Schaffner, and Gill 2017, 3). An additional benefit was that Reddit was outside of disinformation investigations into other large-scale social media companies such as Facebook and Twitter following the 2016 US elections (Breland 2017).

In June 2019, the Atlantic Council's Digital Forensic Research Lab (DFRLabs 2019) identified a disinformation operation that ran across many platforms, including Reddit, across languages and subjects, consistently using the same approach and concealment techniques including fake accounts, forged documents and a multi-platform approach. DFRLabs claim the scale and complexity of the operation indicate that it was conducted by a 'persistent, sophisticated, and well-resourced actor, possibly an intelligence operation.' Reddit's u/worstnerd (2019a) reflected on this attack and Reddit's response noting that over 900% more policy violating content in the first half of 2019 was removed than the same period in 2018, and 99% of that was before it was reported by users. In outlining how Reddit planned to deal with future attacks, especially in the lead up to the 2020 US elections, u/worstnerd notes:

> Bad actors never sleep, and we are always evolving how we identify and mitigate them. But with the upcoming election, we know you want to see more. So we're committing to a quarterly report on content manipulation and account security, with the first to be shared in October 2019.

This first Reddit security report highlights between April – September 2019 over 10 million content manipulation reports in 6 months, over 30 million administration content manipulation removals, over 4 million account sanctions for content manipulation, 6 million third-party breaches and 9 million account security actions (u/KeyserSosa 2019). The following Reddit security report of October 2020 shows over 13 million reports for content manipulation, 67 million administration removals for content manipulation, 19 million account sanctions, 2 million third-party breaches and 4 million account security actions. This security report notes that planning for the 2020 election – with a focus on detection and mitigation strategies – was ongoing since the 2016 Russian influence campaign was brought to light (u/worstnerd 2020b).

In the 2 months following the rollout of new policies on 29 June 2020, Reddit banned nearly 7,000 subreddits (including ban evading subreddits) that had been viewed by approximately 365,000 users each day (u/worstnerd 2020a). The barring of thousands of toxic subreddits, including the pro-Trump r/The_Donald which had over 800,000 subscribers, was described as a major shift in Reddit governance (Copland 2020 ; Copland and Davis 2020; u/worstnerd 2020b). This mass subreddit removal, the largest in Reddit history, came in response to an open letter signed by hundreds of Reddit moderators to Reddit CEO Steve Huffman and Reddit's board demanding changes to the site's policies (Roose 2020). The letter called on Reddit to enact a sitewide policy against racism, slurs and hate speech and to be pro-active in banning users and communities fostering hate (u/DubTeeDub 2020). These bans resulted in a reported 18% reduction in Reddit users posting hateful content, compared to the 2 weeks prior to the ban. Following this mass subreddit removal Reddit revized their content policy with a series of rules. Rule 1 foregrounds 'the human'

Rule 1 states

Remember the human. Reddit is a place for creating community and belonging, not for attacking marginalized or vulnerable groups of people. Everyone has a right to use Reddit free of harassment, bullying, and threats of violence. Communities and users that incite violence or that promote hate based on identity or vulnerability will be banned.

(Reddit's Content Policy and revised rules of October 2020. u/worstnerd 2020a)

Remember the human: digital imagination and platform literacy

The revision of rules and the mass removal of hateful subreddits, along with increased value placed by Reddit of 'community and belonging' and historical opportunities by Reddit's community to drive change offers an opportunity how, within the current structure of the site this change might be re-imagined. With a recent valuation of US $6 billion (Sen, Venkat, and Singh 2021) it is disingenuous to represent Reddit as a commons or some kind of idealized 'social movement'; however, there is a perception by Reddit users that the site sits outside of other digital social monoliths such as Twitter and Facebook (van der Nagel and Frith 2015). This outlier status allows for a different dialogue with and within its community of users. In addition, the greater self-regulation of the site by the Reddit community allows for reflections on how these elements of autopoiesis might be enhanced.

Regulation of user behaviour on Reddit is, as noted by Chandrasekharan et al. (2018, 2), governed by a multi-layered architecture including site-wide content and anti-harassment policies that all subreddits are expected to follow. Posts and comments are moderated by volunteer Redditors who work to enforce Reddit content policies and rules as well as subreddit-specific rules and guidelines. Violating these rules and guidelines can result in a ban of user accounts or even entire subreddits. As Chandrasekharan et al. (2018, 2) note 'rules and norms are loosely coupled on Reddit, with subreddit moderators sometimes turning (often implicit) norms that are enforced behind-the-scenes into rules that face the community.' Drawing on Elinor Ostrom's distinction between rules and norms as articulated in the book *Governing the Commons* (1990), Chandrasekharan et al. (2018, 2) note that 'while rules tend to be explicit, norms are emergent, arise from interaction over time, and respond to current demands on a community.' In the context of collective action, when people organize to enforce their own rules, these rules are more successful than those externally imposed upon them. Costanza-Chock (2019, np) argues it is not technology but people – in communities, in societies – that define and drive change:

> Technology isn't the driver of social movements, it's the other way around. Social movements can drive our development of new communication, organization and mobilization technology.

To caveat this idealism, Sconce points out that accepting the power of the new technologies to 'engineer' new subjectivities and realities implicitly dismisses the social and political mechanisms 'originally posited as producing subjectivity in the first place' (in Turner 2010, 124). Ossewaarde and Reijers (2017) argue that digital commons produce an 'illusion of the commons' giving rise to cynicism and compounding a resignation based in a perception that there are no alternatives. Turner (2010, 125) suggests that a lack of historical imagination, ironically, undermines many of the claims of an historic break, rupture or discontinuity between new media and their predecessors. These arguments bring to mind prior observations by Roberto Unger on 9 January 2014 (in Edmonds and Warburton 2014) who asserted in relation to creating social transformations of institutions and beliefs that:

> The vital element is structural imagination – imagination of how structural change takes place in history and of how we can understand the prevalence of the existing arrangements without vindicating their necessity or their authority.

Unger's point above echoes Turner's concerns that a lack of historical understanding will simply result in creating a false necessity or authority (or the 'false consciousness' of Ossewaarde and Reijers 2017) over what could be an opportunity for re-imagination. The concept of structural imagination can be applied to the mediascape of Reddit – which is re-framed here as 'digital imagination' (Appadurai 1996). Digital imagination shifts attention from individual activities towards practices of collective identification and action and seeks to redress an experience of 'digital resignation' (Draper and Turow 2017, 65). Lovink and Rossiter (2015) argue that one of the defining features of the post-digital era is the normalizing of data infrastructures so that they appear beyond question. Commentators who have theorized a 'post-digital condition' suggest that digital technology has moved on from being a noticeably disruptive force in everyday life, to becoming an unremarkable presence. It is now simply an environment in which we exist (Steyerl 2013, 6). Situated within this environment, Draper and Turow (2017, 65) describe a notion of 'digital resignation',

> By digital resignation we mean the condition created when people desire to control the information and data digital entities such as online marketers have about them, but feel unable to exercise that control.

Overwhelmed by scale, distanced from the humans who have created and control the environment, people feel unable to act, and see no 'possibility of circumvention or resistance' in relation to negotiating how they engage with data infrastructures (Hintz, Dencik, and Wahl-Jorgensen 2019, 117). Digital resignation also emerges from the knowledge that we are being data-mined and manipulated, but there is an unknowability about who is doing the manipulation, how they are doing it and what the effects might be. Carrigan (2018) contends that 'platform literacy' provides a concrete understanding of specific processes and their implications for our agency. Platform literacy is a capacity to understand how platforms such as Reddit shape the action which takes place through them, sometimes in observable and explicit ways but usually in unobservable and implicit ones. It concerns our own (inter)actions and how this context facilitates or frustrates them, as well as the unseen ways in which it subtly moulds them and the responses of others to them. Understanding how community-driven platforms such as Reddit promote user agency is a crucial step in enabling digital imagination. It is through the historical synthesis of Reddit's approach to moderation, shifting rules and regulations in relation to security, and addressing misinformation that this article seeks to make a contribution to this area. Through highlighting a specific example, this opens up new opportunities for future study on how the mediascape (Appadurai 1996) of Reddit has been shaped.

Discussion and conclusion: evidence of platform literacy and digital imagination on Reddit

In the 2020 security report, transparency of Reddit's rule formation and ban process is foregrounded, as is the value of the moderators in reducing exposure to bad actors and their content. Increased auto-moderation and automatic detection are highlighted as important and echo the findings of Jhaver, Bruckman, and Gilbert (2019) that expand explanations for why content removal is worthwhile. While the revision of Reddit's rules and content policy focussed directly on stopping hate showed some efficacy, they do not address many key issues of disinformation campaigns. A Reddit blackout in 2021 protested Reddit employment decisions as well as perceived excessive bannings, automatic and manual deletions and edits of posts and comments. This action showed the capacity of Reddit's users and (volunteer) moderators to resist (paid) Reddit administrator moderation and admin protections.

Sanctions against unverified or compromised accounts are currently an important part of the revised regulation of user behaviour. Increasing moderation, and therefore reach, of bad actors is important and proposed changes by Reddit to auto-moderation (u/worstnerd 2020a) may begin to more effectively target this. Moderator teams use custom bots and custom moderation tools to manage this complex work, creating successor systems that augment reddit's core capabilities through the reddit. Auto-moderation of re-posts and potentially hateful comments along with additional prompts or steps prior to posting allows users time to re-consider as well as placing barriers for bot-posters (until of course smarter bots are built). Increased security for account registration (whether for anonymous or pseudonymous accounts) and even small-time delays between registration and posting and commenting privileges might further diminish bad actor accounts.

However, as long as popularity is incentivized as the primary metric of Reddit visibility the platform will continue to face issues. Importantly, incentivizing new measures of 'popularity' such as rigour, provenance and other metrics around quality of information might further support a shift towards thoughtful posting and focus on quality over quantity. Other social platforms have explored demetrication, such as Instagram hiding the number of likes and recently allowing users to hide likes on their own and others posts (from May 2021), however, rewarding behaviours around well-provenanced information and original content might also prove to effective. As Reddit's revision of moderation practices continues it is important to find ways to archive traces of bad actor behaviour in order to support increased platform literacy by users so that they see and learn these patterns. Community moderators continue to highlight bad actor campaigns (u/LargeSnorlax 2019) and to call for accountability of the Reddit community and the platform as a whole (u/DubTeeDub 2020). Moderators, in this case, embody a critical literacy of Reddit as a platform. Mod-driven critiques are crucial in ensuring that Reddit is seen as a site of shared exploration. By making the invisible visible, by reflecting on new measures and models of incentivization, by increasing transparency, and by fostering a critical reflexivity of Reddit as a platform, this supports enhanced environmental literacy of Reddit by its users and address 'digital resignation' encouraging, instead, digital imagination. No longer is this about digital resignation, drowning within layers of a monolithic platform, it is part of a process of re-organizing space and taking a succession of steps towards a vision of cumulative transformation.

Notes

1. Vote brigading is massively coordinated online voting, often undertaken by bots.
2. Astroturfing refers to creating fake grassroots support. Astroturfing is when an entity – for example a corporation or political party, posts on an online platform pretending to be ordinary, unaffiliated individuals with an opinion about a product, service or even political position. Astroturfing is not limited to advertisers.
3. Shill posting is engaging in covert advertising by posting, commenting or endorsing brands under the guise of personal endorsement (when in fact the user is being paid to post).
4. Karma whoring is when a user posts with the intent to gain Reddit karma, a point system that shows up on a user's Reddit account and increases every time the user receives an upvote. Karmawhores often steal and re-post ideas/ stories/ images (etc) to other subreddits; Or when a user only replies to the top comments in a popular post simply to be seen and upvoted by the majority.

Disclosure statement

No potential conflict of interest was reported by the author(s).

ORCID

Martin Potter http://orcid.org/0000-0002-1681-6341

References

Alexa.com. 2020. "The Top 500 Sites on the Web." *Alexa.com*. Accessed 2021 March 31. https://www.alexa.com/topsites

Appadurai, A. 1996. *Modernity at Large: Cultural Dimensions of Globalization*. Minneapolis: University of Minnesota Press.

Armstrong, B. 2018. "Coordination in a Peer Production Platform: A study of Reddit's /r/Place experiment". Unpublished thesis, University of Waterloo, Waterloo, Ontario, Canada, 2018. https://uwspace.uwaterloo.ca/bitstream/handle/10012/14060/Armstrong_Ben.pdf

Bergstrom, K. 2011. "Don't Feed the Troll": Shutting down Debate about Community Expectations on Reddit.com." *First Monday* 16 (8–1, August). http://firstmonday.org/ojs/index.php/fm/article/view/3498/3029

Boyd, d. 2018. "Media Manipulation, Strategic Amplification, and Responsible Journalism." Data Society: Points, September. Accessed 2021 March 31. https://points.datasociety.net/media-manipulation-strategic-amplification-and-responsible-journalism-95f4d611f462

Breland, A. 2017. Warner sees Reddit as potential target for Russian influence. *The Hill*, 27th September, 2017. https://thehill.com/policy/technology/352584-warner-sees-reddit-as-potential-target-for-russian-influence

Breland, A. 2018. "How Fascist Sympathizers Hijacked Reddit's Libertarian Hangout. Mother Jones : Users Worry the New Moderators' Unprecedented Restrictions Could Boost the Far Right." Mother Jones, Politics, December 20, 2018. Accessed 2021 March 20. https://www.motherjones.com/politics/2018/12/reddit-libertarian-takeover-far-right/

Carman, M., M. Koerber, J. Li, K.R. Choo, and H Ashman. 2018 "Manipulating Visibility of Political and Apolitical Threads on Reddit via Score Boosting." 2018 17th IEEE International Conference On Trust, Security And Privacy In Computing And Communications/ 12th IEEE International Conference On Big Data Science And Engineering (TrustCom/BigDataSE), 184–190, New York, NY, 2018. doi:10.1109/TrustCom/BigDataSE.2018.00037.

Carrigan, M. 2018. "What Is Platform Literacy?" May 13. Accessed 2021 March 18. https://markcarrigan.net/2018/05/13/what-is-platform-literacy/

Chandrasekharan, E., M. Samory, S. Jhaver, H. Charvat, A. Bruckman, C. Lampe, J. Eisenstein, and E. Gilbert. 2018. "The Internet's Hidden Rules: An Empirical Study of Reddit Norm Violations at Micro, Meso, and Macro Scales.„ *Proc. ACM Hum.-Comput. Interact. 2*, CSCW, Article 32 (November 2018): 25. https://doi.org/10.1145/3274301

Constine, J. 2019. "Reddit Confirms $300M Series D Led by China's Tencent at $3B Value in Techcrunch." February 12, 2019. Accessed 2021 March 20. https://techcrunch.com/2019/02/11/reddit-300-million/

Copland, S., and J Davis. 2020. "Reddit Removes Millions of pro-Trump Posts. But Advertisers, Not Values, Rule the Day." *The Conversation*, [Online], July 2, 2020. Accessed 2021 March 20. https://theconversation.com/reddit-removes-millions-of-pro-trump-posts-but-advertisers-not-values-rule-the-day-141703

Costanza-Chock, S. 2019. "'Technology Isn't the Driver of Social Movements, It's the Other Way Around' Interview with Anna Bonet Martínez and Bart Grugeon Plana on 17/ 12/2019, for Internet Interdisciplinary Institute Universitat Obertade Catalunya." Accessed 2020 November 12. uoc.edu/portal/en/news/entrevistes/2019/051-sasha-costanza.html

DFRLabs. 2019. "Top Takes: Suspected Russian Intelligence Operation." Medium, June 23, 2019. Accessed 2021 March 20. https://medium.com/dfrlab/top-takes-suspected-russian-intelligence-operation-39212367d2f0Digital Forensic Research Lab. Ben Nimmo; E. Buziashvili, E.; Sheldon, M.; Karan, K.; Aleksejeva, N.; Bandeira, L.; Andriukaitis, L.; Hibrawi, R.

Draper, N., and J Turow. 2017. "Toward a Sociology of Digital Resignation." Paper presented at the Data Power conference, Ottawa, Canada.

Edmonds, D., and N Warburton. 2014. "Roberto Mangabeira Unger on What Is Wrong with the Social Sciences Today." *Social Science Space*, January 9 2014. Accessed 2020 November 12. http://www.socialsciencespace.com/2014/01/roberto-mangabeira-unger-what-is-wrong-with-the-social-sciences-today/

Farrell, T, M Fernandez, J. Novotny, and A Harith. 2019. "Exploring Misogyny across the Manosphere in Reddit." WebSci '19 Proceedings of the 10th ACM Conference on Web Science, 87–96. Accessed 2021 March 31. doi:10.1145/3292522.3326045.

Freedom House. 2019. "China Media Bulletin: Tencent Complicity, Surveillance Upgrades, Reddit Manipulation (No. 134)." March 26 2019. Accessed 2020 November 12. https://freedomhouse.org/report/china-media-bulletin/china-media-bulletin-tencent-complicity-surveillance-upgrades-reddit

Frontpagemetrics. 2020. "Frontpagemetrics History." [Online]. Accessed 2021 March 31. https://frontpagemetrics.com/history

Hautala, L. 2017. "Reddit Was a Misinformation Hotspot in 2016 Election, Study Says." *CNET News*, December, 19, 2017. 7:34 a.m. PT. Accessed 2021 March 20. https://www.cnet.com/news/reddit-election-misinformation-2016-research/

Hill, K. 2012. "Reddit Co-Founder Alexis Ohanian's Rosy Outlook on the Future of Politics." *Forbes Magazine* [Online], February 2 2012. Accessed 2021 March 31. https://www.forbes.com/sites/kashmirhill/2012/02/02/reddit-co-founder-alexis-ohanians-rosy-outlook-on-the-future-of-politics/#18142d5e5550

Hintz, A., L. Dencik, and K. Wahl-Jorgensen. 2019. *Digital Citizenship in a Datafied Society*. Cambridge, UK: Polity Press.

Horne, B., and S Adali. 2017. "The Impact of Crowds on News Engagement: A Reddit Case Study." *ArXiv Abs/1703.10570*. Accessed 2021 March 20.

Huffman, S., [u/spez]. 2020. "Upcoming Changes to Our Content Policy, Our Board, and Where We're Going from Here." *Reddit Post to r/announcements*, June 6, 2020. Accessed 2021 February 23. https://www.reddit.com/r/announcements/comments/gxas21/upcoming_changes_to_our_content_policy_our_board/

Jhaver, S., A. Bruckman, and E Gilbert. 2019. "Does Transparency in Moderation Really Matter?: User Behavior after Content Removal Explanations on Reddit." *Proceedings of the ACM on Human-Computer Interaction* 3: 27. *CSCW, Article 150 (November 2019)*. Accessed 2021 February 22. 10.1145/3359252

Keller, F., D. Schoch, S. Stier, and J.H. Yang. 2020. "Political Astroturfing on Twitter: How to Coordinate a Disinformation Campaign." *Political Communication* 37 (2): 256–280. doi:10.1080/10584609.2019.1661888.

Kienzle, J. 2016. "The Technological Factors of Reddit: Communication and Identity on Relational Networks." Communication Studies Theses, Dissertations, and Student Research. 38. Accessed 2021 February 22. http://digitalcommons.unl.edu/commstuddiss/38

Kulwin, N. 2015. 'New CEO: Some People on Reddit 'Shouldn't Be Here at All'." *Vox*, July 14, 2015. Accessed 2021 March 12. https://www.vox.com/2015/7/14/11614712/new-ceo-some-people-on-reddit-shouldnt-be-here-at-all

Liao, S. 2019. "Reddit Gets a $150 Million Investment from Tencent and Users are Posting Memes to Mock the Deal." *The Verge*, February 11, 2019. Accessed 2021 February 21. https://www.theverge.com/2019/2/11/18216134/reddit-tencent-investment-deal-memes-amount-winnie-the-pooh-tank-man-china

Lovink, G., and N. Rossiter. 2015. "Network Cultures and the Architecture of Decision." In *Critical Perspectives on Social Media and Protest: Between Control and Emancipation*, edited by L. Dencik and O. Leistert, 219–232. London: Rowman & Littlefield.

Marsh, P. 2019. "Reddit Users Revolt after Reports of Chinese Tech Giant Tencent's Possible Investment." *Australian Broadcasting Corporation News*, February 11 2019, Accessed 12 February 2019. https://www.abc.net.au/news/2019-02-11/reddit-users-revolt-on-news-of-chinese-investment/10798584

Massanari, A. 2015. "#gamergate and the Fappening: How Reddit's Algorithm, Governance, and Culture Support Toxic Technocultures." *New Media & Society* 1461444815608807. doi:10.1177/1461444815608807.

Matias, J. 2016. "Going Dark: Social Factors in Collective Action against Platform Operators in the Reddit Blackout." *CHI '16: Proceedings of the 2016 CHI Conference on Human Factors in Computing Systems May 2016*, 1138–1151. https://doi.org/10.1145/2858036.2858391

McGregor, J. 2016. Reddit for sale: how we made viral fake news for $200. *Forbes Magazine* [Online] December 14th, 2016. https://www.forbes.com/sites/jaymcgregor/2016/12/14/how-we-bought-reddit-for-200/#2c41ed6e44a8

Newman, N. 2019. "Journalism, Media, And Technology Trends And Predictions Digital News Project January 2019." Reuters Institute for the Study of Journalism with the support of the Google Digital News Initiative.

Nithyanand, R., B. Schaffner, and P. Gill. 2017. "Online Political Discourse in the Trump Era." *ArXiv Abs/1711.05303*.

Ossewaarde, M., and W. Reijers. 2017. "The Illusion of the Digital Commons: 'False Consciousness' in Online Alternative Economies." *Organization* 24 (5): 609–628. doi:10.1177/1350508417713217.

Ostrom, E. 1990. *Governing the Commons*. Cambridge: Cambridge university press.

Perez, S. 2019. "Reddit's Monthly Active User Base Grew 30% to Reach 430M in 2019 in Techcrunch." December 5, 2019. Accessed 2021 February 21. https://techcrunch.com/2019/12/04/reddits-monthly-active-user-base-grew-30-to-reach-430m-in-2019/

Redditinc.com. 2020a. redditinc.com home page. Accessed 2021 February 21. https://www.redditinc.com/

Redditinc.com. 2020b. *Transparency Report 2020*. Accessed 2021 February 21. https://www.redditinc.com/policies/transparency-report-2020

Roose, K. 2020. "Reddit's C.E.O. On Why He Banned 'The_donald' Subreddit." *New York Times*, June 30, 2020. Accessed 2021 March 12. https://www.nytimes.com/2020/06/30/us/politics/reddit-bans-steve-huffman.html

Sen, A., R. Venkat, and K Singh. 2021. "Ads, GameStop Raise Reddit Price Tag to $6 Billion in Latest Fundraising." *Reuters*, February 9, 2021. Accessed 2021 March 20. https://www.reuters.com/article/us-reddit-funding-idUSKBN2A9056

Slowe, C., [u/KeyserSosa]. 2017. "An Update on the State of the Reddit/reddit and Reddit/reddit--mobile Repositories." *Reddit*, September 2, 2017. Accessed 2021 February 21. https://www.reddit.com/r/changelog/comments/6xfyfg/an_update_on_the_state_of_the_redditreddit_and/

Stewart, L. G., A. Arif, and K Starbird. 2018. "When Bad Actors Adhere to Group Norms." Workshop paper, CHI'18 Workshop: Understanding Bad Actors. Accessed 2021 February 21.

Steyerl, H. 2013. "Too Much World: Is the Internet Dead?" *e-flux* 49 (November).

TNW Conference. 2016. "Steve Huffman (Reddit) | TNW Conference | Inside the Biggest Online Community." Video published on Youtube, May 28, 2016. Accessed 2021 February 21. https://www.youtube.com/watch?v=uSVqoW1rz6w

Turner, G. 2010. *Ordinary People and the Media the Demotic Turn*. London: Sage publishing.

u/DubTeeDub. 2020. "Open Letter to Steve Huffman and the Board of Directors of Reddit, Inc– If You Believe in Standing up to Hate and Supporting Black Lives, You Need to Act." *Reddit r/AgainstHateSubreddits*, June 9, 2020. Accessed 2021 February 22. https://www.reddit.com/r/AgainstHateSubreddits/comments/gyyqem/open_letter_to_steve_huffman_and_the_board_of/

u/KeyserSosa. 2019. "Reddit Security Report." *Reddit, r/redditsecurity*, October 30, 2019. Accessed 2021 February 22. https://www.reddit.com/r/announcements/comments/dpa8rn/reddit_security_report_october_30_2019/

u/LargeSnorlax. 2019. "User Account Ring - Astroturfing and Multiple Accounts Pushing Narrative on Multiple Subreddits." *Reddit, r/ModSupport* July 3, 2019. Accessed 2021 February 22. https://www.reddit.com/r/ModSupport/comments/c8f6s1/user_account_ring_astroturfing_and_multiple/

u/simbawulf. 2017. *Introducing r/popular on Reddt.com r/ announcements*, February 17, 2017. Accessed 2021 February 22. https://www.reddit.com/r/announcements/comments/5u9pl5/introducing_rpopular/

u/spez. 2015. "Content Policy Update." *AMA Thursday, July 16th, 1pm pst. Reddit, r/ announcements*, June 16, 2105. Accessed 2021 February 23. https://www.reddit.com/r/announcements/comments/3dautm/content_policy_update_ama_thursday_july_16th_1pm/

u/worstnerd. 2019a. "An Update on Content Manipulation… and an Upcoming Report." *Reddit, r/security*, September 20, 2019. Accessed 2021 February 21. https://www.reddit.com/r/redditsecurity/comments/d6l41l/an_update_on_content_manipulation_and_an_upcoming/

u/worstnerd. 2019b. "Suspected Campaign from Russia on Reddit." *Reddit, r/ redditsecurity*, December 7, 2019. Accessed 2021 February 21. https://www.reddit.com/r/redditsecurity/comments/e74nml/suspected_campaign_from_russia_on_reddit/

u/worstnerd. 2020a. "Understanding Hate on Reddit, and the Impact of Our New Policy." *Reddit, r/security*, August 21, 2020. Accessed 2020 March 21. https://www.reddit.com/r/redditsecurity/comments/idclo1/understanding_hate_on_reddit_and_the_impact_of/

u/worstnerd. 2020b. "Reddit Security Report." Reddit, r/security, October 8, 2020. Accessed 2021 February 22. https://www.reddit.com/r/redditsecurity/comments/j7m28f/reddit_security_report_oct_8_2020/

u/yishan. 2015a. "Content Policy Update." *AMA Thursday*, July 16, 2015. Reddit, r/ announcements, June 16th, 2015. Accessed 2021 February 20 https://www.reddit.com/r/announcements/comments/3dautm/content_policy_update_ama_thursday_july_16th_1pm/ct3n7hc/

u/yishan. 2015b. "What's the Best "Long Con" You Ever Pulled?" *Reddit, r/AskReddit*, July 11, 2015. Accessed 2021 February 22. https://www.reddit.com/r/AskReddit/comments/3cs78i/whats_the_best_long_con_you_ever_pulled/cszjqg2/

van der Nagel, E., and J Frith. 2015. "Anonymity, Pseudonymity, and the Agency of Online Identity: Examining the Social Practices of r/Gonewild." *First Monday* 20 (3–2 March). doi:10.5210/fm.v20i3.5615.

Weninger, T., T.J. Johnston, and M Glenski. 2015. "Random Voting Effects in Social-digital Spaces: A Case Study of Reddit Post Submissions." *Proceedings of the 26th ACM Conference on Hypertext & Social Media*, HT, Guzelyurt, TRNC, Cyprus, September 1-4, 2015, 293–297.

Dark, Clear or Brackish? Using Reddit to Break Down the Binary of the Dark and Clear Web

Simon Copland

ABSTRACT
Using Reddit as a case study, this article blurs the boundary between the 'dark' and 'clear' web, arguing that in between these spaces there is what I describe as a 'brackish web', inhabited by 'brackish social spaces'. Reddit, I argue, sits in a murky space between the dark and clear, with its technological rationality, politics, and technological affordances exhibiting elements of both the clear and dark infrastructures. I study these similarities through examining Reddit's relationship to surveillance, arguing that it exhibits similarities to the dark web through a politics of anonymity and its practices of content moderation. Reddit, however, has slowly moved away from some of its 'dark' elements, in particular through a growing reliance on advertising revenue. This has pushed the platform to engage in more surveillance of its users, pushing it away from its dark web politics. This article challenges the dark and clear web binary, further nuancing our understandings of the politics, economics and technological rationality that underpins online digital platforms.

Reddit, a social news platform where users post, share, discuss and rate news, personal stories, political theory and ideas, has been referred to as the 'wild west' of the web (Tierney 2018). Hosting some of the most shocking content on the clear web, Reddit, alongside other clear web platforms such as 4chan and 8kun, is in popular media frequently aligned with the dark web (e.g. Dewey 2015), which is often, unfairly (Jardine, Lindner, and Owenson 2020) defined through a moral lens and seen solely as a space that hosts shocking and 'illegitimate' content.

While rejecting this moral approach (Heemsbergen et al. 2021), this article studies the relationship between Reddit and the dark web. I blur the distinction between the dark and clear web, arguing that instead of working as a distinct binary, sites and platforms in both spaces can exhibit a range of dark and clear characteristics. In between the dark and clear web, there is a 'brackish web', inhabited by 'brackish social spaces'. Like brackish water, the brackish web sits in a murky, interstitial, space in between the dark and clear. Sites and platforms can be brackish in two ways – through their technological affordances (Davis and Chouinard 2016), and their politics, each of which is underpinned by a technological rationality.

I examine the brackish web through studying Reddit, a large social media and news site that exists within the infrastructure of 'platforms' (Murakami Wood and Monahan 2019) on the clear web. Reddit, I argue, has a technological rationality that imbues its politics and affordances with elements of both the clear and dark web. Reddit aligns itself with dark web technologies through its focus on pseudonymity and the ethos of free speech. Despite this, Reddit still diverges strongly with the dark web, primarily through its ongoing surveillance conducted by the platform itself, which has become more prominent in recent years due to a growing reliance on advertising revenue. These similarities and differences with the dark and clear webs are what makes Reddit a 'brackish' social space.

This article challenges the dark and clear web binary, further nuancing our understandings of the politics, economics and technological rationality that underpins online infrastructures.

Reddit's technological rationality

Reddit is a social news platform, where users post, share, discuss and rate news, personal stories, political theory and ideas (Massanari 2015). Registered users of Reddit submit content such as links, text posts and images to the site on themed 'subreddits', which are then 'voted' up or down by other members. Reddit describes itself as the 'front page of the Internet', a space in which users can find the most entertaining, shocking, funny and topical content on the web in one place (Robards 2018).

Reddit is an example of a platform that exists on a clear web infrastructure. The clear web is a form of infrastructure (Gehl and McKelvey 2019) in which 'user requests (connections) are relayed directly to the Internet service provider (ISP) and from there to the desired destination using the shortest possible path' (Barratt, Aldridge, and Maddox 2018, 2). These requests are unencrypted, allowing for network surveillance and/or traffic analysis from companies and the state alike. The clear web therefore facilitates business models in which companies develop content, software and platforms in exchange for access to identifying information and data about users (Barratt, Aldridge, and Maddox 2018).

Within the clear web, there exists a range of sites that theorists and companies themselves describe as 'platforms' (Gillespie 2010). Murakami Wood and Monahan (2019) argue that, while sitting on the infrastructure of the clear web, platforms have become a type of infrastructure in and of themselves, enabling and supporting certain practices while disabling, eroding and resisting others. Gillespie (2018, 18 & 21) defines platforms as "online sites and services that:

- Host, organize, and circulate users' shared content or social interactions for them;
- without having produced or commissioned (the bulk of) that content;
- are built on an infrastructure, beneath the circulation of information, for processing data for customer service, advertising, and profit, and
- do, and must, moderate the content and activity of users, using some logistics of detection, review, and enforcement".

Platforms are 'multisided digital frameworks that shape the terms in which participants interact with each other' (Kenney and Zysman 2016, 61). As infrastructure, digital platforms are involved in material development, such as through funding large undersea cabling (Murakami Wood and Monahan 2019) or the development of 'the cloud', a space in which entire markets and ecosystems operate (Kenney and Zysman 2016). Platforms also change socio-technical relations, including facilitating social activity and connection online, as well as fundamentally changing systems of production through the creation of the gig economy (Kenney and Zysman 2016; Murakami Wood and Monahan 2019). Platforms are achieving a scale and indispensability that competes with a range of other public and private infrastructures (Plantin and Punathambekar 2019).

Platforms are driven by a 'technological rationality' (Marcuse 1964), describing 'those forms of reason that are embedded within technological design and practices' (Salter 2018, 256). Technological rationality is underpinned by politics (Gillespie 2010; Massanari 2017) and economics (Srnicek 2017), which drive the development of platforms, the people who are attracted to them, and the activities and culture that occur within. Clear web social media platforms, of which Reddit is one, have two, at times seemingly contradictory, rationalities. First, they are spaces in which users are seen as not just consumers, but producers as well – or prosumers (Van Dijck 2009; Fisher 2010). Platforms sell themselves directly to users as spaces through which they can speak, trade and consume as they wish, with this approach being central to gaining attention and large user bases (Gillespie 2010). For social media platforms like Reddit, this means creating a space in which the majority of content is created and shared by users rather than the platform itself. This is true of both clear and dark web platforms, which both drive to hand over control to users.

Second, aligned with Zuboff's (2019) notion of 'surveillance capitalism', clear web platforms are underpinned 'platform surveillance' (Murakami Wood and Monahan 2019). Platforms work to 'fundamentally transform social practices and relations, recasting them as surveillant exchanges whose coordination must be technologically mediated and therefore made exploitable as data (Murakami Wood and Monahan 2019, 1)'. Platform surveillance is driven primarily through the collection of user data, which is used to predict, influence and modify behaviours in order to increase profit (Srnicek 2017; Zuboff 2019). Surveillance and data are used to target the sale of advertisements (Srnicek 2017), encourage shifts in behaviours to, for example, reduce the risk of insurance claims (Sadowski 2020), and to monitor and moderate content to ensure ongoing legitimacy of sites with advertisers, users, other companies and lawmakers (Gillespie 2018).

In its initial years, Reddit focused heavily on the first of these rationalities, creating a platform designed to hand over control to users. I study this briefly here, connecting this to the rationality of the dark web in the next section. I then look at how a growing reliance on the second of these rationalities – surveillance – has led to greater divergence between Reddit and the dark web.

Reddit was established in 2005 by college friends Alexis Ohanian and Steve Huffman (Ohanian 2013). In its early stages, Reddit operated through an acquisition and growth model (Peitz and Valletti 2015; Noreen et al. 2018), relying primarily on funding from investors to establish, develop, grow and gain attention – an integral part of how platforms survive and thrive economically (Terranova 2012).

To gain this attention, in its early stages, Reddit was driven by a desire to remove hierarchies and democratize access to information and the ability to speak. As described by Ohanian (2013) for example, the inspiration for Reddit came from Slashdot, a news website with heavy editorial oversight and moderation practices, and del.icio.us, a site that allowed people to bookmark websites, and which also included a sub-page that aggregated the most popular bookmarked URLs across the site at a given time. Ohanian and Huffman set out to build a site that merged these ideas, building a platform in which 'readers, not editors, would determine the front page of what's new and interesting by submitting links to be voted on by the community' (Ohanian 2013, 42). The 'prosumer' was therefore central to the platform. As Ohanian articulates, this was based on a desire to build a community platform that broke down hierarchies:

> The Internet is a democratic network where all links are created equal. And when such networks get hierarchies forced upon them, they break. They start looking a lot more like the gatekeepers and bureaucracies that stifle great ideas and people in the physical world. That's why we fight so hard to keep them the way they are – open – so any idea that's good enough can flourish without having to ask anyone's permission (Ohanian 2013, 10-11).

Ohanian and Huffman achieved this through shaping Reddit as a 'community of communities' (Potts and Harrison 2013), driven by a key feature of the platform – the subreddit. Ohanian and Huffman turned Reddit into 'platform for online communities' (Ohanian 2013, 43) allowing individuals to create their own subreddits on any topic they liked, with subreddits being regulated by users themselves. In a blog post in 2008, when subreddits were still simply called 'reddits', Ohanian said:

> We learned a long time ago that there are things you all as a community can do that we — as a team of five — couldn't possibly do. Creating different verticals for reddit is just one more area where we know our community can do a better job identifying and growing successful reddits.
>
> Now we're just taking ourselves out of the equation. (Ohanian 2008, cited in Robertson 2015, np).

Reddit hands power to users in multiple ways, including giving them control of content, making the platform's code open source (Massanari 2015), and through a community-wide project called *Rediquette – an* 'informal expression of the values of many redditors, as written by redditors themselves' (Reddit 2021).

Similar to many other clear web platforms therefore, Reddit is built upon a technological rationality of community, driven by the underlying ethos of the 'prosumer'. This rationality is facilitated to drive attention to the platform, building a large audience to make Reddit viable. This mass attention brought some initial revenue in the early years, primarily from small amounts of advertising as well as sign ups to a premium service called Reddit Gold, which allowed the platform to defray its server costs (Massanari 2017). Over a number of funding rounds, the platform also attracted investors – ranging from companies Andreessen Horowitz to Sequoia Capital to the celebrities Snoop Dogg and Jared Leto – who provided finance to allow the platform to keep operating and building (Castillo 2018).

Reddit as a case study of the brackish web

In this section, I examine how Reddit's rationality of handing over control aligns it with the dark web. Reddit aligns strongly with the dark web through both its technological infrastructure itself and the political rationality that underpins this infrastructure.

While, as described above, the clear web facilitates surveillance (Zuboff 2019; Murakami Wood and Monahan 2019), the dark web works to circumvent it. While the dark is often defined through a moral lens, which treats it as a space in which 'illegitimate', or 'dark' activities occur (Bartlett 2014), similar to my approach to the clear web, I define it instead as an infrastructure (Gehl and McKelvey 2019). The dark web consists of 'websites with standard web technologies (HTML, CSS, server-side scripting languages, hosting software) that can be viewed with a standard web browser, such as Firefox or Chrome, which is routed through special routing software packages' (Gehl 2018, 5). These routing technologies conceal the identity and location of users and producers of content (Harrison and Roberts 2016). Dark web platforms oppose structural surveillance (Heemsbergen et al. 2021) with technological affordances deliberately developed in resistance to both the openness (i.e. viewability) and censorship of the clear web. The dark web is established to provide relief from the digital light that exists on the clear web, aiming to subvert practices within platforms that encourage the collection of data, influencing the behaviour and moderation of content.

As infrastructures, however, the dark and clear webs are not binary opposites but are deeply interconnected (Barratt, Aldridge, and Maddox 2018). For example, the dark web browser, 'Tor', acts as an overlay network on the clear web, using standard Internet infrastructure to 'relay' a user's website traffic through a minimum of three randomly selected nodes (Jardine 2019). Tor can also be used to browse websites on the clear web, allowing users to search clear websites without their location being tracked (Barratt, Aldridge, and Maddox 2018). The dark-web clear web binary is also murky when it comes to user behaviour. Reddit, my case study for the brackish web, acts as a bridging site between the dark and clear webs, with, for example, both sellers and buyers in dark web cryptomarkets using the platform as a space for discussion (Kwon and Shao 2020).

While the above infrastructural discussion illustrates the entwined and murky nature of dark and clear web, the subsequent discussion will delve deeper into the ways the political rationality of Reddit illustrates the brackish web. Reddit's rationality aligns with the dark web in two ways – through the affordances and politics of anonymity; and through a politics of free speech, which has historically been implemented through community-based moderation policies. I argue that, while the rationality behind Reddit is in some ways different to that of dark web platforms, it has still driven a form of 'dark' technological affordances and politics. Reddit, however, still diverges from the dark web through a growing alignment with the practices of platform surveillance.

Anonymity and privacy

While Reddit does not sit behind routing software – the key delineation between it and the dark web – anonymity still forms a core part of the politics of the platform. This aligns with Reddit's commitment to breaking down hierarchies, with anonymity spoken about (from executives to users alike) as a feature to allow people to speak freely on the platform without fear (Van der Nagel and Frith 2015).

Reddit, and users within the platform, enforce anonymity and pseudonymity through a number of technological, culture and political practices. Unlike platforms, such as Facebook, when users register to Reddit, they are not required, or even able, to provide any demographic information. Instead, they are only able to provide an email address and username. Similarly, unlike platforms, such as Twitter, Reddit's affordances do not encourage (Davis and Chouinard 2016) users to post photos or any demographic data on their profile. This limits the data available to Reddit, restricting the capacity for the platform to target users with advertising (Rowley 2015). Additionally, Reddit allows users to create multiple accounts through the same email address, facilitating a culture in which users create 'throwaway accounts' in order to post more controversial or salacious material away from their main account (Van der Nagel and Frith 2015). All of these affordances limit the ability for external surveillance.

Culturally, pseudonymity is also an expectation within the platform (Kilgo et al. 2018). While users are required to create usernames, it is generally expected they do not include any personal identifiers (Massanari 2015). This allows users to remain functionally anonymous, facilitating a culture of free speech and expression.

Similarly, while Reddit does not have rules against individuals posting their own information, they have strong policies against doxing – the posting of other people's personal data. This is also an activity shunned on many dark web platforms. The previous community manager Kristine Fasnacht of Reddit articulated this policy:

> DO NOT POST USERS' PERSONAL INFORMATION. EVER. NO phone numbers, NO email addresses, NO real names, NO blood types, NO SSN's, NO facebook pics or profiles, NO mothers' maiden names, NOTHING. This is a ban-on-sight offense, and lately we have banned multiple users for posting personal info.

Posting personal information is the Internet version of vandalism and abuse and will not be tolerated (cited in Robertson 2015, np).

Reddit therefore aims to maintain a cultural practice of anonymity, but within a clear-web context. This politics of anonymity, similar to that of the dark web, is designed to limit surveillance of users, allowing for the flourishing of free speech and community within the platform.

Freedom of speech and resistance to hierarchies

An examination of technological rationality can provide further insights into the similarities and differences between the dark and clear webs, bolstering the analysis of Reddit as a brackish platform. Both the clear and dark webs have a rationality based on libertarian politics and a focus on free speech, which are highlighted by the platform's respective approaches to content moderation.

As already noted, underpinning the politics of the dark web is an overarching belief in freedom of speech and expression, with a particular resistance of the surveillance and censorship of speech from the state and large corporations (Gehl 2016). This has manifested in a distinct libertarian politics within dark web platforms. The Silk Road cryptomarket for example was historically dominated by libertarian discourses (Munksgaard and Demant 2016), one which 'resonates with traditional beliefs about the purpose and meaning of the Internet to change society through radical reconfiguring of relations of power …' (Maddox et al. 2016, 112). This resistance to surveillance and censorship has allowed a range of controversial activities (Jardine 2019) to flourish on the dark web, including black markets (Maddox et al. 2016), terrorism (Weimann 2016), child pornography and sexual abuse, and other forms of illegal activity (Gehl 2018), all of which remains uncensored by the technology providers.

This ethos aligns strongly with the libertarian politics of Reddit, which, as discussed earlier, was established as a space designed to radically democratize information accessibility and the ability to speak, and to redistribute power. Similar to that of the dark web, this has resulted in Reddit gaining a reputation of hosting some of the most shocking content on the clear web (Robards 2018), including communities dedicated to racism, sexism, homophobia, the hatred of fat people, and even of the sharing of pics of underage kids. Reddit has also been a space that has hosted discussion of dark web cryptomarkets, becoming a space in which sellers can engage in self-promotion and buyers can share personal experiences about vendors, products, and safe practices for ordering and delivery (Kwon and Shao 2020).

This politics plays out through moderation policies. Through libertarian politics both Reddit and dark web platforms rely on community-based moderation, rejecting top-down, hierarchical approaches.

Dark web infrastructures do not engage in censorship. Tor, for example, argues that all people involved in the project are united by a common belief: 'internet users should have private access to an uncensored web' (Tor 2021). Users instead engage in community-based moderation. Gehl (2016) identifies that DWSN, a social network on the onion router, has strict controls on child pornography, ones that are enforced rigorously by moderators. However, this is driven by the community, rather than coming from the top-down. Dark web users react against centralized surveillance and controls, instead relying on their own practices in order to manage content (Gehl 2016).

With its leaders arguing that it is a space for free speech (Robertson 2015) Reddit has historically engaged in similar politics, seeking to distinguish between community and top-down moderation. Similar to parts of the dark web, Reddit is built on a decentralized system of content moderation, maintaining an approach that relies heavily on community and volunteer moderators to decide what is, and is not, okay (Matias 2019). In defending the existence of racism on the platform in 2018, for example, Reddit co-founder and CEO Steve Huffman said:

> Our approach to governance is that communities can set appropriate standards around language for themselves. Many communities have rules around speech that are more restrictive than our own, and we fully support those rules. (Huffman, cited in Statt 2018, np)

In 2014, the then CEO of Reddit, Yisham Wong, similarly described this ethos:

> We uphold the ideal of free speech on reddit as much as possible not because we are legally bound to, but because we believe that you — the user — has the right to choose between right and wrong, good and evil, and that it is your responsibility to do so (cited in Robertson 2015, np).

This does not mean, however, that Reddit has never banned content, an approach of top-down surveillance that distinguishes it from the dark web. From its early stages, Reddit implemented policies banning illegal material, and even some hate speech (Statt 2018). The above quote from Wong came after Reddit was pushed to ban the subreddit r/thefappening, which grew rapidly after a trove of illegally accessed photos of high-profile female celebrities was released online (Massanari 2017). But Reddit executives have historically been hesitant to engage in such moderation, often only acting after being pushed by outside forces (Massanari 2017). This aligns strongly with the ethos of the dark web, which both allow for localized moderation of content, but resists moderation occurring in a centralized manner.

Reddit, however, sits in an uncomfortable position, straddling between allowing free speech, while at the same time meeting the needs (regulatory, social, etc.) of clear-web platforms. As we will see in the next section, Reddit's ability to maintain this balance has becoming increasingly difficult. This, I argue, highlights the major difference between the dark and clear web – that of their respective relationships to surveillance.

Reddit: becoming more 'clear'?

Reddit therefore exists as a 'brackish social space', a platform that, through its technological rationality, politics, and affordances exhibit elements of both the clear and dark web. Its existence as a brackish social space drove initial attention to Reddit, helping it establish itself as one of the largest platforms in the world. In recent years, however, Reddit has begun to change some of its approaches, particularly becoming more active in surveillance due to a greater reliance on advertising.

As noted earlier, Reddit was initially established under an acquisition and growth model, relying on seed funding and investors for operations. Such a model, however, is not sustainable in the long term, as platforms are required to transition towards more ongoing funding sources (Peitz and Vallett 2015; Noreen et al. 2018). Reddit has shifted its funding model. In 2017, the company raised $200 million in a funding round, with investors ranging from large companies Andreessen Horowitz and Sequoia Capital to the celebrities Snoop Dogg and Jared Leto. This funding round placed increased pressure on Reddit to commit to revenue growth (Castillo 2018), with the platform turning to advertising. Reddit has begun to provide broader advertising offerings, including the provision of banner ads and sponsored posts (Castillo 2018), as well as autoplay in-stream videos and a function called 'Top Post Takeover', in which brands are able to take over the front page of the platform with their ads for a period of time (eMarketer 2019). In 2019, Reddit raised $119 million in advertising revenue, an increase by 54.7% based on the year before (eMarketer 2019).

This shift to advertising has brought challenges to Reddit's libertarian politics, with the company pursuing greater surveillance to provide more detail about its user base for potential advertisers. Reddit's website now features an in-depth portal for companies and individuals to set up advertising. This includes a number of 'white papers' targeted at advertisers that provide details about the platform's audience, as well as case studies from the companies Welch's, Poshmark, L'Oreal and Audi. Reddit has begun to invest in research of their community, providing detailed analysis of users and individual spaces for advertisers (Reddit.com 2021bb). This analysis allows advertisers to target users within the site via categories, such as their interests, community connections, devices and location (Reddit.com 2021cc). While this research and advertiser targeting does not override users pseudonymity, it has increased surveillance of the community and users alike for the needs of advertisers.

In addition, driven by perceptions of their image, Reddit has become more engaged in top-down moderation. Advertisers have been cautious about Reddit's free-speech ethos, with concerns about being associated with hateful and other distasteful material (eMarketer 2019). Working to keep advertisers and their user base together, Reddit has therefore begun to attempt to clean up its image, slowly changing its content policies and becoming more active in banning particular content and communities (Copland 2020). It has changed its policies to ban any suggestive or sexual content featuring minors (u/reddit 2012), the sharing of nude photos without the subject's consent (u/kn0thing 2015), 'attacks and harassment of individuals' (u/5days et al. 2015), the incitement of violence (u/landoflobsters 2017), and attacks and harassment of broad social groups (u/landoflobsters 2019). These shifts have become more intense in recent years as Reddit, with Reddit becoming more active in the surveillance of its users in order to maintain strong relationships with advertisers. Reddit has become more active in 'quarantining' and banning particular subreddits (Copland 2020). The platform has quarantined and banned men's rights subreddits and in July 2020 undertook a large clean-up of the platform, banning 2,000 subreddits, including the most prominent subreddit in support of the US President Donald Trump, r/The_Donald (Copland 2020).

Notably, this has often occurred, while Reddit's executives were still trying to defend the free-speech ethos of the site. The quote from the previous section, for example, in which founder Steve Huffman defended the existence of racism on the platform, occurred only a year before it had banned attacks and harassment of broad social groups. Huffman himself received significant pushback from the statement, resulting in him backtracking somewhat (Statt 2018). This follows a similar pattern to other moderation changes in the platform, which have often only come after significant external pressure (Massanari 2017).

These changing practices have highlighted the major difference between clear platforms and the dark web, and the challenges faced by Reddit as a 'brackish' space. While some of the technological rationalities of Reddit and the dark web are similar, they have growing divergent relationships with surveillance. In the early stages of Reddit as a platform, rationality of free speech and lax moderation was essential in building a large user base. In more recent years, however, as it has turned its attention towards advertising in order to increase profit, Reddit has become more engrained in the structures of surveillance that underpin clear web platforms.

This profit-driven rationality is less prominent in the dark web, with creators of this infrastructure instead driven by social justice causes, which have been driven by an antagonistic relationship with surveillance. Tor, for example, was developed and run by a non-profit organization that conducts research and development into online privacy. Tor defines its project as one based on a politics of privacy and human rights, stating on their 'about' page:

> "We believe everyone should be able to explore the internet with privacy ... We advance human rights and defend your privacy online through free software and open networks. (Tor 2021bb, np)"

Through having less of a focus on profits, dark web infrastructures have less motivation towards surveillance, instead acting as a space that is shielded from surveillance.

Technological rationality is driven by different motivations, with clear web platforms using surveillance techniques to further profit-making ventures. Dark web platforms, however, sit outside these systems, being established and driven specifically to circumvent the surveillance of the clear web. As highlighted by this article, these differing motivations and rationality have shaped similarities between the dark and clear web, while at the same time facilitating fundamental differences between the two.

Conclusion: the consequences of being a brackish space

This article has sought the challenge the binary between the dark and clear webs. In this binary, the dark web is a form of infrastructure that uses routing technologies to avoid surveillance, while the clear web sits in the light, viewable to all. I have used Reddit as an example to show, however, that the distinction between dark and clear is in fact not particularly clear.

Reddit is a platform that exhibits both clear and dark features. Reddit's underlying rationality is similar to other clear web platforms, with its founders trying to make a community platform in which users – or 'prosumers' (Van Dijck 2009; Fisher 2010) have control. This was designed to break down the hierarchies of the web, and society overall. In doing so, Reddit is a platform that has included a focus on anonymity, pseudonymity, and an internal politics that resists top-down moderation, elements that strongly align it with the dark web. Reddit sits in a brackish space, in between dark and clear. As I have shown with recent changes driven by an increasing focus on advertising, Reddit has slowly moved away from some of its 'dark' elements. It has begun to engage more heavily in surveillance in order to appeal to a greater range of advertisers.

This article presents a nuanced engagement with the dark/clear binary. While a technological definition provides a strong basis, we can only fully understand the difference between dark and clear platforms by examining the rationality that underpins their development. This rationality, driven by platform's respective positions either within or on the edge/outside of systems of platform surveillance, fundamentally influences how they are designed, the users attracted to them, and the politics that occur within.

Disclosure statement

No potential conflict of interest was reported by the author(s).

References

Barratt, M. J., J. Aldridge, and A Maddox. 2018. ""Dark Web."." In *Sage Encyclopedia of the Internet*, edited by B Warf, 185–188. Thousand Oaks: SAGE Publications, .
Bartlett, J. 2014. *The Dark Net: Inside the Digital Underworld*. London: William Heinemann.

Castillo, M. 2018. "Reddit – One of the World's Most Popular Websites - Is Trying to Cash in through Advertising." *CNBC*. July 5. Accessed 21 September 2021. https://www.cnbc.com/2018/06/29/how-reddit-plans-to-make-money-through-advertising.html

Copland, S. 2020. ""Reddit Quarantined: Can Changing Platform Affordances Reduce Hateful Material Online?"." *Internet Policy Review* 9 (4). doi:10.14763/2020.4.1516.

Davis, J. L., and J. Chouinard. 2016. ""Theorizing Affordances: From Request to Refuse."." *Bulletin of Science, Technology & Society* 36 (4): 241–248. doi:10.1177/0270467617714944.

Dewey, C. 2015. "In Search of the Darkest, Most Disturbing Content on the Internet." *The Washington Post*. September 3. Accessed 21 September 2021. https://www.washingtonpost.com/news/the-intersect/wp/2015/09/02/in-search-of-the-darkest-most-disturbing-content-on-the-internet/

eMarketer. 2019. "Reddit to cross $100 million in ad revenues in 2019". eMarketer.com. 26 March. Accessed 21 September 2021. https://www.emarketer.com/content/reddit-to-cross-100-million-in-ad-revenues-in-2019

Fisher, E. 2010. *Media and New Capitalism in the Digital Age*. New York: Palgrave MacMillan.

Gehl, R. 2016. "Power/freedom on the Dark Web: A Digital Ethnography of the Dark Web Social Network." *New Media & Society* 18 (7): 1219–1235. doi:10.1177/1461444814554900.

Gehl, R. 2018. *Weaving the Dark Web: Legitimacy on Freenet, Tor and I2P*. Cambridge and London: MIT Press.

Gehl, R., and F. McKelvey. 2019. "Bugging out: darknets as parasites of large-scale media objects". *Media, Culture & Society* 41 (2): 219–235. https://doi.org/10.1177/0163443718818379

Gillespie, T. 2010. "The Politics of 'Platforms." *New Media and Society* 12 (3): 347–364. doi:10.1177/1461444809342738.

Gillespie, T. 2018. *Custodians of the Internet: platforms, content moderation, and the hidden decisions that shape social media*. New Haven and London: Yale University Press.

Harrison, J., and D. Roberts. 2016. "Assessing the Extent and Nature of Wildlife Trade on the Dark Web." *Conversation Biology* 30 (4): 900–904.

Heemsbergen, L. J., A. Maddox, T Cinque, A Johns, and R Gehl. 2021. "Dark." *M/C Journal* 24 (2). doi:10.5204/mcj.2791.

Jardine, E. 2019. "Online Content Moderation and the Dark Web: Policy Responses to Radicalizing Hate Speech and Malicious Content on the Darknet." *First Monday*, 24 (12).

Jardine, E., A. Lindner, and G Owenson. 2020. "The Potential Harms of the Tor Anonymity Network Cluster Disproportionately in Free Countries." *PNAS* 117 (50): 31. doi:10.1073/pnas.2011893117.

Kenney, M., and J. Zysman. 2016. "The Rise of the Platform Economy." *Issues in Science and Technology* xxxii (3): 61–69.

Kilgo, D., Y. Ng, M Riedl, and I Lacasa-Mas. 2018. "Reddit's Veil of Anonymity: Predictors of Engagement and Participation in Media Environments with Hostile Reputations." *Social Media + Society*. 1–9

Kwon, H., and C. Shao. 2020. "Communicative Constitution of Illicit Online Trade Collectives: An Exploration of Darkweb Market Subreddits." *SMSociety '20*, July 22–24, 2020, Toronto, ON, Canada.

Maddox, A., M. Barratt, M Allen, and S Lenton. 2016. "Constructive Activism in the Dark Web: Cryptomarkets and Illicit Drugs in the Digital 'Demimonde." *Information, Communication & Society* 19 (1): 111–126. doi:10.1080/1369118X.2015.1093531.

Marcuse, H. 1964. *One-Dimensional Man: Studies in the Ideology of Advanced Industrial Society*. London: Routledge.

Massanari, A. 2015. *Participatory Culture, Community, and Play*. New York: Peter Lang Publishing.

Massanari, A. 2017. "Gamergate and the Fappening: How Reddit's Algorithm, Governance, and Culture Support Toxic Technocultures." *New Media and Society* 19 (3): 329–346. doi:10.1177/1461444815608807.

Matias, N. 2019. "The Civic Labour of Volunteer Moderators Online." *Social Media + Society* 1–12.

Munksgaard, R., and J. Demant. 2016. "Mixing Politics and Crime – The Prevalence and Decline of Political Discourse on the Cryptomarket." *International Journal of Drug Policy* 35: 77–83. doi:10.1016/j.drugpo.2016.04.021.

Murakami Wood, D., and T. Monahan. 2019. "Platform Surveillance." *Surveillance & Society* 17 (1/2): 1–6. doi:10.24908/ss.v17i1/2.13237.

Noreen, P., N. Van Gorp, N van Eijk, and R. Ó Fathaigh. 2018. "Should We Regulate Digital Platforms? A New Framework for Evaluating Policy Options." *Policy and Internet* 10 (3): 264–301. doi:10.1002/poi3.177.

Ohanian, A. 2013. *"Without Their Permission: How the 21st Century Will Be Made, Not Managed.* Business Plus".

Peitz, M., and T. Vallett. 2015. "Reassessing Competition Concerns in Electronic Communications Markets." *Telecommunications Policy* 39 (10): 896–912. doi:10.1016/j.telpol.2015.07.012.

Plantin, J., and A. Punathambekar. 2019. "Digital Media Infrastructures: Pipes, Platforms, and Politics." *Media, Culture & Society* 41 (2): 163–174. doi:10.1177/0163443718818376.

Potts, L., and A. Harrison. 2013. "Interfaces as Rhetorical Constructions: Reddit and 4chan during the Boston Marathon Bombings." SIGDOC '13: Proceedings of the 31st ACM international conference on Design of communication, Greenville North Carolina USA. Accessed 21 September 2021. https://dl.acm.org/doi/10.1145/2507065.2507079

Reddit.com. 2021. "Reddiquette". Accessed 21 September 2021. https://www.reddithelp.com/en/categories/reddit-101/reddit-basics/reddiquette

Reddit.com. 2021b. "Audience". Accessed 21 September 2021. https://www.redditinc.com/advertising/audience

Reddit.com. 2021c. "Targeting". Accessed 21 September 2021. https://advertising.reddithelp.com/en/categories/targeting

Robards, B. 2018. "'Totally Straight': Contested Sexual Identities on Social Media Site Reddit." *Sexualities* 21 (1–2): 49–67. doi:10.1177/1363460716678563.

Robertson, A. 2015. "Was Reddit Always about Free Speech? Yes, and No." *The Verge*. July 15. Accessed 21 September 2021. https://www.theverge.com/2015/7/15/8964995/reddit-free-speech-history

Rowley, L. 2015. "Walking the Razor's Edge: Reddit Tries to Figure Out Its Ad Business." *Ad Exchanger*. 13 July. Accessed 21 September 2021. https://www.adexchanger.com/featured-2/walking-the-razors-edge-reddit-tries-to-figure-out-its-ad-business/

Sadowski, J. 2020. *Too Smart: How Digital Capitalism Is Extracting Data, Controlling Our Lives, and Taking over the World*. Cambridge: MIT Press.

Salter, M. 2018. "From Geek Masculinity to Gamergate: The Technological Rationality of Online Abuse." *Crime, Media, Culture* 14 (2): 247–264. doi:10.1177/1741659017690893.

Srnicek, N. 2017. *Platform Capitalism*. Cambridge, UK: Polity Press.

Statt, N. 2018. "Reddit CEO Says Racism Is Permitted on the Platform, and Users are up in Arms". 11 April. Accessed 21 September 2021. https://www.theverge.com/2018/4/11/17226416/reddit-ceo-steve-huffman-racism-racist-slurs-are-okay

Terranova, T. 2012. "Attention, Economy and the Brain." *Culture Machine* 13: 1–19.

Tierney, E. 2018. "The Wild West of the Internet – Reddit May Be Your Brand's Secret Weapon". *Marketing Mag*. 7 August. Accessed 21 September 2021. https://www.marketingmag.com.au/hubs-c/opinion-erin-tierney-wild-reddit/

Tor. 2021. "*History*". Tor. Accessed 21 September 2021. https://www.torproject.org/about/history/

Tor. 2021b. "*Browse Privately. Explore Freely*". Tor. Accessed 21 September 2021. https://www.torproject.org/

u/5days, u/ekjp, and u/kn0thing. 2015. "Promote Ideas, Protect People [Blog Post]". *Reddit Blog*. 14 May. Accessed 21 September 2021. https://redditblog.com/2015/05/14/promote-ideas-protect-people/

u/kn0thing. 2015. "From 1 to 9,000 Communities, Now Taking Steps to Grow Reddit to 90,000 Communities (And Beyond!) [Post]". *Reddit*. 25 February. Accessed 21 September 2021. https://www.reddit.com/r/announcements/comments/2x0g9v/from_1_to_9000_communities_now_taking_steps_to/

u/landoflobsters. 2017. "Update on Site-wide Rules regarding Violent Content [Post]". *Reddit*. 26 October. Accessed 21 September 2021. https://www.reddit.com/r/modnews/comments/78p7bz/update_on_sitewide_rules_regarding_violent_content/

u/landoflobsters. 2019. "Changes to Our Policy against Bullying and Harassment [Post]". *Reddit*. 1 October. Accessed 21 September 2021. https://www.reddit.com/r/announcements/comments/dbf9nj/changes_to_our_policy_against_bullying_and/

u/reddit. 2012. "A Necessary Change in Policy [Post]". *Reddit*. 13 February. Accessed 21 September 2021. https://www.reddit.com/r/blog/comments/pmj7f/a_necessary_change_in_policy/

Van der Nagel, E, and J. Frith. 2015. "Anonymity, Pseudonymity, and the Agency of Online Identity: Examining the Social Practices of r/Gonewild." *First Monday* 20: 3.

Van Dijck, J. 2009. "Users like You? Theorizing Agency in User-generated Content." *Media, Culture & Society* 31 (1): 41–58. doi:10.1177/0163443708098245.

Weimann, G. 2016. "Going Dark: Terrorism on the Dark Web." *Studies in Conflict & Terrorism* 39 (3): 195–206. doi:10.1080/1057610X.2015.1119546.

Zuboff, S. 2019. *The Age of Surveillance Capitalism: The Fight for a Human Future at the New Frontier of Power*. London: Profile Books.

The Affective Pressures of WhatsApp: From Safe Spaces to Conspiratorial Publics

Amelia Johns and Niki Cheong

ABSTRACT
In this paper we bring together media logics, affordances and affect theory to ask how conspiracy theory moves through WhatsApp groups and moves people through their encounters with these contents towards 'conspiracy thinking'. Firstly, we draw upon media logic theory to examine the extent to which WhatsApp's architecture, design and technical functions 'steer' users' towards particular communication and behaviours. Second, we use affordance theory to examine how communities incorporate platform affordances into their tactics to resist, subvert or circumvent institutional power. Finally, we use theories of affect to understand whether the shared emotions and intensities that arise through encounters between digital environments and bodies of users drive experiences that bypass human cognition and representation to create 'affective atmospheres'. We apply this integrated framework to ask whether WhatsApp's closed infrastructure, end-to-end encryption and social features such as 'Groups' and the 'forward' button – with the embodied practices of users – shape affective environments which normalize conspiracy thinking.

Introduction

In this paper we bring together media logics (Van Dijck and Poell 2013; Agur 2019), affordances (McVeigh-Schultz and Baym 2015; Hanckel et al. 2019) and affect theory (Lupton 2017) to ask how conspiracy theory moves through WhatsApp groups and moves people through these encounters towards 'conspiracy thinking' (Onderco and Stoeckel 2020). Firstly, we draw upon media logic theory to examine the extent to which WhatsApp's architecture, design and technical functions 'steer' users' towards particular communication and behaviours (Van Dijck and Poell 2013). Second, we use affordance theory to examine how communities incorporate platform affordances into their tactics to resist, subvert or circumvent institutional power. Finally, we use theories of affect to understand whether the shared emotions and intensities that arise through encounters between digital environments and bodies drive experiences that bypass human cognition and representation to create 'affective atmospheres' (Lupton 2017, 2). We apply this integrated framework to ask whether WhatsApp's closed infrastructure, end-to-end encryption and social features such as 'Groups' and the 'forward' button – with the embodied practices of users – shape affective environments which normalize conspiracy thinking.

We draw upon findings from a study conducted between 2016 and 2018 in Malaysia, which included interviews with young political and LGBT activists,[1] about their digital, civic and political practices in the lead up to the 2018 Malaysian General Election (GE14). The findings highlight the significance of WhatsApp's end-to-end encryption and closed architecture to the civic and political repertoires of activists and everyday users. This was particularly so within a broader media ecology, where censorship, surveillance and manipulation of social media publics fuelled perceptions that WhatsApp's end-to-end encrypted group chats (and opt-in encrypted messaging platforms like Telegram) provided a 'safe space'. However, participants also described other affective responses to the groups they participated in, with the same features (encryption, closed groups) and social functions (message forwarding) being associated with an uptick of misinformation and conspiracy thinking.

Addressing the theme of the special issue, the findings highlight the ambivalent experiences of users of 'dark social' technologies.[2] The architecture and affordances of WhatsApp and other messaging platforms allow a range of actors to subvert, resist and evade the logics of surveillance and publicness embedded in social networking platforms and the regimes of state censorship and control that benefit from them. These findings support the work of dark web scholars such as Gehl (2018) and Maddox et al. (2016), who critique the 'moral' registers used to understand dark social spaces and the actors who inhabit them. One of the main findings of this study was that 'dark social' technologies enabled activist safety from 'digital light' defined in relation to processes of datafication, state, and platform surveillance. Nonetheless we want to complicate framings that would suggest digital darkness is always productive and progressive; rather the dark social shapes 'affective atmospheres' that are contingent, context-dependent and dynamic, and which can move users from one affective state to another.

Background

In 2018, Malaysia's internet space was declared 'Partly Free' (Freedom House 2018). Freedom House noted – following Malaysia's 14th General Election (GE14) and the first government change in over 60 years – that 'there are hopes that restrictions will lessen'. The restrictions referred to included blocking of online news portals and blogs including *Sarawak Report*, and *Medium*, after they reported allegations of political corruption involving former Prime Minister Najib Razak, who misappropriated funds from the government-operated 1Malaysia Development Berhad (1MDB) strategic development corporation.

The blocking was imposed by the Malaysian Communication and Multimedia Commission (MCMC) that regulates media and communications industries. Over the years, the MCMC has been involved in efforts to censor and manage online information by instructing websites and users to remove 'offensive' content (Johns and Cheong 2019). This is enabled by laws, including the Communications and Multimedia Act 1998 and the colonial legacies embedded in the Sedition Act (in 2015, updated to cover online communication), the now-repealed Internal Security Act, and the Printing Presses and Publications Act – all of which have been used to control speech in the country (Case 1993).

Nonetheless, these laws did not suppress growing anti-government expressions in an online space dubbed 'the opposition playground' (Cheong 2020). In response, the Najib administration first turned to the mobilization of 'cybertroopers', that is, covert online actors engaging in political trolling against government's critics. It has been argued that the use of cybertroopers, alongside repressive laws, were part of the administration's efforts to 'exploit and manipulate' networked affect to dampen the progress of social movements in Malaysia (Johns and Cheong 2019, 10).

Another tactic adopted by the government was to steamroll an Anti-Fake News Bill through Parliament pre–GE14, which targeted opposition politicians, media outlets and WhatsApp group admins. The law identified 'fake news' as 'any news, information, data and reports that are whole or partly false' (Fernandez 2019, 179). The vagueness of the definition was likely because, as Lim (2020, 8) argues, 'there has never been a clear legal or public sense of what constitutes 'fake news in Malaysia', considering that 'false and misleading content is already criminalized under other legislation'.

Scholars have offered various terms to capture the types of information and content that can be considered 'fake news' or 'problematic information'. As explained by Jack (2017, 1): 'Some information ... is inaccurate, misleading, inappropriately attributed, or altogether fabricated'. Further, misinformation and disinformation, including rumours and conspiracy theories, describe contents intended to deceive or mislead (disinformation) or are shared without knowledge of the falsehood they contain (misinformation). This interpretation is consistent with the ways participants in this study referred to 'fake news'. Tapsell (2018) has further highlighted 'gossip, rumours and conspiracy' circulating through WhatsApp groups ahead of GE14 as a 'weapon of the weak', which generates feelings of empowerment for citizens otherwise disempowered through normative forms of political participation. We acknowledge this, but also seek to understand how the digital environment itself shapes user experiences, emotions and behaviour. We specifically want to see if 'conspiratorial thinking' – a pattern of thinking (and feeling) where actors 'dismiss authoritative accounts of political events and instead believe in "hidden, malevolent groups secretly perpetuating political plots and social calamities to further their own nefarious goals"' (Oliver and Wood 2014, cited in Onderco and Stoeckel 2020, 1) – may be fostered by WhatsApp's affective environment.

Theoretical framework

To understand and theorize the ambivalent but often shared thoughts and feelings aroused through participation in WhatsApp groups, in this paper we bring together media logics, affordance theory and theories of affective atmospheres, and examine how they fit within the broader literature on messaging platforms and digital activism.

WhatsApp, Telegram, Signal and other instant messaging applications which have closed architectures; default or opt-in end-to-end encryption for group communication; and affordances which allow media content to be shared between users and groups, have, since their introduction, been identified by activists, journalists, and whistleblowers as platforms which arouse different communication styles and logics to those on social media, as well as a different set of emotions and feelings. They have been identified as spaces which promote safety, intimacy and authenticity (away from the reputational dynamics and datafication of user-interactions on social networking media platforms, see Van Dijck and Poell 2013; Baym and Boyd 2012), and retreat from heavily censored and manipulated mainstream media and social media ecologies. They are also associated with emerging communicative logics, enabling flexible, real-time protest communication and micro-coordination (Ling and Lai 2016; Treré 2015; Lee and Ting 2015).

Treré (2015) argues that too much attention has been paid in the digital activism and social movements literature to the affordances of social media (i.e. Facebook and Twitter) which connect and mobilize 'networked publics', and where publicly available data make these movements easier to analyse at scale. He claims that this focus comes at the expense of research on messaging platforms like WhatsApp, where the closed architecture of the platform prompts different logics focused on internal communication, social cohesion, solidarity and trust building. While Treré uses a media ecologies approach to analyse the movement of activists between the social media 'front stage' (Twitter and Facebook) and 'backstage' (WhatsApp and Facebook Messenger), he stresses how use of closed messaging groups does not just foster new communication styles but also produces shared feelings of safety, retreat and protection, or 'digital comfort zones' (911).

Lee and Ting (2015) adopt a 'media logics' lens to centre platforms, their technical features and design which steer social practices and communication of activists, while also shaping broader media industries, cultures and institutional practices. Agur (2019) also documents the importance of closed messaging platforms for journalistic information gathering in South–East Asian contexts. Drawing on Altheide and Snow's classic approach, Agur (2019, 181) identifies how 'media formats . . . organise and technologically structure content and audience expectations'. He argues that connecting with sources in these contexts require that journalists use messaging platforms, such as WhatsApp, Telegram, Line, and others. This is because of their broad use and popularity, but he also notes how the platform structures logics of 'connectedness' and 'insularity': 'interactions that take place within closed groups and, over time, become isolated in terms of participants and content. Insularity is the result not only of social practices but also of codes, data, algorithms, and interface design' (183). This introduces new ethical considerations for journalists connecting with sources given that users tend to only trust known (internal) contacts and harbour suspicion towards outsiders.

LGBT activists and community members in Southeast Asian contexts also use closed messaging groups in line with these logics. Hanckel et al. (2019) emphasized how closed groups generate feelings of safety, intimacy and trust for young LGBT people. This is because there is considerable risk for them to safely navigate social networking platforms that, by their design, reward visibility and publicness (see also Cho 2018). In choosing closed messaging groups then, they consciously eschew social media logics in favour of safety and 'control of their experience of using the app' (Hanckel et al. 2019). The study draws upon theories of affordances (McVeigh-Schultz and Baym 2015) to understand queer young people's navigation of digital publicness, and their social media strategies which include strategic retreats to closed messaging apps to circumvent risk and create conditions of safety.

Attention has also turned recently to the role that platforms like WhatsApp play in circulating problematic information, primarily misinformation, rumour, conspiracy theory and hate speech. Scholars have focused on the way the use of the app increases the potential for election manipulation, as in the case of the 2018 Brazilian election (Pereira and Bojzcuk 2018) and GE14 in Malaysia (Tapsell 2018). In these cases, mass messaging through WhatsApp groups enabled by the forward function, and where messages are difficult to trace owing to end-to-end encryption has allowed inauthentic behaviour to gain a presence among WhatsApp groups discussing the election (Cheong 2020, 78; Pereira and Bojzcuk 2018).

Tapsell provides an account of how rumour and conspiracy focused on PM Najib's wife, Rosmah, spread like wildfire through WhatsApp groups in the lead up to GE14, a phenomenon he associated with political parties' use of WhatsApp for campaigning, as well as the desire for the 'weak' to seek tools which amplify speech that harms the powerful, while not having repercussions for user communities (Tapsell 2018, 19). In a different register, and not exclusively focused on messaging platforms, Whyte (2020) provides insight into the role played by Reddit, Discord and 4Chan in the election of Donald Trump in 2016. He argues that despite much literature being dedicated to the 'democracy hacking' and manipulation of Facebook and Twitter via bots and false accounts during the 2016 US election campaign, that 'closed, conspiratorial communications' were fundamental to Trump's disinformation machine. Whyte argues that content circulating in these platforms and forums is 'characterized by conspiracy-oriented discursive practices that discourage critical thought, "meme-ify" controversial content and encourage hostile rebuttal of external criticism', and that these contents and practices often act as the anchor point and feeder source for algorithmic modes of manipulation.

In this paper we will bring these different scholarly insights – considering closed and default or opt-in encrypted messaging platforms as safe spaces for activists, as well as conspiracy thinking amplifiers – by drawing together theories of media logics, affordances and 'affective atmospheres' (Lupton 2017). We will use theories of 'affective atmospheres' to identify gaps in the aforementioned literature. Rather than locating emotional states and feelings in the rational or conscious interaction of users with digital technologies and affordances, we will reference theories that call attention to how human and non-human interactions in digital environments are 'often felt or sensed by humans entering a place rather than directly observed or represented', which 'can have profound effects on the ways in which people think and feel about and sense the spaces they inhabit and through which they move' (Lupton 2017, 1). This framework will be operationalized to analyse informant responses to WhatsApp, and to a lesser extent, Telegram use in 2016 and the lead up to GE14 (2018).

Methods

The data informing the study is drawn from two field trips to Kuala Lumpur between 2016 and 2018, a time of dramatic upheaval in Malaysia's political structure (Johns and Cheong 2019). This was also a time when participation in encrypted chats on Facebook Messenger, Telegram, and WhatsApp was recognized as a game changer, subverting Malaysian authorities' efforts to curb political activism through surveillance and laws.

The sample for this paper consisted of 29 informants of Malaysian-Chinese ethnicity, aged 18–24, who were recruited using targeted as well as convenience sampling. Advertisements were placed in known activist social media (including by invitation to closed WhatsApp groups), as well as university student association Facebook groups and social media. Malaysian-Chinese young people were purposively recruited into the study owing to media accounts that this community was crucial to online movements and activism to change Malaysia's leadership (Tapsell 2018).

In keeping with best practice working with digital communities who resist intrusion (Swart, Peters, and Broersma 2018) WhatsApp and Facebook group admins were contacted and permission sought to monitor closed communications. In addition, semi-structured interviews of 60-min duration were undertaken with 21 informants in 2016 using techniques to open up interviews beyond structured questioning, i.e. use of video and screen capture to elicit responses from participants as they scrolled through their feeds, demonstrating daily social media routines and habits. Further 8 informants were interviewed in 2018, including follow-up interviews with 4 original participants.

Findings

The safety of WhatsApp

Among the activists we interviewed half were LGBT activists whose focus was on more than changing the political structure though this was also a concern. Because of the social stigma attached to this community, combined with fears that communication on public social media might incur the surveillance and legal machinery of the state, the 'default publicness' (Cho 2018) of platforms like Facebook was eschewed, and WhatsApp or opt-in encrypted chats on Telegram were preferred. One informant also discussed 'secret groups' on Facebook, and on Messenger:

> Usually secret groups are highly sensitive or things that you don't want other people who are not in the group to know... closed groups are sort of like I don't mind being in the group but I don't want people to read unless they are in the group. Open is public. (Phillip, LGBT activist, 21).

Julian, a student activist, expressed a preference for Telegram but identified WhatsApp as a more popular platform in Malaysia owing to the way messaging apps were marketed and taken up in this context (Ling and Lai 2016); he particularly discussed the politics surrounding encryption, with Facebook's entry into this market in 2016:

> Informant: everyone's on 3 different chat apps at once, because Singapore and Malaysia got hit 3 ways at the same time. So they've had WhatsApp for a while and then WeChat came in from China and then Viber ... now there's like Telegram for paranoid people.
>
> Interviewer: So why is Telegram for paranoid people? WhatsApp's got end-to-end encryption too?
>
> Informant: It does now. And at the time they were all saying, 'Oh Facebook's going to buy WhatsApp, we're all going to be screwed, they're going to suck in our phone numbers and our profiles against our will and we'll have to delete everything manually.' So I was freaking out ... except our worst fears have not come to pass somehow and they've also introduced encryption. So we are at least safe from the government, but not necessary from Facebook (Julian, 24).

While Julian describes concerns regarding surveillance by digital platforms, nonetheless, the end-to-end encryption guarantee of WhatsApp and Telegram was identified as a form of protection from government surveillance. This affordance was discussed in the context of a spate of arrests that had caused fear among politically engaged young people in 2016, a period of time when the Sedition Act and other legal measures were being used to curb contentious speech:

> People are being arrested just because they posted something that insults the government or Prime Minister. A few weeks back, the founder of Seksualiti Merdeka and a few of his friends were arrested. (Steven, 23).

As scholars have noted, the growth in popularity of encrypted by default or opt-in encrypted messaging applications, particularly WhatsApp and Telegram in Malaysia, has, in part, been due to a tightening of the regulatory environment for social media participation and speech since the 2013 election. This is also reflected in non-activist informant accounts, where topics or postings that could be considered at risk of coming under scrutiny by MCMC led them to seek the most secure and protected spaces they could.

Ben (21) was on numerous political WhatsApp groups, but never engaged in political chat on Facebook for fear of legal repercussions and reputational damage to him and his family. He cited the Sedition Act as a reason why many Malaysian-Chinese people felt unsafe on open social networks, as he felt it was used by the government to suppress criticism of special *Bumiputera* rights in Malaysia and increasing Islamization of the public sphere, both topics considered contentious and incurring claims of sedition:

> It's an invisible box, and we call that box the Sedition Act ... it is omnipresent, always in the background waiting for you to make some sort of statement that you can get hauled away for. And I think a lot of people do live in perpetual fear of that (Ben, 18).

Rhys, a law student, who also discussed being on multiple WhatsApp groups for political discussion, described WhatsApp as 'safer' than social networking platforms like Twitter, where even if account settings were set to private, the actions of other people in the network made it easier to access information:

> I think [WhatsApp] was somewhat safer ... safe for me to discuss politics, rather than discussing it publicly ... because there are always people watching even if you've set your settings to private. (Rhys, 24).

The latter comment referred to a friend of his who was doxed on Twitter despite having a private account. Some activists felt a compulsion to share their political views on Facebook status updates and on Twitter or Instagram, so as not to be silenced; but they also discussed the importance of encrypted group chats in a manner which reflected Treré's analysis of WhatsApp as a social media 'backstage' (Treré 2015). Billy, who worked for an NGO seeking an end to political corruption and Simone, who volunteered for a WhatsApp group who provided legal assistance to citizens arrested under sedition charges, spoke about the types of communication that these platforms afforded

> It's one of our primary communication methods internally, for staff and committee members. To mobilize for example, we have a whole bunch of groups. So, the last by-elections, we form WhatsApp groups for the volunteers; to disseminate information, or mobilize people for certain things, it's just a matter of mass communicating (Billy, 26).

> Like when someone gets arrested for any posting, they'll post it here and then they will contact that person's family or that person directly, and offer legal assistance. (Simone, 19).

In thinking through the experiences informants had of using WhatsApp and Telegram, the architecture and design of these platforms, and particularly the feature of end-to-end encryption seemed to make this a preferred option for privacy conscious activists and everyday users, and mention was often made of it being 'safer' than public social media communications (Agur 2019). Of course, this was also informed by broader media ecologies where surveillance of networked publics and laws to censor speech and arrest users made retreats to the social media 'backstage' more urgent.

The type of communication logic steered by closed, encrypted chat also reflects Treré's discussion of WhatsApp as a 'digital comfort zone' (Treré 2015) where the focus is on internal cohesion building, intimacy and trust. Despite Billy arguing that WhatsApp is used by organizers to mobilize volunteers for specific campaigns, mirroring the communicative logics more commonly associated with social media platforms; the dominant takeaway from informant responses was the feeling of 'safety' that encrypted chats offered, even if it was ephemeral and in some cases illusory as the next section reveals.

Spies and rumours

Despite WhatsApp providing assurances to activists, journalists and citizens that their conversations were able to be kept safe in the 'dark', in 2016–2018, high-profile cases where WhatsApp group conversations were leaked or compromised raised alarm and began to replace perceptions of WhatsApp as a 'safe space'. In one case the arrest of a 76-year-old 'uncle' in a WhatsApp group where he shared an image that caused 'offence' to the Prime Minister, reverberated through activist communities:

> Recently one man was arrested if I'm not mistaken ... for posting things on WhatsApp that were insulting to the Prime Minister (Steven).

The broad assumption seemed to be that government informants, or police, had infiltrated the group by requesting invitation under a pseudonym, making end-to-end encryption redundant. Once in, they could share screenshots with authorities:

> Because even though no matter how secure it is people can simply screenshot and give it to the police or give it to the administrative of the school (Hai Yang, 22).

> I wouldn't give it [political opinion] in WhatsApp or any recorded setting. Because it's not good to keep records ... words become very sensitive. ... There are news that police tend to catch people who are spreading the rumours on WhatsApp (Anita, 22).

The findings show that human-centred methods of collecting and sharing information outside a closed chat could not be stopped by encryption guarantees, despite their aura of impenetrability. Julian also claimed that several activist groups he belonged to have been compromised by spies:

> We would try to use WhatsApp and Telegram encrypted platforms in order to avoid espionage from government, but of course the technology is only as strong as the human link. So there were cases that came up in the year previous to the election where there were student groups that were affected where the government would simply insert one of their agents into the group ... You have no protection from the encryption at that point. (Julian).

Nonetheless, given that activists and pro-opposition supporters held a world-view where they were suspicious of government and public institutions (Tapsell 2018) it was not difficult to see how real though isolated cases could be escalated into a conspiracy that spies lurked everywhere, particularly given the logics of 'insularity' and suspicion towards outsiders noted by Agur (2019). As Julian admitted, much of the rumour circulating in WhatsApp groups leading up to GE14 began with distrust of government then anxieties grew in the dark, and echoed through WhatsApp's closed though connected groups.

This is a key point that warrants attention. For the insular and closed, though connected (as Agur suggests) WhatsApp public, the lack of platform moderation (Matamoros-Fernández 2020) combined with the social function of the forward button enabled rumours to be forwarded easily. Julian recalled how the groups he was plugged into in the lead up to GE14 reflected these types of mediated anxiety and paranoia:

> I was plugged into a group of diaspora members in Melbourne and ... every evening there would be one coming in. There would be like, 'this person has been corrupt – how much money they have embezzled – they are doing this – they are scheming this'. Like it switches an opinion in favour of certain political figures or parties - no-one really knows who is sending out these messages. No-one really knows if they are true or not. The people believe it because of course the government is visibly corrupt (Julian).

This analysis shows that beyond the strategic and rational retreat of actors to WhatsApp and Telegram – where the architecture and affordances of these platforms are understood to shield users from the digital light – in some contexts, feelings of suspicion towards outsiders and anxiety regarding 'spies' or fabricated claims about politicians can also grow. This, combined with the forward function and the ease with which contents can be shared between groups facilitates affective states in some communities of users, where pre-formed suspicions interact with the 'haptic' qualities of the platform, primarily the forward button, driving forms of anxiety that are 'more than human' and which can help spurious claims gain legitimacy and normalize belief that secret plots are everywhere.

Fakery and conspiracy

The belief in WhatsApp as a 'safe space' was further challenged by informants who we interviewed after GE14 – including those who in 2016 expressed a view that WhatsApp was a safe and progressive discursive space, but who in 2018 expressed concerns that WhatsApp had become a source of 'fake news':

> I am very cautious about information on WhatsApp. I did have a family group ...... cousins and relatives sharing like – oh you could say like fake photos (of politicians) (Anita, 24).

Cassie, a journalist who in 2016 used a WhatsApp group for work but felt uneasy about the private groups she was in – because she felt that the closed architecture had a tendency to produce echo chambers among her social group (predominantly anti-government) – had her feelings confirmed in 2018, when she claimed that the circulation of misinformation and rumour was rife, with much of it seeming to suggest government conspiracies were afoot. In the interview, Cassie showed us a message she had received which insinuated that the government were in 'secret talks' for PM Najib to stand down to try to save votes for BN (see Figure 1). She particularly described the amplifying function of the forward button, which made it easy for anxious or non-digitally literate users to forward content, with messages getting 'forwarded and forwarded' (see Figure 2):

Here, the haptic function of the forward button and the emotive contents of some of the messages detected by informants as 'fake news' resonates with Lupton's work on 'affective atmospheres' created in the digital health space where Lupton argues that: 'Affective atmospheres are shaped by their multisensory properties: how spaces and places are physically encountered via their visual, haptic, aural, olfactory and taste

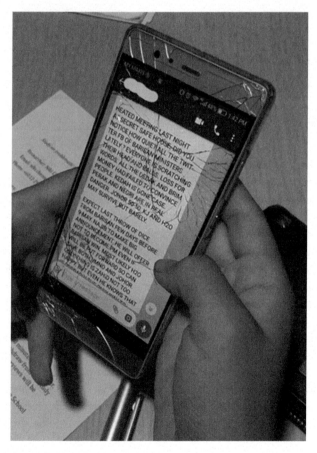

Figure 1. WhatsApp chain mail.

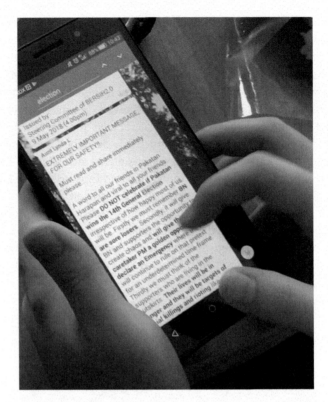

Figure 2. Chain mail message.

properties is central to the feelings they generate', which in relation to digital health technologies, Lupton likens to wearables which vibrate, buzz or 'tap' users, prompting affective reactions and states of feeling such as happiness or anxiety (Lupton 2017, 1, 7).

The content of the messages discussed here also generated affective responses. The messages themselves, according to informants, appeared in 'long text message' format often including capitalized characters, and had instructions that warned participants that an emergency was unfolding and for their own or their loved one's safety they needed to forward it on. This was referred to as being like 'chain mail'.

Simon (22), a non-politically active informant, spoke of several examples of messages he received through WhatsApp family groups (Figure 3):

He acknowledged the way that these contents manipulated people like his father, who shared not just because of panic, but because of love and care for his family and a feeling he was helping. However, even in this scenario Simon claimed that the suspension of rational thought and the 'affective atmosphere' of WhatsApp also competed with quite rational behaviours, i.e. recognition that the messages were hidden from authorities and largely unmoderated. As a result he felt his dad did not think twice about sharing:

> They don't kind of think they're being watched at all or it could possibly come back to them … (Simon)

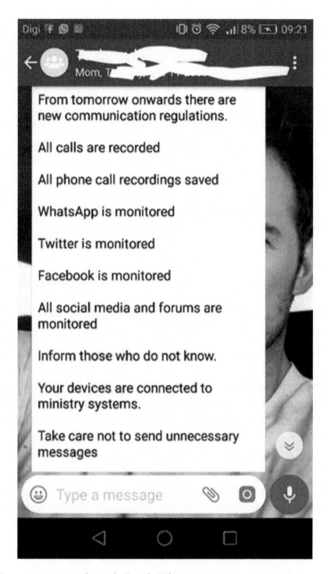

Figure 3. Alarmist message sent through Family WhatsApp group.

Conclusion

As discussed by informants, the closed architecture and guarantee of end-to-end encryption has made WhatsApp an essential 'backstage' for activists, enabling communities to resist and subvert state-based practices of surveillance and control of public conversations on social media. Informants also supported claims that communicative logics of 'insularity', trust and authenticity associated with the closed architecture and the encryption guarantee of WhatsApp and Telegram (Agur 2019; Johns 2020) differed from social media logics of connectivity, publicness, visibility, datafication (Van Dijck and Poell 2013) and audience management to protect reputation and identity (Baym and Boyd 2012). These newer logics were commonly identified with increased feelings of safety and trust among users and between users and the platform. Nonetheless, some informants discussed more ambivalent feelings even as early as 2016. By 2018, in the lead up to GE14, this ambivalence had increased with some informants believing that pressures to determine validity and quality of information on more public-facing social media fell away on WhatsApp, with lack of moderation and inability for authorities to access conversations leading problematic information to circulate.

The logic of insularity (Agur 2019) is interesting to the current study as it explains the retreat of activist and other political communities to these platforms, where concerns about surveillance and being subject to 'moderating mechanisms' by corrupt semi-authoritarian governments (for example, via sedition laws and communications and multimedia act) structures retreats to 'safe spaces' where members can avoid censorship, allowing a free exchange of ideas critical to democracy (Treré 2015). However, the insularity of members within a closed 'socio-technical system', also steers practices that can lead users to only trust insiders and believe mainstream news and 'official' accounts to be inauthentic and fake. This allows problematic information that contradicts official information, including rumours and conspiracy, to flow more freely through WhatsApp groups.

We also gave more consideration to how users connect, create and share content differently in closed and encrypted messaging platforms but also to consider how this contributed towards shared feelings and perceptions. We drew on theories of affect and 'affective atmospheres' (Lupton 2017) to consider how, away from the institutional light and visibility of social media platforms, information that is false, often deliberately so, can be shared more easily. For example, receiving information from a known, trusted contact increases our willingness to believe in its validity and to forward it on. If this information creates a sense of anxiety and urgency this can also move users to share and suspend rational judgement. Informants in this study suggested that the emotive content of messages they identified as 'fake news', i.e. warning of dark, secretive plots that would harm society, combined with the haptic qualities of the forward function and the assurance from end-to-end encryption generated feelings that moved users to anxiously share. The constant attention being paid to these contents which were 'forwarded and forwarded' between groups were shown in some informants' view to reinforce and normalize belief in the conspiratorial content of the messages.

While more research is required, we believe that affect theory can help us to account for these contingent, and sometimes quite unexpected shifts in the shared, embodied feelings and beliefs that arise from users' encounters with dark social technologies, encouraging researchers to avoid framing user behaviour and practices as being influenced either purely by the technologies or the rational decisions of actors. Rather in this paper we have considered how effective atmospheres account for the 'more than human' interactions that occur beyond this limiting dyad.

Notes

1. Lesbian, Gay, Bisexual, Transgender. This was the most commonly used terminology among participants.
2. 'dark social' refers to social traffic or shares that do not contain information referring back to a source, and can't be traced. So, unlike shares from social media platforms, dark social refers to sharing of contents through private channels, like email, SMS and messaging platforms.

Acknowledgments

We would like to acknowledge Deakin University, who provided seed funding for the project, our informants and the organizations who assisted with recruitment.

Disclosure statement

No potential conflict of interest was reported by the author(s).

ORCID

Amelia Johns http://orcid.org/0000-0002-3946-7869
Niki Cheong http://orcid.org/0000-0002-4402-0738

References

Agur, C. 2019. "Insularized Connectedness: Mobile Chat Applications and News Production." *Media and Communication* 7 (1): 179–188. doi:10.17645/mac.v7i1.1802.

Baym, N., and D. Boyd. 2012. "Socially Mediated Publicness: An Introduction." *Journal of Broadcasting & Electronic Media* 56 (3): 320–329. doi:10.1080/08838151.2012.705200.

Case, W. 1993. "Semi-Democracy in Malaysia: Withstanding the Pressures for Regime Change." *Pacific Affairs* 66 (2): 183–205. doi:10.2307/2759366.

Cheong, N. 2020. "Disinformation as a Response to the 'Opposition Playground' in Malaysia." In *From Grassroots Activism to Disinformation: Social Media in Southeast Asia*, edited by Aim Sinpeng and Ross Tapsell, 63–85. Singapore: ISEAS Publishing.

Cho, A. 2018. "Default Publicness: Queer Youth of Color, Social Media, and Being Outed by the Machine." *New Media & Society* 20 (9): 3183–3200. doi:10.1177/1461444817744784.

Fernandez, J. 2019. "Malaysia's Anti-Fake News Act." *Pacific Journalism Review* 25 (1 & 2): 173–192. doi:10.24135/pjr.v25i1.474.

Freedom House. 2018. "Freedom of the Net 2018: Malaysia." Accessed 18 April 2021. https://freedomhouse.org/country/malaysia/freedom-world/2018

Gehl, R. W. 2018. *Weaving the Dark Web: Legitimacy on Freenet, Tor, and I2P*. Cambridge, MA: MIT Press.

Hanckel, B., S. Vivienne, P. Byron, B. Robards, and C. Churchill. 2019. "'That's Not Necessarily for Them': LGBTIQ+ Young People, Social Media Platform Affordances and Identity Curation." *Media, Culture & Society* 41 (8): 1–18. doi:10.1177/0163443719846612.

Jack, C. 2017. "Lexicon of lies : terms for problematic information." Accessed 21 May 2021." https://datasociety.net/output/lexicon-of-lies/

Johns, A. (2020)."'This will be the WhatsApp election': Crypto-publics and digital citizenship in Malaysia's GE14 election" *First Monday* 25 (12). doi: 10.5210/fm.v25i12.10381.

Johns, A, and N. Cheong. 2019. "Feeling the Chill: Bersih 2.0, State Censorship, and 'Networked Affect' on Malaysian Social Media 2012–2018." *Social Media + Society* 5 (2): 1–12. doi:10.1177/2056305118821801.

Lee, A.Y. L., and K.W. Ting. 2015. "Media and Information Praxis of Young Activists in the Umbrella Movement." *Chinese Journal of Communication* 8 (4): 376–392. doi:10.1080/17544750.2015.1086399.

Lim, G. 2020. "Securitize/counter-securitize: the life and death of Malaysia's anti-fake news act." Accessed 21 May 2021." https://datasociety.net/library/securitize-counter-securitize/

Ling, R, and C. H. Lai. 2016. "Microcoordination 2.0: Social Coordination in the Age of Smartphones and Messaging Apps." *Journal of Communication* 66 (5): 834–856. doi:10.1111/jcom.12251.

Lupton, D. 2017. "How Does Health Feel? Towards Research on the Affective Atmospheres of Digital Health." *Digital Health, No* 3: 1–11. doi:10.1177/2055207617701276.

Maddox, A, M. J. Barratt, M Allen, and S. Lenton. 2016. "Constructive Activism in the Dark Web: Cryptomarkets and Illicit Drugs in the Digital 'Demimonde.'." *Information, Communication & Society* 19 (1): 111–126. doi:10.1080/1369118X.2015.1093531.

Matamoros-Fernández, A. 2020. "'El Negro De WhatsApp' Meme, Digital Blackface, and Racism on Social Media." *First Monday* 25: 12. doi:10.5210/fm.v25i12.10420.

McVeigh-Schultz, J, and N. K. Baym. 2015. "Thinking of You: Vernacular Affordance in the Context of the Microsocial Relationship App, Couple." *Social Media + Society* 1 (2): 1–13. doi:10.1177/2056305115604649.

Onderco, M, and F. Stoeckel. 2020. "Conspiratorial Thinking and Foreign Policy Views: Evidence from Central Europe." *Journal of Elections, Public Opinion and Parties* 1–15. doi:10.1080/17457289.2020.1814309.

Pereira, G., and I. Bojzcuk. 2018. "Zap zap, who's there? WhatsApp and the spread of fake news during the 2018 elections in Brazil – global media technologies and cultures lab." Accessed 19 January 2021. http://globalmedia.mit.edu/2018/11/09/zap-zap-whos-there-whatsapp-and-the-spread-of-fake-news-during-the-2018-elections-in-brazil/

Swart, J., C. Peters, and M. Broersma. 2018. "Shedding Light on the Dark Social: The Connective Role of News and Journalism in Social Media Communities." *New Media & Society* 20 (11): 4329–4345. doi:10.1177/1461444818772063.

Tapsell, Ross. 2018. "The Smartphone as the 'Weapon of the Weak': Assessing the Role of Communication Technologies in Malaysia's Regime Change." *Journal of Current Southeast Asian Affairs* 37 (3): 9–29. doi:10.1177/186810341803700302.

Treré, E. 2015. "Reclaiming, Proclaiming, and Maintaining Collective Identity in the #yosoy132 Movement in Mexico: An Examination of Digital Frontstage and Backstage Activism through Social Media and Instant Messaging Platforms." *Information, Communication & Society* 18 (8): 901–915. doi:10.1080/1369118X.2015.1043744.

Van Dijck, J., and T. Poell. 2013. "Understanding Social Media Logic." *Media and Communication* 1 (1): 2–14. doi:10.12924/mac2013.01010002.

Whyte, C. 2020. "View of Of Commissars, Cults and Conspiratorial Communities: The Role of Countercultural Spaces in "Democracy Hacking" Campaigns." *First Monday* 25 (4). doi:10.5210/fm.v25i4.10241.

Great AI Divides? Automated Decision-Making Technologies and Dreams of Development

Jolynna Sinanan and Thomas McNamara

ABSTRACT
A growing body of scholarship is combining studies of automated decision-making's potential to alleviate challenges of development with critical perspectives on discourses and deployment of technologies in developing contexts. This article builds on this literature by drawing links between 'dreams of development' and the imaginings and aspirations surrounding automated decision making in the Global South. The article explores how three classic development imaginaries are reframed, altered and ultimately reinforced by policy recommendations at the global level by the World Bank: alleviating poverty and the creation of wealth, good governance, and social inclusion. We bring into sharper focus the interplay between international narratives about the emancipatory potential of AI and unpack co-created moral discourses around the responsibility over the provision, use and consequences of automated decision-making technologies. Themes of intentionality and the uptake of AI technologies become even more contentious in the Global South, where populations have arguably been subject to consecutive projects described as development, which have resulted in further entrenchment of systemic inequalities.

Introduction

Increasing internet affordability and literacies have inspired discussions of the potential for e-commerce, e-governance and education to address specific economic, political and social challenges in the developing world, or countries in the Global South. Development's uncomfortable early 2000s entwinement of market logics and participatory ideals proved fertile ground for the relationship between internet technologies and social transformation, echoing observations made by media and cultural studies scholars (Castells 2004; Wellman 2018). The World Bank's *World Development Report 2000/01: Attacking Poverty* employed the digital positivist rhetoric associated with the social potentials of internet technologies by: increasing participation, building partnerships, building social capital and increasing access to markets. In the two decades that have followed, these ideas have taken different iterations from building a knowledge-based economy or society, closing digital divides and increasing digital inclusion (see Walsham 2017). ICT for development (ICT4D) scholarship has critically engaged with the implementation of development initiatives that focus on the potential of internet and more recently, digital technologies and has provided in-depth details of the cultural encounter that follows (see Irani 2019; Noske-Turner 2017). Such ethnographically grounded research has illustrated that in the face of development programmes and experts, cultural and social adoption of technologies reveal the negotiation strategies and creativity that characterize the making-do practices of daily life (Rangaswamy and Arora 2016).

Most recently, a growing body of scholarship has drawn together two literatures into deeper discussion: the first is around the impacts of automated decision-making and its potential to alleviate challenges of development, and the second takes critical perspectives towards discourses and deployment of technologies in developing contexts. AI technologies have been analysed as 'backroads' of uneven development, where McDuie-Ra and Gulson 2020, 628) argue that interest in AI from highly influential bodies in setting the agenda for international development such as the World Bank is symptomatic of how AI is becoming incorporated into thinking about mainstream development at the global level. As 'another digital divide', the ways that digital technologies transform spatial relations can perpetuate 'divisions between classes, urban locations and nations' (Ash, Kitchin, and Leszczynski 2018, 30). As these scholars observe, the relationship between the growth of automated decision-making infrastructures and the precursors to these (through digital platforms, smartphones and cloud-based data storage and sharing services) and regional contexts in the Global South remains under investigated.

This article takes a cue from this emerging body of research that critically discusses the nascent agenda concerning the role of AI in international development. We build on this scholarship by linking and drawing parallels between imaginings and aspirations surrounding automated decision-making in the developing world and 'dreams of development'; where the visibility of development signifies an uncritical desire for an unrealizable development (De Vries 2007). By extrapolating great AI divides, the article explores how three classic imaginaries in development studies are reframed, altered and ultimately reinforced in the ICT for development space: the first is around alleviating poverty and the creation of wealth, the second is good governance, and finally, social inclusion. Through select, regional examples from the Global South, we bring into sharper focus the interplay between international narratives about the emancipatory potential of AI and distinct contexts, unpacking co-created moral discourses around the responsibility for the provision, use and consequences of the precursor technologies to automated decision-making. This article contributes to the themes of the *Continuum* Special Issue 'The Dark Social: Online Practices of Resistance, Motility and Power' by integrating these streams of scholarship to develop a critical, theoretical perspective on discourses surrounding AI technologies in developing contexts, and foregrounds the ongoing inequities that pervade both technological access and North-South relations.

In the sections that follow, we introduce De Vries' call for analysing development interventions as a set of often anti-political ideas about social change, and about the relationship between the Global North and South (2007, 27). We then draw on key positions by the World Bank and regional policy recommendations that emphasize the potential of automated decision-making technologies for addressing long-standing challenges in development: increasing wealth, depoliticization and social transformation. We have selected and analysed framings from the World Bank's World Development Report

2016: *Digital Dividends* as a key text of recent recommendations the international institution has put forward for the potentials of digital and automated technologies at a global policy level. We interrogate the framings of AI and provide regionally-based examples of how populations in locally-bound contexts counter, reinforce or navigate these experiences of ICT for Development and the potentials of AI.

Dreams of development: technologization and divides

From the World Bank's structural adjustment agenda to inclusive liberalism, major development institutions' narratives link market-driven economic growth, North-South technological transfer and Global South social change (Kothari and Minogue 2002). Challenging these assumptions, post-development perspectives have drawn attention to the kinds of citizenships development projects and narratives encourage. The 'problems' of poverty as economically lacking are inextricable from systemic and structural forces that guide the inter-and-intra-national based on inequality gender, class and ethnicity, which directly affect 'quality of life' (Nussbaum and Sen 1993).

International institutions' dominance of the vision and implementation of development and its consequences for the Global South is the subject of James Ferguson's seminal: *The Anti-Politics Machine* (1994). Through ethnographic research conducted over nearly ten years with World Bank projects in Lesotho, Ferguson defines anti-politics through two key arguments that resonate with ICT4D today. Firstly, development is envisioned by international actors and implemented through organizational and technocratic means. It therefore decontextualizes and dehistoricizes the political creation and maintenance of structural challenges of poverty. Secondly, through the development machinery, external, internationally-led projects exacerbate existing intra-national inequalities and consolidate power structures that continue to cause conflict within locally-bound social relations. Ferguson (1994) argues an unintended effect is development, implemented as a seemingly neutral and apolitical project, is deeply political and is contested and recreated through intensified local imaginaries and cultural vernacular. As we explore further, these well-established arguments in development studies are rearticulated through engagements with AI.

De Vries (2007) expands upon Ferguson's (1994) thinking by engaging with the dreams and desires of the societies who are positioned as the subjects and beneficiaries of development. Inspired by Deleuze and Guattari (1987) he depicts development as a desiring machine, where small amounts of externally provisioned development, and the presence of signifiers like ICT devices shape *intra*-community aspirations for development. The meanings of development and its pursuit should therefore be considered in relation to and emerging from the desires for development in specific contexts and the promises development organizations – both overtly and inadvertently – make to development recipients (De Vries 2007, 26). By taking seriously the desires for development as locally driven, the outcome will draw from, but may not be, consistent with the vision for development as conceived by international actors. More importantly for De Vries (2007), the idea of development itself relies on the production of desires, which development cannot fulfil. Within literature describing technological visions and ICT utilization, we see parallels where digital technologies, as designed and marketed according to imagined practices in the Western countries in the Global North inadvertently promise a 'development' of wealth and technological advancement, without inter-or-intra-national redistributions of resources and power (Gumucio-Dagron and Tufte 2006; Lennie and Tacchi 2013).

The scholarship of locative and mobile media increasingly emphasizes the need to explore practices beyond the Global North (Miller et al. 2016). Although they do not use language associated with development, these scholars point towards the ways in which mobile phone use by populations in the Global South demonstrates innovation, creativity and intricate practices of making do (Wilken, Goggin, and Horst 2019, 5). Ethnographic studies in developing regions illustrate how digital technologies are subject to wide variations, adaptations and appropriations, in response to cultural and religious norms or infrastructural, financial and social challenges (Horst and Miller 2006). The literature based on primary research in developing regions foregrounds that although digital technologies are designed according to the imaginaries, assumptions and standpoints of corporations located in the Global North, the ultimate form of adoption is rarely uniform (Goggin 2011). By doing do, these studies of technologies perhaps demonstrate a deeper appreciation for the ways that uses of digital technologies counter the visions from which they have emerged. As we discuss further, the visions for digital technologies and for the capacities of AI in particular are framed in terms of their potential for economic development in the Global South. We argue that such a position extends and replicates the long-standing discourse of technology as an avenue for a technology-driven, apolitical development.

Of the many precursor technologies invoked to justify the liberating potential of AI, the most common is machine learning, where machines take large data sets, identify patterns and 'learn' from these, with little input from humans (Nilsson 2010; Russell and Norvig 2009). Within these definitions, machine learning combines large volumes of data with computing power to allow abilities such as reasoning, language, perception, vision and spatial processing, based on automated decision-making. Machine learning combined with precursor technologies to demonstrate the supposed potential for meeting the challenges of development appears across two areas. First is within the administrative level of organizations, such as for the improvement of digital infrastructures, and; the second is within personal use of digital devices such as smartphones. In the sections that follow, we outline the World Bank's endorsements for integrating digital technologies into an 'internet economy' in the *World Development Report 2016: Digital Dividends*. The 2016 WDR includes several examples of how internet technologies promote inclusion, efficiency and innovation under the rubrics of businesses, people and governments. However, the narratives of examples provided are predominantly expressed through metrics indicating increase or decrease of implementation, or through vignettes that describe the mechanisms of inclusion, efficiency and innovation, largely devoid of the contextual factors that facilitate or challenge these mechanisms. We introduce examples of how regional policy recommendations for AI adoption echoes those of the World Bank and provide illustrations from empirical case studies of how contextually driven factors influence how locally-bound populations navigate the promises of development that are associated with technologization and eventually AI.

Alleviating poverty and creating wealth

Digital technologies supposedly facilitate inclusion by increasing trade and job opportunities, create efficiency by maximizing capital utilization and labour productivity and driving innovation by increasing competitiveness (World Bank 2016, 12). The WDR (2016, 12) report emphasizes the value of 'better information' and argues that 'the greatest contribution to growth comes from the internet's lowering of costs and thus from raising efficiency and labour productivity in practically all economic sectors'. Organizations that influence regional policy making such as the International Finance Corporation and the United Nations Economic and Social Commission for Asia and the Pacific reiterate the World Bank's position through statements such as 'Productivity improvements also stem from more investment in human capital thanks to automation' (Strusani and Houngbonon 2019, 4) and 'Encouraging businesses to embrace the power of digital technology, therefore, should be an imperative of governments' (Economic and Social Commission for Asia and the Pacific 2017, 6).

Financial technology (FinTech) and mobile money have become exemplars of the potential for automated decision-making and digital devices for alleviating poverty in developing regions. One of the most novel innovations for smartphones is in regard to mobile money and allowing the storing and sending of small amounts of 'money' (in reality, digital information) from individual mobile phones using SMS. This is without the need for a bank account or internet connection, presenting an opportunity for those without the capacity to secure these prerequisites for exchanging larger amounts of money. In the Caribbean, for example, mobile phone provider Digicel facilitates mobile money exchanges through SMS-based menus. In their study of mobile money users in Haiti, Taylor and Horst argue that its rapid uptake was due to two interconnected factors (2013). Firstly, following the Haiti earthquake, mobile phone infrastructure was quicker to recover than other financial, communications and transport infrastructure and secondly, given Haiti's large mobile working population, money through mobile technologies often moved alongside people and objects. Given these contextual factors, mobile money operated within existing economic and social practices, that were facilitated by digital platforms and were not caused by them (Taylor and Horst 2013, 89).

In examples of successful mobile technology interventions, Kenyan mobile service provider Safaricom's mobile money transfer service M-Pesa frequently appears as a positive case study of technological innovation to address challenges of financial inclusion for rural populations in sub-Saharan African societies (Suri and William 2016). For Kenyan smallholders who cannot afford bank accounts or lack sufficient savings, M-Pesa offers credit viability and stores and transfer funds, therefore enabling better risk management and allocation of resources and labour (Suri and William 2016; Abdulhamid 2020). This enables short-term but not long-term poverty alleviation for M-Pesa users, who are still hampered by shortcomings in financial literacy and burdened with financial risk (Abdulhamid 2020; Bateman, Duvendack, and Loubere 2019).

The promotion and critique of fin-tech echo debates made some fifteen years ago about microcredit (Ames and Ames 2012; Burkett 2007: Fernando 2006). Within this scholarship, it is well established that outcomes of microfinance and other poverty alleviation strategies vary from context to context and are inextricable from existing social and economic resources and literacies. Significant to the arguments of this article, the appeal that microfinance holds over the imagination of development approaches is the ideological position that emphasizes the engagement of individuals' responsibility in becoming active economic citizens, which is why microfinance receives wide support from large-scale corporate funding (Burkett 2007, 152). Bateman, Duvendack, and Loubere (2019, 3) explicitly address these parallels by arguing 'the rapid popularization of fin-tech as a developmental solution is, in many respects, premised on the continued prominence of the quintessential local development intervention associated with the neoliberal revolution: microcredit and the broader concept of financial inclusion'.

Innovations in FinTech is often used to invoke dreams of AI-driven development. It is envisaged that data generated through smartphones can enable mobile AI apps to deliver microlending, targeted education and medical and health communication (Strusani and Houngbonon 2019, 4). As McDuie-Ra and Gulson (2020, 629) argue, a key assumption is that poverty alleviation can be achieved from afar with greater precision achieved by algorithmic decision-making. Similar to its role in commerce, the internet was expected to usher in a new era of accountability and political empowerment, with citizens participating in policy making and forming self-organized virtual communities to hold government to account, narratives that echo earlier enthusiastic visions for internet technologies such as those of Howard Rheingold (Rheingold 1993; World Bank 2016, 23). Yet, as we have seen, the role of smartphone technologies and social media platforms in governance and political accountability has been highly contentious (Suzor, Van Geelen, and Myers West 2018). Despite its potentials, the concerns for the role of AI in depoliticization have increased alongside the lack of coordinated policies for deploying AI ethically (Walsh 2020).

Good governance

Building social capital and utilizing social networks have been core to the inclusive liberal approach in development since the 2000s (Amin 2005). Building civil society is hoped to instil better judgements and values, and through this the better management of social and economic resources. However, as Craig and Porter (2006, 71) have argued, the assumption of harnessing social resources implies that people will conform to externally determined 'better decisions'. Within areas of civic engagement, governance and political organization, AI is perceived to facilitate transparency and increase efficiency in the provision of information. For service delivery from government and administrative bodies, 'the internet raises efficiency and productivity through automation and data-driven management' (World Bank 2016, 17). Yet, despite its optimism, the World Bank has observed that political participation and engagement of populations living on low income has remained limited, while in many countries digital technologies has disproportionately benefitted political elites and increased the governments' capacity to influence social and political discourse (2016, 24).

Within the literature on big data, the algorithmic turn and digital citizenship, the role of digital technologies in political and democratic processes is burgeoning with critiques and empirically-based studies countering techno optimism (Dencik et al. 2019; Hintz, Dencik, and Wahl-Jorgensen 2018; Milan and Treré 2019; Singh and Gurumurthy 2013; Treré 2016). Yet, Henman (2019) observes that although algorithms have been in use by governments for policy and service delivery for decades, most prominently in the Global North and technological hubs in Asia, issues of governance in service delivery apps and digital advice is fairly recent and has received little attention.

Drawing on earlier proponents for computerizing government services, Henman (2019) observes the constant argument in favour of automation and algorithmic government is that by automating public policy processes, they become accelerated, reducing the need for human resources and the costs associated with them. Indeed, the World Bank (2016, 8) reiterates these aspirations by arguing that lowering information costs and creating information goods, data driven automated decision making can facilitate searching, matching and sharing of information, enabling greater organization and cross-sector collaboration across several sectors. Digitizing government services is perceived to enable greater efficiency, lower costs, higher-quality services and enhanced government accountability and transparency (Chopra 2014).

The recent Cambodian context is illustrative in this respect. Following the civil conflict, rebuilding fixed-line telecommunications infrastructure was not as effective as establishing a wider mobile phone network. Beschorner et al. (2018, 8) observe that by 'jumpstarting it's telecommunications infrastructure with mobile phones', one result is that by 2016, Cambodia had one of the highest levels of increase in mobile phone subscriptions in Asia and was categorized as a middle-income country by the World Bank. Cambodia has seen a dramatic change in its state of digital technologies uptake and empirical studies reveal that Cambodians use them in original and innovative ways that fit their needs but also respond to the challenges of their environment (Jack 2020; Noske-Turner 2017). However, at the national government level, digital technologies for the provision of services through apps remains limited. Currently, Cambodia does not have a centralized national government portal, only independently developed websites without standardization in appearance, platform or security (Beschorner et al. 2018, 14).

Significant commentary about digital government assumes that digital technologies facilitate democracy, transparency and accountability by making it easier for citizens to engage with the government (Henman 2019, 84; World Bank 2016, 156). Yet, as we have seen in Western, developed countries, this has not been the case and there is sufficient basis to argue that AI might already be exacerbating problems of government accountability and transparency. Automated processing of candidate profiles for employment and credit scoring may reduce time and cost, but the profiling of individuals and targeting of policies and services may result in differential treatment towards individuals. Such differences that may result from predictive profiling represent a fundamental shift in policy and service delivery rationales and risks deepening social inequalities and divisions where some people are treated very different to others (Henman 2019, 2010). To counter the potential consequences of surveillance through data collection that informs automated decision-making and subsequent misuse through political influence, the need for ethical considerations in the development of intelligent interactive systems has led to several government, non-government and research initiatives such as non-profit research organization Data & Society's AI on the Ground project (Singh 2021; Andrejevic, Hearn, and Kennedy 2015; Dignum 2018).

Beyond its currency for corporate and government interests, 'big data' is like other buzzwords that have gained momentum referring to interconnected social, economic and technological phenomena, where the emphasis is placed on benefits and challenges

(Treré 2016). Cornwall (2007) offers a sharp critique of the uses of buzzwords in development practice (which are often drawn from economistic and technological discourses). She argues 'development's buzzwords gain their purchase and power through their vague and euphemistic qualities, their capacity to embrace a multitude of possible meanings, and their normative resonance' (Cornwall 2007, 472). Buzzwords such as poverty reduction and good governance as catch-terms influence how development is practiced, for whom and by whom and they impact on processes from funding to expertise. While precursor technologies to AI are increasingly integrated into strategies for achieving goals of development, the promise of AI driven development risks becoming part of existing pitfalls within the challenges of development. We consider these arguments in our final section that focuses on social transformation.

Social inclusion

Treré (2016) argues that the literature on social movements and digital technologies often reduces diverse complex socio-technical configurations and cultural contexts to more simplistic Twitter or Facebook 'revolutions'. While these movements have involved long-term strategies by activists and their networks for gaining momentum and enhanced by algorithms within social media platforms that steer collective public action (often in problematic ways), platforms are already under scrutiny for their impacts on social configurations in the Global South (Milan 2015).

Many Global South populations primarily experience the internet as Facebook, where social media platforms are accessed through low-cost smartphones and mobile data through pay-as-you-go plans (Miller et al. 2016; Sinanan 2017). A consequence is that social media forms a part of daily routines more than web informational resources extending the possibilities of everyday life (Hughes and Eng 2019). In this final section, we focus on a long-standing theme in the goals of development for social transformation and how AI is becoming integrated into discussions of development strategies. The specific focus here is on technological mechanisms for gender empowerment.

Development through inclusive liberalism featured several critiques that 'gender', 'culture' and 'community' as espoused by influential policy bodies are reduced to economistic problems that need to be addressed, rather than being recognized for their full social complexities (Jackson 1996; Mohan and Stokke 2000). Schech and Vas Dev (2007, 15) describe that 'rather than facilitating a rigorous analysis of poverty, for example, the World Development Report 2000/01 frames the poor in the gendered language of vulnerability and disempowerment and presents them in need of capacity building and of non-poor coalitions and leadership'. More recently, technological means have been touted to address challenges under the umbrella term of 'gender'. The World Bank applies 'a gender lens' to digital technologies and economic opportunities, identifying three opportunities (2016). Digital technologies are perceived to facilitate 'connecting women to work, and generating new opportunities in online work, e-commerce, and the sharing economy' (World Bank 2016, 134). The report further argues that 'women are well positioned to gain from a shift in employment toward nonroutine occupations, and away from physical work' and 'digital technologies also impact women's voice and agency. Increased access to information can affect gender norms and affect aspirations, often faster than expected' (ibid).

Significant case studies counter the assumptions behind these perceptions (above). In detail, most directly in the areas of app-enabled casualized work and the consequences for women of different demographics who exercise their voices in digital spaces (Duffy 2016; Vickery and Everbach 2018). Further, Vinuesa et al. (2020) problematize the role of AI in the context of Sustainable Development Goal 5: Achieve gender equality and empower all women and girls, arguing that machine-learning algorithms inadvertently learn and reproduce societal biases against women and girls (Vinuesa et al. 2020, 3). Research drawing on a feminist approach to AI design and uptake makes a significant critical contribution to discussions on the ways in which AI technologies might address the challenges for women in developing countries. Nanditha (2021) for example draws attention to algorithms that influence visibility on Twitter in her analysis of #MeToo in India. She argues that consequences of existing design include excluding the voices of marginalized groups of women at the intersection of caste and class and instead amplifies the voices of more elite groups (Nanditha 2021). Existing gender disparities based on structures of ethnicity, class have already proven to be consequential for past development initiatives, historically (Kothari and Minogue 2002). Microfinance for example might alleviate challenges of household income, but does not address gender disparities in the household that undermines women's labour (Ames and Ames 2012).

The literature and empirically based studies that focus on gender and development is beyond the scope of this article. However, we have drawn attention to the World Bank's framing of technological potentials and have countered them by drawing on perspectives that consider a gendered perspective in the consequences of AI uptake to emphasize the need to draw a closer conversation between these bodies of research. The World Development Reports are not just policy documents but rather, they play a critical role in shaping the boundaries and the nature of debates in development and therefore justify a closer reading (Schech and Vas Dev 2007). And as McDuie-Ra and Gulson 2020, 632) have argued, further research needs to map the ways AI is emerging in the national politics of developing countries, where many are still navigating previous disruptions, from imperialism to outsourcing.

Conclusion

In this article, we have argued that automated technologies have inspired new 'dreams of development' for all including women in the Global South. These narratives carry an explicit moral position that the Global North institutions of development will use depoliticized, market-driven technologies to improve societies in the Global South. We have focused on existing precursor technologies, each of which is linked to a vision of AI as enabling poverty alleviation, good governance and social inclusion. By linking and drawing parallels between imaginings and aspirations surrounding automated decision-making in the developing world and dominant themes in development, we have shown that the dreams of AI obfuscate the global inequalities at the heart of international development.

De Vries (2007) has long argued for a radical shift in development subjectivity, where desires for development are locally-driven and taken seriously by the 'Western' world. Instead of being an economic, and technologization project conceived of, directed and implemented from the Global North, development initiatives need more than consultation and nominal inclusion on behalf of countries in the Global South. The majority of research that addresses AI applications for development comes from regions where AI researchers live and work, which are higher income, technologically advanced environments (Vinuesa et al. 2020). These researchers are often those who have benefitted from North–South power dynamics and from technological advancement, and often experience the latter obfuscating the former (Dignum 2018, 1).

Interventions that use AI and automated technologies as a strategy for development are the most recent trend in a long line of projects and programs that have attempted to use Global North technological dominance to 'modernize' populations and societies in the Global South (Lewis and Mosse 2006). The outcomes of this have been uneven at best, potentially deepening structural inequalities and exacerbated economic, politic and social exclusion (Enghel and Noske-Turner 2018). The assumptions behind designing, implementing and the perceived uptake of AI are predicated upon assumptions about efficiency and effectiveness, which undermines the creative capacities and making-do practices of women and 'the poor'. The emphasis on efficiency and effectiveness also neglects to recognize that social bonding, leisure, and entertainment are integral to routines and maintaining good relationships associated with everyday life, where social relations are in many ways a more reliable safety net than other economic activities espoused by development initiatives (Bebbington and Kothari 2006; Narotzky and Besnier 2014).

Data, algorithms and digital infrastructure in the Global North are already under scrutiny for embedding forms of discrimination, oppression and social exclusion in their day to operation. Such investigations are becoming increasingly important in contemporary discussions of how much power and privacy is entrusted to digital media, cloud storage and automation (Boczkowski and Lievrouw 2008; Gillespie 2016; Gillespie, Boczkowski, and Foot 2014; Lievrouw 2014; McKelvey 2018).

There is only very recent discussion emerging around ethical principles that should be applied to the implementation of automated technologies globally. However, although there is some convergence around the principles of transparency, justice and fairness, non-maleficence, responsibility and privacy; there is substantive divergence in how these principles are interpreted, which actors are responsible for upholding them and how they should be implemented (Jobin et al. 2019). These conversations are also led by countries in the Global North, with little representation of countries in the Global South in international or supranational organizations. We have outlined why closer scrutiny between the visions and implementations for AI and automated technologies and development narratives historically need deeper consideration to map the emergence of the ways in which they are imagined, implemented and navigated in developing countries.

Acknowledgments

The authors wish to express their gratitude to the Special Issue editors and reviewers, the Socio-Tech Futures Lab in the Department of Media and Communications at the University of Sydney and to the Intelligence in Singapore Society module students at Tembusu College for constructive discussion in developing this article.

Disclosure statement

No potential conflict of interest was reported by the author(s).

ORCID

Jolynna Sinanan http://orcid.org/0000-0002-4423-8972
Tom McNamara http://orcid.org/0000-0002-8589-5194

References

Abdulhamid, N. 2020. "Disruptive Technology, Mobile Money, and Financial Mobilization in Africa: M-Pesa as Kenya's Solution to Global Financial Exclusion." In *Disruptive Technologies, Innovation and Development in Africa*, edited by P. Arthur, K. Hanson, and K. Puplampu, 187–202. Cham: Palgrave Macmillan.

Ames, A., and T. Ames. 2012. "The Effects of Microfinance on the Orang Asli of Malaysia." In *Southeast Asia's Credit Revolution: From Moneylenders to Microfinance*, edited by A. Goenka and D. Henley, 141–155. Oxford: Routledge.

Amin, A. 2005. "Local Community on Trial." *Economy and Society* 34 (4): 612–633. doi:10.1080/03085140500277211.

Andrejevic, M., A. Hearn, and H. Kennedy. 2015. "Cultural Studies of Data Mining: Introduction." *European Journal of Cultural Studies* 18 (4–5): 379–394. doi:10.1177/1367549415577395.

Ash, J., R. Kitchin, and A. Leszczynski. 2018. "Digital Turn, Digital Geographies?" *Progress in Human Geography* 42 (1): 25–43. doi:10.1177/0309132516664800.

Bateman, M., M. Duvendack, and N. Loubere. 2019. "Is Fin-tech the New Panacea for Poverty Alleviation and Local Development? Contesting Suri and Jack's M-Pesa Findings Published in Science." *Review of African Political Economy* 46 (161): 480–495. doi:10.1080/03056244.2019.1614552.

Bebbington, A., and U. Kothari. 2006. "Transnational Development Networks." *Environment & Planning A* 38 (5): 849–866. doi:10.1068/a37213.

Beschorner, N., J. Neumann, M. Sanchez Martin, and B. Larson. 2018. *Benefiting from the Digital Economy: Cambodia Policy Note*. New York: World Bank.

Boczkowski, P., and L. Lievrouw. 2008. "Bridging STS and Communication Studies: Research on Media and Information Technologies." In *The Handbook of Science and Technologies Studies*, edited by E. Hackett, O. Amsterdamska, M. Lynch, and J. Wacjman, 949–978. Cambridge: MIT Press.

Burkett, I. 2007. "Globalized Microfinance: Economic Empowerment or Just Debt?" In *Revitalising Communities in a Globalising World*, edited by L. Dominelli, 151–160. London: Routledge.

Castells, M. 2004. *The Network Society: A Cross-cultural Perspective*. Cheltenham: Edward Elgar.

Chopra, A. 2014. *Innovative State: How New Technologies Can Transform Government*. Grove: Atlantic

Cornwall, A. 2007. "Buzzwords and Fuzzwords: Deconstructing Development Discourse." *Development in Practice* 17 (4–5): 471–484. doi:10.1080/09614520701469302.

Craig, D., and D. Porter. 2006. *Development beyond Neoliberalism? Governance, Poverty Reduction and Political Economy*. London: Routledge.

De Vries, P. 2007. "Don't Compromise Your Desire for Development! A Lacanian/Deleuzian Rethinking of the Anti-politics Machine." *Third World Quarterly* 28 (1): 25–43. doi:10.1080/01436590601081765.

Deleuze, G, and F. Guattari. 1987. *A Thousand Plateaus: Capitalism and Schizophrenia*. Minneapolis: University of Minnesota Press.

Dencik, L., A. Hintz, J. Redden, and E. Treré. 2019. "Exploring Data Justice: Conceptions, Applications and Directions." *Information, Communication & Society* 22 (7): 873–881. doi:10.1080/1369118X.2019.1606268.

Dignum, V. 2018. "Ethics in Artificial Intelligence: Introduction to the Special Issue." *Ethics and Information Technology* 20: 1–3. doi:10.1007/s10676-018-9450-z.

Duffy, B. 2016. "The Romance of Work: Gender and Aspirational Labour in the Digital Culture Industries." *International Journal of Cultural Studies* 19 (4): 441–457. doi:10.1177/1367877915572186.

Economic and Social Commission for Asia and the Pacific. 2017. *Artificial Intelligence in Asia and the Pacific*. Bangkok: United Nations.

Enghel, F., and J. Noske-Turner, eds. 2018. *Communication in International Development: Doing Good or Looking Good?* London: Routledge.

Ferguson, J. 1994. *The Anti-Politics Machine: 'Development', Depoliticization, and Bureaucratic Power in Lesotho*. Minneapolis: University of Minnesota Press.

Fernando, J. 2006. *Microfinance: Perils and Prospects*. London: Routledge.

Gillespie, T. 2016. "# Trendingistrending: When Algorithms Become Culture." In *Algorithmic Cultures: Essays on Meaning, Performance and New Technologies*, edited by R. Seyfert and J. Roberge, 64–87. London: Routledge.

Gillespie, T., P. Boczkowski, and K. Foot, eds. 2014. *Media Technologies: Essays on Communication, Materiality, and Society*. Cambridge: MIT Press.

Goggin, G. 2011. "Going Mobile." In *The Handbook of Media Audiences*, edited by V. Nightingale, 128–146. Malden: Wiley Blackwell.

Gumucio-Dagron, A., and T. Tufte. 2006. *Communication for Social Change Anthology: Historical and Contemporary Readings*. South Orange: Communication for Social Change Consortium.

Henman, P. 2010. *Governing Electronically: E-government and the Reconfiguration of Public Administration, Policy and Power*. London: Palgrave.

Henman, P. 2019. "Of Algorithms, Apps and Advice: Digital Social Policy and Service Delivery." *Journal of Asian Public Policy* 12 (1): 71–89. doi:10.1080/17516234.2018.1495885.

Hintz, A., L. Dencik, and K. Wahl-Jorgensen. 2018. *Digital Citizenship in a Datafied Society*. New Jersey: John Wiley & Sons.

Horst, H., and D. Miller. 2006. *The Cell Phone: An Anthropology of Communication*. Oxford: Berg.

Hughes, C., and N. Eng. 2019. "Facebook, Contestation and Poor People's Politics: Spanning the Urban–Rural Divide in Cambodia?" *Journal of Contemporary Asia* 49 (3): 365–388. doi:10.1080/00472336.2018.1520910.

Irani, L. 2019. *Chasing Innovation: Making Entrepreneurial Citizens in Modern India*. Vol. 22. Princeton: Princeton University Press.

Jack, M. 2020. "The Socio-spatial Installed Base: Ride-hailing Applications, Parking Associations, and Precarity in Tuk Tuk Driving in Phnom Penh, Cambodia." *The Information Society* 36 (5): 1–14.

Jackson, C. 1996. "Rescuing Gender from the Poverty Trap." *World Development* 24 (3): 489–504. doi:10.1016/0305-750X(95)00150-B.

Jobin, A., M. Ienca, and E. Vayena. 2019. "The global landscape of AI ethics guidelines„. *Nature, Machine, Intelligence* 1 (9): 389–399.

Kothari, U., and M. Minogue, eds. 2002. *Critical Perspectives in Development Theory and Practice*. Basingstoke: Macmillan.

Lennie, J., and J. Tacchi. 2013. *Evaluating Communication for Development: A Framework for Social Change*. London: Routledge.

Lewis, D., and D. Mosse. 2006. *Development Brokers and Translators: The Ethnography of Aid and Agencies*. Bloomfield: Kumarian Press.

Lievrouw, L. 2014. "Materiality and Media in Communication and Technology Studies: An Unfinished Project." In *Media Technologies: Essays on Communication, Materiality, and Society*, edited by T. Gillespie, P. Boczkowski, and K. Foot, 21–51. Cambridge: MIT Press.

McDuie-Ra, D., and K. Gulson. 2020. "The Backroads of AI: The Uneven Geographies of Artificial Intelligence and Development." *Area* 52 (3): 626–633. doi:10.1111/area.12602.

McKelvey, F. 2018. *Internet Daemons: Digital Communications Possessed*. Minneapolis: University of Minnesota Press.

Milan, S. 2015. "When Algorithms Shape Collective Action: Social Media and the Dynamics of Cloud Protesting." *Social Media+ Society* 1 (2): 2056305115622481.

Milan, S., and E. Treré. 2019. "Big Data from the South (s): Beyond Data Iniversalism." *Television & New Media* 20 (4): 319–335. doi:10.1177/1527476419837739.

Miller, D., E. Costa, N. Haynes, T. McDonald, R. Nicolescu, J. Sinanan, J. Spyer, S. Venkatramen, and X. Wang. 2016. *How the World Changed Social Media*. London: UCL Press.

Mohan, G., and K. Stokke. 2000. "Participatory Development and Empowerment: The Dangers of Localism." *Third World Quarterly* 21 (2): 247–268. doi:10.1080/01436590050004346.

Nanditha, N. 2021. "Exclusion in #metoo India: Rethinking Inclusivity and Intersectionality in Indian Digital Feminist Movements." *Feminist Media Studies*. doi:10.1080/14680777.2021.1913432.

Narotzky, S., and N. Besnier. 2014. "Crisis, Value, and Hope: Rethinking the Economy: An Introduction to Supplement 9." *Current Anthropology* 55 (S9): S4–S16. doi:10.1086/676327.

Nilsson, N. 2010. *The Quest for Artificial Intelligence: A History of Ideas and Achievements*. Cambridge: Cambridge University Press.

Noske-Turner, J. 2017. *Rethinking Media Development Through Evaluation: Beyond Freedom*. Cham: Springer.

Nussbaum, M., and A. Sen, eds. 1993. *The Quality of Life*. Oxford: Oxford University Press.

Rangaswamy, N., and P. Arora. 2016. "The Mobile Internet in the Wild and Every Day: Digital Leisure in the Slums of Urban India." *International Journal of Cultural Studies* 19 (6): 611–626. doi:10.1177/1367877915576538.

Rheingold, H. 1993. "A Slice of Life in My Virtual Community." In *Global Networks: Computers and International Communication*, edited by L. Harasim, 57–80. Cambridge: MIT Press.

Russell, S., and P. Norvig. 2009. *Artificial Intelligence: A Modern Approach*. New Jersey: Pearson.

Schech, S., and S. Vas Dev. 2007. "Gender Justice: The World Bank's New Approach to the Poor?" *Development in Practice* 17 (1): 14–26. doi:10.1080/09614520601092451.

Sinanan, Jolynna. 2017. *Social Media in Trinidad: Values and Visibility*. London: UCL Press.

Singh, P., and A. Gurumurthy. 2013. "Establishing Public-ness in the Network: New Moorings for Development—A Critique of the Concepts of Openness and Open Development." In *Open Development: Networked Innovations in International Development*, edited by M. Smith and K. Reilly, 173–196. Cambridge: MIT Press.

Singh, R. 2021. "Mapping AI in the Global South: A New Project to Identify Sites and Vocabularies of Digital IDs and AI". Accessed 2 February 2021. https://points.datasociety.net/ai-in-the-global-south-sites-and-vocabularies-e3b67d631508

Strusani, D., and G. Houngbonon. 2019. *The Role of Artificial Intelligence in Supporting Development in Emerging Markets*. New York: International Finance Corporation.

Suri, T., and J. William. 2016. "The Long-run Poverty and Gender Impacts of Mobile Money." *Science* 354 (6317): 1288–1292. doi:10.1126/science.aah5309.

Suzor, N., T. Van Geelen, and S. Myers West. 2018. "Evaluating the Legitimacy of Platform Governance: A Review of Research and A Shared Research Agenda." *International Communication Gazette* 80 (4): 385–400. doi:10.1177/1748048518757142.

Taylor, E., and H. Horst. 2013. "From Street to Satellite: Mixing Methods to Understand Mobile Money Users." *Ethnographic Praxis in Industry Conference Proceedings* 2013 (1): 88–102. doi:10.1111/j.1559-8918.2013.00008.x.

Treré, E. 2016. "The Dark Side of Digital Politics: Understanding the Algorithmic Manufacturing of Consent and the Hindering of Online Dissidence." *IDS Bulletin* 47 (1): 127–138. doi:10.19088/1968-2016.111.

Vickery, J., and T. Everbach. 2018. *Mediating Misogyny*. Cham: Springer.

Vinuesa, R., H. Azizpour, I. Leite, M. Balaam, V. Dignum, S. Domisch, A. Felländer, S. Langhans, M. Tegmark, and F. Nerini. 2020. "The Role of Artificial Intelligence in Achieving the Sustainable Development Goals." *Nature Communications* 11 (1): 1–10. doi:10.1038/s41467-019-14108-y.

Walsh, T. 2020. "A Pebble in the AI Race." *arXiv Preprint arXiv:2003.13861,* Mar 30: 1–5.

Walsham, G. 2017. "ICT4D Research: Reflections on History and Future Agenda." *Information Technology for Development* 23 (1): 18–41. doi:10.1080/02681102.2016.1246406.

Wellman, B. 2018. *Networks in the Global Village: Life in Contemporary Communities*. London: Routledge.

Wilken, R., G. Goggin, and H. Horst, eds. 2019. *Location Technologies in an International Context*. London and New York: Routledge.

World Bank. 2016. *World Development Report 2016: Digital Dividends*. New York: OUP.

Shedding Light on "Dark" Ads

Verity Trott, Luzhou Li, Robbie Fordyce and Mark Andrejevic

ABSTRACT
Targeted advertising lies at the heart of digital economic models and has been scrutinized with respect to the potential pathologies of discriminatory job and housing advertising along with concerns about harmful forms of manipulation and the invasive character of online data harvesting. This article takes as its focus the non-transparent forms of cultural association reproduced by targeted advertising. We call into question the ready distinction between editorial content and advertising that treats news content as a public interest good and advertising as primarily a matter of private interest and personal taste. In online media environments, it has become difficult to interrogate advertising due to their 'dark' nature (they are only visible to those to whom they are targeted) allowing them to avoid public scrutiny. This project puts forward a prototype for a tool that may be used to advance accountability discussions further by providing insight into how targeted advertising takes place across demographic categories. This article describes the pilot test of such a tool – one that can be deployed to reveal and illuminate patterns that emerge from targeted and dark advertising practices.

Shortly before the 2016 Presidential election in the United States, the leader of Donald Trump's media team boasted to reporters about its strategy for depressing Democratic voter turnout by targeting African-American voters with ads claiming that Hillary Clinton had implied Black youth were 'super predators' when supporting her husband's crime bill in 1996. The strategy relied on the ability to use Facebook to serve so-called 'dark ads' – non-public posts whose viewership the campaign controls – to targeted audiences. As the campaign's Digital Director, Brad Parscale, put it, 'only the people we want to see it, see it.' (Green and Issenberg 2016). In the era of electronic media, this capability marks an epochal shift in the ability to micro-target in real time on a mass scale. Parscale claimed to have run between 50,000 and 60,000 micro-targeted ads daily during the run up to the election. Similarly, in the UK, the 'pro-leave' campaign reportedly served more than a billion targeted ads over a period of just ten weeks (Wong 2018).

These numbers demonstrate the challenge posed by automated forms of customization and targeting. Keeping track of hundreds of thousands of ads that are continually modified based on changing campaign strategies and ongoing testing would pose a logistical challenge even if the ads were publicly available. It is the difficulty in monitoring such advertisements that have earned them the moniker 'dark ads,' because of the complementary forms of opacity that characterize them. It is difficult for any but those who have received these ads to see their content – *and* even those who have received them cannot see who *else* is receiving the ads. Lynch 2017) distinguishes between targeted ads, which are 'often shared by friend-to-friend activity' and dark ads which are, '*only* shown to users meeting very specific demographic parameters.' We would add to this formulation that dark ads pose a specific set of logistical challenges unique to digital platforms with respect to transparency and accountability because of their number, their addressability to individual users and devices, and their digital ephemerality.

With these limitations in mind, we set out to develop a prototype for a tool that might advance the accountability discussion a bit further by providing some insight into how targeting takes place across demographic categories. This article describes the pilot test of such a tool – one that can be deployed across all categories of advertising to reveal targeting patterns. The following sections develop the key social concerns raised by dark advertising in order to frame a description of the development and implementation of a new Facebook ad tool that builds on what has been accomplished so far. We also provide the results of our pilot test of the project and consider its potential and its limitations. Until and unless Facebook is required to reveal details about how it targets ads to an independent oversight board, it will be impossible to provide complete visibility into its practices, but it is urgently important to provide some level of accountability for a process that is rapidly becoming the dominant online advertising model.

Background: the social role of advertising

Advertising, as media scholars have long argued, played a central role in the rise of mass consumer society in the 20th century. As the historian TJ Jackson Lears contends, advertising has collaborated with other social institutions to promote, 'dominant aspirations, anxieties, even notions of personal identity' (1995, 2). In addition to its role in mobilizing consumption to keep pace with the productivity of industrialized mass production, advertising thus has a broader cultural significance. As Michael Schudson argues advertising, 'may shape our sense of values even under conditions where it does not greatly corrupt our buying habits" (1984, 23). For Schudson, the symbolic power of advertising comes from the way ads 'make us mind, make us focus – and on some things rather than on others. Ads do not "merely" reinforce existing social trends: they re-enforce social trends, and some trends and not others' (1984, 24). In this respect, he notes, 'Advertising, whether or not it sells cars or chocolate, surrounds us and enters into us, so that when we speak we may speak in or with reference to the language of advertising and when we see we may see through schemata that advertising has made salient for us' (Schudson 1984, 210).

Given its central cultural role in shaping attention and reinforcing social trends, much work has been done on the role played by advertising in reproducing stereotypes, preconceptions, and dominant meanings and associations. Scholars and researchers have explored the role played by advertising in shaping attitudes towards female body image and beauty (Kilbourne 1990); racial preconceptions and prejudices (Wilson, Clint, and Gutiérrez 1995); and class (Marchand 1985), among other areas of social life. As ads come to permeate contemporary life, the values and attitudes they select and reinforce become a core component of the informational atmosphere through which we move, in combination with the influence of the family, schools, and other arenas of meaning making and cultural production. The strategies and systems that shape this atmosphere, then, bear close scrutiny – especially during a time when advertising is undergoing profound shifts in its mode of production and distribution.

The origins of targeted advertising have a history over a century old. Webber (2013) locates the earliest targeted advertising as emerging in the Midwestern United States in the late 19th Century as a part of the origins of direct marketing. For Webber, the effectiveness of this approach relied on a combination of widespread consumer literacy, and the development of appropriate communications systems – specifically a reliable postal system, commercial newspapers, and quality printing. In the UK in the 1970s, the Royal Mail provided commercial advertisers with access to postcode data that linked consumers' addresses to socioeconomic status, allowing high degrees of advertising segmentation based on wealth and class (297).

The rise of dark ads and their changing structure

In 2017, digital ad revenues surpassed television for the first time (Slefo 2017). Last year, Facebook reported $55 billion in ad revenue while Google reported $116.3 billion (Facebook 2019; Wodinsky 2019). Together, the digital duopoly accounted for 60.1% of the total digital ad spending in the US in 2018 and was forecast to continue reigning over the ad world for the foreseeable future (Spangler 2018; Wodinsky 2019). This shift is arguably disruptive partly because digital entities like Facebook and Google, unlike their traditional counterparts, do not produce content themselves, although there are signs that things are changing. Rather, these platforms rely on their participatory, interactive structure, to solicit content – above all, via contribution from ordinary users (that is, UGC) and curation. During this process, platforms trace people's web use, extract user data, and ultimately analyse and use that data to sell ads in a highly customized way and meanwhile to improve the architectural traits of the websites so as to encourage more user participation and contribution (Wu and Taneja 2019). In this emerging new media business model which they consider a major shift both in the communications field and in the social and economic order at large, Turow and Couldry (2018, 415) note that these 'data-extraction-and-analysis technologies' have increasingly relegated 'traditional content genres to a supporting role in a larger arena of knowledge production'. Elsewhere, these digital entities are referred to as 'advertising platforms' (Srnicek 2017), as 'service/data-profile/advertising complex' (Lovink and Tkacz 2015, 15), as '"rentiers" of the network' (O'Dwyer 2015, 234) for they collect 'rents' – above all, advertising revenue – from data analytics and automated forms of ad customization and targeting, or as 'socio-technical intermediaries' in marketing exchanges that participate in processes of capitalization (Langley and Leyshon 2017).

All these terms point to 'new advertising and data-processing development' (Turow and Couldry 2018, 415) that come under the umbrella of 'platform' logics (Gillespie 2017). In the pre-digital media environment, advertisers (usually through advertising agencies) buy ad space on media, which produce content to attract audience attention and sell that attention to advertisers. Even in the online context, the practice of ad buying and selling remained direct and manual for a while as with traditional media, simply because advertisers continued to buy ad space from digital publishers directly and manually.

Things began to change largely, if not entirely, because of the growing scale of internet use: 'voluminous amounts of data appeared and so did the opportunity to use it for finding and targeting specific online consumers' (MIT Technology Review Insights 2013). Ad networks such as Google AdSense and Facebook Audience Network were born into that context as an intermediating layer of service providers to broker online marketing exchange between numerous publishers/websites who had accumulated and wanted to sell billions of impressions, the currency of the digital ad world measuring the number of times an ad is viewed, and numerous advertisers who desired to reach the 'right' consumers.

One of the under-appreciated and under-studied drawbacks of commercial targeting online from a social and cultural perspective is the fact that it renders a significant and influential part of culture socially opaque. This opacity is a stubborn one because it remains, from a commercial perspective, seemingly advantageous to marketers, advertisers, and campaign strategists. The ability to avoid public scrutiny frees up advertisers to develop and implement strategies that would have been objectionable and caused public and legal backlash were they subjected to shared public scrutiny. As the independent media outlet *ProPublica* discovered, for example, Facebook's automated ad targeting system made it possible, in theory, for advertisers to discriminate by race in the delivery of ads for jobs and housing – violating Federal law. *ProPublica* was able to prove this by setting up their own ad buy, however, they could not determine whether this feature had been put to use in the past by advertisers, precisely because there is no public record of the range of ads served to Facebook users over the years (Angwin et al. 2017).

With respect to gender, it is worth noting that recent research reveals Facebook's own algorithms may reinforce stereotyping by introducing gender bias into the distribution of online ads (Ali et al. 2019). This research found that even when advertisers do not specifically target a particular gender, the algorithm might 'decide' based on the success of past campaigns, that a particular ad is more likely to receive clicks from one or another gender. It will then distribute those ads accordingly, resulting in, 'potentially discriminatory ad delivery, even when advertisers set their targeting parameters to be highly inclusive' (Ali et al. 2019). The combined result of the strategic use of 'dark ads' by marketers and the perpetuation of gendered, racialized, or classed stereotypes by automated systems is the prospect of new configurations of stereotyping, discrimination, and the promulgation of unaccountable forms of potentially socially harmful cultural messaging.

The opacity of dark advertising cuts two ways: programmatic advertising, which relies on data-driven systems to seek out the most likely targets, can also be non-transparent to the companies who pay for ad placement; that is, they may not know which media outlets are hosting their ads. The activist organization Sleeping Giants has sought to shed light on this process by notifying large ad buyers when their ads crop up on outlets with which they might not want to be associated. Ad buyers can specify which outlets to include and exclude from their ad buy. Such accountability processes force advertisers to balance the expected payoff of algorithmic targeting against the potential cost of negative publicity.

The forms of targeting and segmentation enabled by the datafied intermediation of advertising is taking place at unprecedented 'speed, scale, and intensity' (Turow and Couldry 2018). Researchers have demonstrated the ability of advertisers to use platforms like Facebook to discriminate against protected categories of consumers, including age, race, and gender (Angwin et al. 2017) and the tendency of Facebook's automated ad optimization to discriminate (Ali et al. 2019). Empirically, there is also a nascent literature suggesting data-based social discrimination in online ad delivery. For example, Sweeney (2013) shows that a greater percentage of background check service ads appeared for black-identifying first names than for white-identifying first names in searches on Google and Reuters which hosts Google AdSense ads. Similarly, Datta, Tschantz, and Datta (2015)'s study of Google Ad Settings found that setting the gender to female resulted in getting fewer ads related to high paying jobs than setting it to male.

The big challenge is to try to reverse engineer forms of opaque targeting that take place on a mass scale and are stubbornly difficult to study. Insufficient transparency has always been an issue plaguing the industry. Advertisers do not know where their ads are placed and who really see their ads, and publishers do not know who exactly buys their ad space or inventories. Our purpose here is not to probe into this blackbox as researchers in computer science and machine learning have done. Rather, we tackle the issue of opacity from consumers' perspectives, focusing on their interactions with targeting systems.

Dark ad accountability

A number of independent efforts have emerged to address the reluctance of platforms to provide accountability for their new advertising model. The independent investigative journalists at *ProPublica* developed a tool in 2017 to collect political advertising on Facebook and provide insight into the less publicly accountable form of messaging enabled by the platform (Larson, Angwin, and Jennifer 2017). Independent accountability organizations such as the Tech Transparency Project have set up social media accounts that follow extremist groups to see what kind of ads they are receiving, and New York University's Ad Observatory Project uses a tool similar to *ProPublica*'s to collect and analyse politics ads.

There are, however, significant limits to what such tools can accomplish. The *ProPublica* project, like the NYU project provides important insight into political messaging – a core concern for democracy – but not into more general advertising patterns that might be cause for concern. The Tech Transparency Project, for example, discovered that Facebook was serving ads for military gear alongside posts about the 2020 US Capitol insurrection (Mac and Silverman 2021). It is perhaps good business for advertisers to market military equipment to those interested in violent anti-democratic activity – but perhaps not good for democracy itself. In the *ProPublica* project, there was no information about who received the targeted ads; in the Tech Transparency Project no sense of the overall targeting pattern.

In the wake of public concern about targeted political messaging, Facebook made a symbolic attempt to create a political ad library in some countries, including the United States, but researchers have noted that this approach has been plagued with problems. As *The New York Times* reported in 2019, 'The social network's new ad library is so flawed, researchers say, that it is effectively useless as a way to track political messaging' (Rosenberg 2019). The non-functionality of the Facebook ad library is unlikely to be an accident, given the demand on the part of advertisers engaging in strategies that rely on dark ads. From the perspective of political campaigns and a range of other advertisers, the ability to reach particular individuals or groups without being subject to public accountability is a feature, not a flaw, of the online advertising proposition.

Methodological approach

Our prototype advertising accountability tool builds on existing systems for ad scraping – and, in particular on the publicly available Facebook Political Ad Collector originally developed by ProPublica (Larson, Angwin, and Jennifer 2017). This tool combined a Chrome extension that scans for and collects sponsored ads in users' news feeds and then automatically extracts political ads. There is a tradeoff in any accountability system that attempts to lift the veil on dark ad strategies: how to protect privacy while also determining how ads are targeted. The virtue of ProPublica's tool is that it protects user privacy by stripping any identifying information from the ads, thus rendering visibility to dark ads, but making it impossible to see how these are targeted. The tool did capture the information provided to Facebook users by the 'Why Am I Seeing This Ad' functionality. This tool does not outline the terms of the actual ad buy and is unlikely to show any information that might reveal the types of strategies that are of central concern to an ad accountability system. It is unlikely, for example, that the 2016 Trump ad campaign revealed to recipients of the Clinton ad that they were being targeted because they were African American voters in key electoral districts.

With these considerations in mind, we developed a tool built around some compromises: we would not be able to reveal all the targeting details that shape the ad environment, as this would require in-depth behavioural tracking, as well as monitoring and modelling social networks. What we could do is ask users to provide some basic demographic information when they installed the browser extension. This information would not be enough to reverse engineer an individual user's identity but would make it possible to gain an overview of how different combinations of demographic variables might shape the type of ads users experience. The potential virtue of such an approach is that it could enable us to see some of the patterns that emerge as the cumulative result of Facebook's targeting system. We could, in principle, see, for example if particular ad categories were being shown primarily to men or women, to people in certain age groups, to particular ethnicities, or to some combination of these variables. While it does not get to the intent of advertisers or the platform, the accountability tool allows us, in principle, to see the end result, which is one of the operative accountability mechanisms in anti-discrimination regulations (Datta et al. 2018).

One of the significant determinants of what ads people see is their recent online search behaviour – which is not captured by the ad scraping tool. The other major limitation of such a tool is that it is costly to deploy at scale. To get a representative sample, we used a market research company for our pilot project, at a cost of $100 per participant for up to six weeks in two stages, a pilot of 30 participants and a subsequent larger group of 200. Not all of the participants successfully installed the extension, leaving us with 167 unique accounts that successfully contributed data to our project. We conducted follow-up interviews with selected participants who generated the most ads. The interviews asked participants to reflect on how the ads may have been shaped by their online activities, and how they felt about the level of targeting apparent in the stream of ads they received. The following section provides a detailed view of the research tool and its capabilities.

Anatomy of an ad transparency system

Like the ProPublica tool, our ad collection system makes it relatively easy to instal the browser extension, which is available on the Chrome store. Participants are sent a solicitation which includes a link to a Web page that provides installation instructions, information about the project, an ethics sign off, and the request to provide basic demographic information. Participants can choose which categories of information they are comfortable with sharing prior to installing the extension. Once in place, participants need to use Facebook on Chrome in order to generate ads. The tool scans for new ads at brief intervals, and these are generated as users navigate the site – new ads are served with each refresh. The data collected was limited to the ad's image file (a still image in the event of a video), the ad's text and target URL, and the advertiser's name and page icon. This allows us to identify individual ads and click through to the target – as long as the link is still operational.

There are two ways available for processing the ad data, once collected, we can directly sort the database using data analytics tools, including image and text classifiers, and we have created a user-friendly interface that allows users and members of the public to explore the database. We describe the user-facing database in detail, because it provides some of the functionality that might be used to promote the more widespread use of the tool. The public facing interface for the ad scraping project allows members of the public to experiment with the data by selecting different combinations of demographic variables to see how this changes the array of ads collected (see Figure 1).

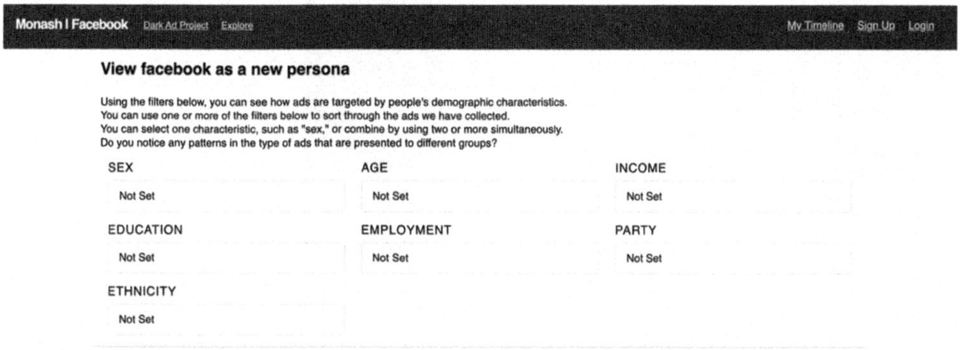

Figure 1. Platform interface.

In the current iteration of the interface, visitors to the site are invited to select a combination of variables to create an online 'persona' in order to see what types of ads people with the selected attributes have encountered on Facebook. In subsequent workshops we have conducted with the tool, we have found from some people experimenting with the database that when they enter their own demographic information, they encounter many of the same ads that they have seen in their own feeds. The result is that they tend to notice how they are associated with a particular cluster – and the type of messaging with which this cluster is associated. Of course, this finding depends a lot on a match with the database. Because of the limited initial sample, there is not broad coverage of demographic groups (for example, one Asian male in his 20s reported that he could not find any ads that matched his demographic profile in the pilot database). Much depends on the ability to recruit a broad-ranging group of participants to instal and use the accountability tool.

Advertising patterns emerge via the tool's interface when the demographic filters are varied to see how the content and form of the collected ads change. Consider for example the selection of ads in Figure 2, which arrays side-by-side a short selection of ads varied by gender. A brief selection like this is only suggestive, since the ads are displayed in the order in which they are received, which means they may cluster by users (it is likely, for example that each set came from the same person during a particular browsing session). Nevertheless, even in a small sample, varying the filter can yield some indicative patterns, both in terms of content and form. We noticed, in our pilot group, a strong skew of gambling, tech, and military recruitment ads (by gender: primarily male), as well as of craft, clothing, cooking, and birth control ads (primarily female). Such associations are not necessarily surprising given the gendered sets of expectations and biases that are

Figure 2. A short selection of ads varied by gender (self-designated 'male' on the left and 'female' on the right).

reproduced by advertising logics. Some other patterns are perhaps less obvious, such as the gender skew in certain forms of business and entrepreneurial self-help programmes (depending on what might be read into these ads).

We also include, in Figure 3, a short selection of ads varied by educational level. These images provide some sense of the experience of exploring the tool's user interface, which we envision as a potentially useful tool for anyone interested in investigating the patterns that emerge from ad targeting processes, including educators, researchers, activists, and policy makers. It is not difficult to note some salient differences, even in a short selection of ads. There are some ready-to-hand associations between reading material and education level – with publications like The New York Times and the New Yorker targeted towards the group with a higher stated level of educational attainment, and loan savings services to those with lower levels of education attainment. Even a relatively cursory investigation of our pilot database provides a range of suggestions for considering how demographic variables are correlated with cultural associations. While it is not possible to make systematic generalizations from our small sample size, the findings open up avenues for public concern and scrutiny. The short selection in Figure 4, which shows the results of varying the search filters by party preference displays some potentially familiar sets of lifestyle associations – the Greens party preference coupled with yoga and fitness ads (highly gendered, in this case) and the connection between right-wing politics and the military. But, again, these are anecdotal findings based on a small sample size. The goal of a transparency database would be to extract patterns that appear robust over time and groups of users.

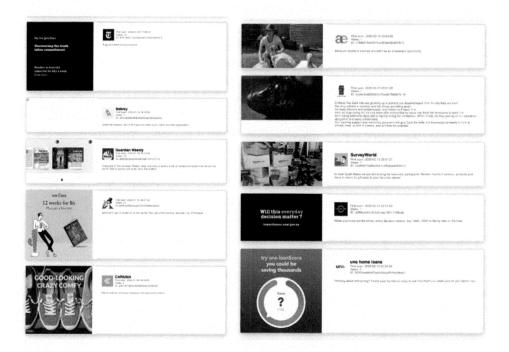

Figure 3. A short selection of results from the ad database comparing different values for the education filter. The figure on the left shows results from entering the variable 'doctorate' in the filter; that on the right from entering 'less than year 12 or equivalent'.

Figure 4. A brief selection of adds varied by party preference. The image on the left shows the results for entering "Australian Greans" in the preference filter. That on the right shows the results for entering "Pauline Hansen's One Nation" – A right-wing, anti-immigration party.

One of the challenges posed by implementing the tool at scale is making sense of large volumes of ads. Our pilot project involved only 167 people for a brief period of time, with the understanding that participants varied in the regularity of their Facebook use. Even so, we collected more than 13,000 ads. Any systematic claims about advertising patterns on a significantly larger scale would likely require automated forms of preliminary analysis using image classification and natural language processing. However, the public interface has the potential to be used for educational purposes and for raising awareness about the issues posed by the forms of non-transparent nichification and stereotyping associated with the targeted advertising model.

Discussion

The preliminary findings are suggestive only insofar as they start to make the case for what might be described as the advertising 'filter bubble' – the way that consumers are hemmed in by ads that reproduce a data-driven conception not just of their consumer preferences, but of the cultural associations that condition these. Much digital ink has been spilled on the notion of the so-called filter bubble in the realm of news and information (for an introduction to this concept, see Pariser 2011; for a critical overview, see Bruns 2019). However, less attention has been paid to the filter bubble in the realm of advertising and marketing – which, as the literature on the social role of advertising suggests – has an important role to play in the formation of social attitudes and tastes. Moreover, there may be attitudinal links between advertising and news that are masked by the tendency of research to focus on one or the other. It may be difficult to separate hyper-customization and targeting of information commodities from one another, since advertising is not simply about private tastes and preferences but is also about messaging that reinforces and reproduces the cultural values that underpin social relations. This latter point is confirmed by historical experience wherein ads that once seemed acceptable (at least to the groups that created and promulgated them) reveal their racist, sexist, and imperialist assumptions against the background of contemporary sensibilities. Ads are not exempt from the ideological forms of messaging that directly impact questions of power and social relations that are central to the process of democratic deliberation and participation. More recently, of course, the decision by brands to drop racist signifiers such as Uncle Ben's and Aunt Jemima concede the cultural and political impact of denigrating stereotypes. It seems odd to have to emphasize this point, but we do so because of the recurring tendency of critiques of customization to focus on editorial content. The importance of ad transparency is highlighted by the role that harmful stereotypes in advertising play in reinforcing historical forms of discrimination and oppression. What, other than public scrutiny, stands in the way of renewed and rehabilitated forms of stereotyping making their way back into the informational byways of targeted advertising?

Conclusion

Providing accountability of the activities of huge global platforms like Facebook and Google poses numerous, seemingly insurmountable challenges. Perhaps we need not replicate their size and wealth to do so – if it were possible to envision some kind of collective, crowd-sourced response. This may be a slim hope, but it is perhaps one of the few remaining available strategies. The ad accountability tool developed by our team is meant to highlight both the potentials and challenges of such an approach. It envisions the possibility of constructing a collaborative tool that people could freely contribute to by providing access to the ads they receive. To make something like this work on a broader scale would require regulations that enabled this type of scrutiny to take place. The tool we created faces several limitations, including Facebook's deliberate attempts to thwart transparency tools. Our tool, for example, only works on laptop and desktop computers running Chrome (although it could also be extended to Firefox and perhaps other browsers). This has implications for the possible global uptake of the tool and for ad accountability in countries that largely rely on mobile access to digital platforms (e.g. Southeast Asian countries). It only works on Facebook and not on other social media platforms. So far, we have had to update the tool three times because of attempts by Facebook to deliberately obscure the ways in which ads are tagged. On the other hand, an accountability tool needn't be comprehensive. There is an amplifying logic of uncertainty at work – if it is possible that a particular ad might be unearthed online, and this possibility is increased by accountability tools, that might help serve as a deterrent for strategies unlikely to withstand public scrutiny.

The prototype we developed showcases some possible attributes of a public accountability system for dark ads, should it be possible to deploy such a system more widely. It is freely available and open to the public who can inspect the ads seen by others and, if they wish, can scrutinize the unique stream of ads directed to them over time. Our tool allows people who instal it to use a unique identifier, available only to them, to retrieve the ads sourced from their news feed. The prototype is collaborative and scalable – with the caveat that a system for automated analysis of ad content is necessitated as the database increases in size. The tool also serves as a possible resource for public and educational scrutiny of the advertising environment and for raising awareness of the societal challenges posed by the rise of dark ads. Finally, it helps raise questions about the broader economy of customization and individualization that characterizes the economic model we have created for our online environment – the net result of which is to foster misrecognition of the forms of interdependence and commonality that shape our social world.

Disclosure statement

No potential conflict of interest was reported by the author(s).

Funding

The funder is the Australian Communications Consumer Action Network (ACCAN) and the grant ID: 2019009

References

Ali, Muhammad, Piotr Sapiezynski, Miranda Bogen, Aleksandra Korolova, Alan Mislove, and Aaron Rieke. 2019. "Discrimination through Optimization: How Facebook's Ad Delivery Can Lead to Skewed Outcomes." *ArXiv* preprint arXiv:1904.02095.
Angwin, Julia, Ariana Tobin, and Madeleine Varner. 2017. "Facebook (Still) Letting Housing Advertisers Exclude Users by Race." *ProPublica*. Accessed 21 November 2017. https://www.propublica.org/article/facebook-advertising-discrimination-housing-race-sex-national-origin
Bruns, Axel. 2019. *Are Filter Bubbles Real?* Cambridge: Polity Press.
Datta, Amit, Anupam Datta, Jael Makagon, Deirdre K. Mulligan, and Michael Carl Tschantz. 2018. "Discrimination in Online Personalization: A Multidisciplinary Inquiry." *FAT* 81: 20–34.

Datta, Amit, Michael Carl Tschantz, and Anupam Datta. 2015. "Automated Experiments on Ad Privacy Settings." *Proceedings on Privacy Enhancing Technologies* 2015 (1): 92–112. doi:10.1515/popets-2015-0007.

Facebook. 2019. "Facebook Reports Fourth Quarter and Full Year 2018 Results." *Facebook*. Accessed 30 January 2019. https://investor.fb.com/investor-news/press-release-details/2019/Facebook-Reports-Fourth-Quarter-and-Full-Year-2018-Results/default.aspx

Gillespie, Tarleton. 2017. "Governance of and by Platforms." In *Sage Handbook of Social Media*, edited by Jean Burgess, Thomas Poell, and Alice Marwick, 254–278. London: Sage.

Green, Joshua, and Sasha Issenberg. 2016. "Inside the Trump Bunker, with Days to Go." *Bloomberg Business*. Accessed 27 October 2016. https://www.bloomberg.com/news/articles/2016-10-27/inside-the-trump-bunker-with-12-days-to-go

Kilbourne, Jean. 1990. "Beauty and the Beast in Advertising." In *Women in Culture: An Intersectional Anthology for Gender and Women's Studies*, edited by Bonnie Kime Scott, Susan E. Cayleff, Anne Donadey, and Irene Lara, 183–186, John Wiley & Sons: West Sussex, UK.

Langley, Paul, and Andrew Leyshon. 2017. "Platform Capitalism: The Intermediation and Capitalisation of Digital Economic Circulation." *Finance and Society* 3 (1): 11–31. doi:10.2218/finsoc.v3i1.1936.

Larson, Jeff, Julia Angwin, and Valentino-DeVreis Jennifer. 2017. "How We are Monitoring Political Ads on Facebook." *ProPublica* Accessed 5 December 2017. https://www.propublica.org/article/how-we-are-monitoring-political-ads-on-facebook.

Lears, Jackson. 1995. *Fables of Abundance: A Cultural History of Advertising in America*. Basic Books: New York.

Lovink, Geert, and Nathaniel Tkacz. 2015. "Moneylab: Sprouting New Digital-economic Forms." In *Moneylab Reader: An Intervention in Digital Economy*, edited by G. Lovink, N. Tkacz, and P. De Vries, 13–18. Amsterdam: Institute of Network Cultures.

Lynch, Clifford. 2017. "Stewardship in the Age of Algorithms." *First Monday* 22(12): n.p.

Mac, Ryan, and Craig Silverman. 2021. "Facebook Has Been Showing Military Gear Ads Next to Insurrection Posts." *BuzzFeedNews.com*. Accessed January 13. https://www.buzzfeednews.com/article/ryanmac/facebook-profits-military-gear-ads-capitol-riot.

Marchand, Roland. 1985. *Advertising the American Dream: Making Way for Modernity, 1920-1940*. Vol. 53. University of California Press: Berkeley and Los Angeles, California.

MIT Technology Review Insights. 2013. "The Evolution of Ad Tech." *MIT Technology Review* Accessed 5 September 2013. https://www.technologyreview.com/s/518551/the-evolution-of-ad-tech/.

O'Dwyer, Rachel. 2015. "Money Talks: The Enclosure of Mobile Payments." In *MoneyLab Reader: An Intervention in Digital Economy*, edited by G. Lovink, N. Tkacz, and P. De Vries, 230–244. Amsterdam: Institute of Network Cultures.

Pariser, Eli. 2011. *The filter bubble: What the Internet is hiding from you*. Penguin Books: London.

Rosenberg, Matthew. 2019. "Ad Tool Facebook Built to Fight Disinformation Doesn't Work as Advertised." *The New York Times*. Accessed 25 July 2019. https://www.nytimes.com/2019/07/25/technology/facebook-ad-library.html

Schudson, Michael. 1984. *Advertising, the Uneasy Persuasion*. Basic Books: Milton Park, Abingdon, Oxon.

Slefo, George P. 2017. "Desktop and Mobile Ad Revenue Surpasses TV for the First Time." *AdAge*. Accessed 26 April 2017. https://adage.com/article/digital/digital-ad-revenue-surpasses-tv-desktop-iab/308808

Spangler, Todd. 2018. "Amazon on Track to Be No. 3 In U.S. Digital Ad Revenue but Still Way behind Google, Facebook." *Variety*. Accessed 19 September 2018. https://variety.com/2018/digital/news/amazon-us-digital-ad-revenue-google-facebook-1202947923/

Srnicek, Nick. 2017. *Platform Capitalism*. John Wiley & Sons: Cambridge, UK.

Sweeney, Latanya. 2013. "Discrimination in Online Ad Delivery." *arXiv* preprint arXiv:1301.6822.

Turow, Joseph, and Nick Couldry. 2018. "Media as Data Extraction: Towards a New Map of a Transformed Communications Field." *Journal of Communication* 68 (2): 415–423. doi:10.1093/joc/jqx011.

Webber, Richard. 2013. "The Evolution of Direct, Data and Digital Marketing." *Journal of Direct, Data and Digital Marketing Practice* 14 (4): 291–309. doi:10.1057/dddmp.2013.20.

Wilson, II, C Clint, and FF Gutiérrez. 1995. *Race, Multiculturalism, and the Media: From Mass to Class Communication*. Sage Publications: Michigan, US.

Wodinsky, Shoshana. 2019. "The Digital Duopoly Still Reigns the Ad World, according to a New Report." *AdWeek*. Accessed 22 March 2019. https://www.adweek.com/programmatic/the-digital-duopoly-still-reigns-the-ad-world-according-to-a-new-report/

Wong, Julia Carrie. 2018. "'It Might Work Too Well': The Dark Art of Political Advertising Online." *The Guardian*. Accessed 19 March 2018. Available at: https://www.theguardian.com/technology/2018/mar/19/facebook-political-ads-social-media-history-online-democracy

Wu, Angela Xiao, and Harsh Taneja. 2019. "How Did the Data Extraction Business Model Come to Dominate? Changes in the Web Use Ecosystem before Mobiles Surpassed Personal Computers." *The Information Society* 35 (5): 272–285.

Critical Data Provenance as a Methodology for Studying How Language Conceals Data Ethics

Robbie Fordyce and Suneel Jethani

ABSTRACT
This paper contributes to a project that maps the concept of 'data provenance' into qualitative data research. Data provenance is a concept from computer science that allows us to trace the history of sets of data to determine the accuracy and validity of a database. We transform this into a critical concept by arguing that data provenance can be used to trace the acts of governance and rhetoric. We then analyse the forms of discursive power that shape transactions in data. Our approach can create a history of the governance and justifications that are used to build and assemble datasets from multiple sources. Presently, data often lacks this information about its own discursive origins, unlike other forms of data provenance. Critical data provenance gives us a model for thinking about how governance could be mapped onto data. And thus, critical data provenance is also a framework for critiquing the justifications used when dataset owners acquire data – for instance, whether data stewards or users are encouraged to be 'open', to 'share', or be 'transparent'. To this end, we demonstrate this model of thinking and provide the analytical tools necessary to redeploy these ideas into new contexts.

We, unh, it-, it-, unh, It's the age of access rather than the age of transfer [...] Data is a, unh, incredibly powerful; it's the new oil.

Christopher Wylie, Testimony to Congress regarding Cambridge Analytica, 16 May 2018

Introduction

This paper contributes to research into how language is used to describe data movements, and argues that the role of words such as sharing, openness, release, and access creates a murky context for the ethical analysis of data transactions. Specifically, we are gesturing to the insufficiency of this language in describing individual cases of data transactions in a critical way, obscuring ethical complications at the same time. We argue that, for humanities and social sciences (HASS) disciplines, there is value in incorporating and developing the language of 'data provenance' from computer science to understand concepts such as sharing, access, openness and safety with greater nuance.

This analysis is deeply intellectually indebted to the work of Carol Bacchi (2000; 2009), whose problem-representation approach informs our analysis of language. Bacchi provides us with the conceptual tools to interrogate the terms we use to describe how we exchange information, and to interrogate what is happening 'behind' this language.

Christopher Wylie's observation, noted in the epigraph, refers to two common aphorisms about data (Guardian News 2018). The latter – that 'data is the new oil' – stems from Clive Humby's speech of the same name (2006) and is a metaphor that has generated debate over what our correct metaphor should be, if any. However, it is the former comment that we wish to use as our point of departure: the corrective that 'we live in the age of access' denotes a problem in understanding the circulation of data in our present moment. We will explore this line of thinking in this article. When heard in the context of his testimony, Wylie's pithy summary of Jeremy Rifkin's *The Age of Access* (2000) has a clear subtext: massified transfer of data is no longer standard (or even feasible), if it ever even was. Instead, data stewards provide access to data in a gated and incomplete manner: data is provided in partial form and accessed through diverse mechanisms. This includes APIs,[1] passwords, biometrics, and types of log-ins; but also policy processes such as security clearances, Freedom of Information requests, and other mechanisms. These might be freely available, subscription-based, bought, government-mandated, stolen, leaked, or otherwise. Against this, Wylie's secondary observation is important, the perceived value of data means that there are pressures to copy, collate, and absorb data from all manner of sources. It would be easy enough to point to the obvious commercial imperative: despite critiques to the contrary (see Martínez 2019), data is very much the new oil if we consider how it is treated by those who profit from it. We are far from alone in this position as Sadowski has already accounted for the capitalist imperatives around data in great detail (2019). We would, however, argue that these capitalist imperatives only assess part of the picture and are not enough in themselves to fully explain attempts to intensively capture data and the different motivations that may be involved, from the mundane to the creepy: researchers, hobbyists, activists, leakers, whistleblowers, stalkers, and abusive ex-partners.

The virtues of information freedom

The HASS disciplines tend to conceive of the different types of data transactions in terms of words such as 'sharing', 'openness', 'release', 'access'. These words may seek to highlight a meaningful social component of any data sharing; but this terminology may also come from the corporations that own these services, whether their source is public relations campaigns or the various platform interfaces. To any attentive reader, there is an immediate problem. These words describe online practices that have *prima facie* positive social connotations, while concealing a deeper level of complications that are specific to the event in question. Within the language of data transactions there is a variety of impacts for different users involved in any transaction. This is true whether describing crime scene photos released onto Tor onion services,[2] accumulation of COVID data by *the Atlantic* becoming the de facto official source of US coronavirus data (Meyer and Madrigal 2021), police officers publishing to Facebook groups (see Statt 2019), or Facebook user data shared by Aleksandr Kogan with Cambridge Analytica.

This tradition of openness as a positive social force for democracy stems from the liberalizing of world trade during the Cold War, when openness was framed as a civic virtue of honest governments, polarized against the USSR. The Free Flow of Information was installed as the pioneering communications concept of globalization, established during the United Nations Declaration of Human Rights conferences of 1946. During the Cold War, the idea of information sharing as central both to ideal societies and to democracy itself was baked into Western societies. The US and UK rejected attempts to critically evaluate the accuracy of this idea, such as through the MacBride report (MacBride et al 1980), MacLean located this disagreement as the basis for the US/UK withdrawal from UNESCO (MacLean 2011, 53). While other language is used – for instance 'leaking', 'theft', 'hacking' – our interest is in those terms that imply liberal concepts of a socially harmonious 'goo", because it is this language that complicates ethical analysis. The history of information flows in Western nations is a history that has often privileged the free flow of information as an uncritical normative ideal, and we now see that this same endless sharing of everything is at the core of the capitalization of social interactions by private companies.

The terminology associated with these practices describes the mode of transaction but says very little about how data has been obtained in the first place, and how it will be used by the receiving party. The goal is not to understand what these terms 'really' mean as if that were possible; indeed, many of the scholars we cite note that words such as 'sharing' remain slippery. This results in a conceptual ambiguity that is sometimes to do with the ideological trajectory these terms are set on, and other times by rhetorical shifts that take terms from a communal logic to a corporate one. These terms have such traction because they emerge from a set of related discourses used in industry and government to explain transactions that have been subject to significant critical attention. Even our own attempt to use a suitably generic term – transaction – is insufficient because it evacuates important social implications from the discussion, yet at the same time, these terms allow for greater attention to the economic and technical capacities of movements of data.

Data provenance as used in computer science is a framework for auditing databases that focuses on understanding where data comes from and why it is structured in a particular way. We argue that this framework can be expanded beyond the technical to act as an analytical ethics tool for thinking about transactions in data and their consequences. By pulling in existing critical research on data we can create a simple heuristic for thinking about data with an eye to ethics and justice. Our heuristic expands from the 'where' and 'why' provenance mapped by Buneman, Khanna, and Tan (2001), Dai et al. (2008), and Glavic (2012) to include questions of 'who', 'what', 'when' and 'how'. This deliberately simple approach is to encourage a heuristic that is both memorable and extensible. While we write this for an academic context, the framework is readily deployable in other contexts where data ethics reviews are necessary. Our concept is not exhaustive, and–by its nature–involves informed speculation on information gathered by diverse methodologies and is still being mapped out (see Jethani and Fordyce 2021, and also; Ford and Graham 2016).

Provenance as an illuminating method

Virginia Eubanks, in *Automating Inequality*, proposes that ethical thinking about data will require 'flexing our imaginations and asking entirely different kinds of questions' (2018, n. p.) of data-driven sociotechnical systems. Picking up on the call for 'greater conceptual work' (Kitchin and Lauriault 2014) in the field of critical data studies (see: boyd and Crawford 2012; Dalton et al. 2016; Iliadis and Russo 2016; Michael and Lupton 2016), our work contributes to data provenance in terms of expanding on how data is *used* rhetorically. Informed by these calls for a richer critical lexicon, data provenance can be developed as a way of thinking about data from a HASS perspective. We understand data here in a broad sense, including well-structured data housed in a relational database or accessed via API methods; but also, data that are linked with other sources, corrupted or partial, leaked, abandoned, or encrypted. Indeed, we can even consider data that is non-digital or non-computational (Pool 2016).

Data provenance is important because any data transaction or decision in data cannot be reduced to purely a technical exchange. We can make data provenance critical and ethical by questioning not just the consequences of database construction and composition, but also what a database outputs–whether resources, decisions, or dollars, investigating the discursive construction of these moments as we progress. Multiple decisions, motivations, and intentions shape data transactions, and provenance is an approach for mapping these. We assume that, firstly, data is political. Data can circulate as evidence to be contested, and serve political ends, they can be 'of' the body politic; data is political in how it is used. Data exists in a world where its gathering and use have effects that are never neutral. Secondly, datasets are epistemological objects. They represent and cohere information, they are a product of a method, and thus of an epistemology. Thirdly, data are mutable. They can gain or lose types of information. Data can be sent, received and recombined. Even in relational databases, data can appear in dataframes that can be redefined, depreciated, misplaced, deleted, or released. For instance, the specifications for the common XML[3] data format have been designed to allow data structures to be defined and redefined arbitrarily. All of these aspects facilitate data being decontextualized or recontextualized in forms that are totally foreign to their original purpose, losing their epistemological context along the way.

Data provenance was first proposed by Buneman, Khanna, and Tan (2000) to explore data in two forms: *where*-provenance, as in 'where did it come from?' and *why*-provenance, as in 'why is it here?' Buneman et al. frame provenance as focused on understanding what decisions have fed into the creation of a database that audits the system down to the impact of a single entry. Data provenance is also an evaluation of the *a priori* assumptions that shape database queries. In the context of the computational sciences, data provenance is raised specifically as a way to test the reliability of data in terms of how they are included in a dataset (or not) as well as mapping impacts on how data are extracted from a database (Buneman, Khanna, and Tan 2000, 89, 2001, 8–14). Computational data provenance identifies technical questions of inputs and outputs.

'Where-provenance' questions how data is affected by other data. Matters of where-provenance are often recorded to ensure that scripted queries of a database are logically coherent. Where-provenance emphasis how the structure of a database may trace the history of a particular piece of data. Within this context, where-provenance has an important role in systems such as banking, immigration, electronic voting, and other contexts where the presence and origins of a highly valued resource (such as money or votes) must be accounted for. If a database allows multiple records with the same number, then any attempt to find or trace data may be confounded. Why-provenance is more interested in understanding how the content of a database affects what data can be collected.

To illustrate these principles, imagine teaching a class of nine students with a normal distribution of scores. To demonstrate where-provenance, imagine examining a table of student grades to see students in the top 20% of the class. Adding students below this threshold would change who is calculated in the sample and how many, even though the added students would not be represented in the output. An example of why provenance would be someone searching this spreadsheet for a student's name and stopping when they find it; data provenance would suggest ensuring that the sheet is filtered for identical names. The where-/why- approaches are important and necessary but take us in a different path to our research goal, which is to address a different kind of provenance around how data is politicized in its transactions.

Increasing data availability

In 2016, Scott Morrison (then Treasurer, presently Prime Minister of Australia and federal leader of the Liberal Party) commissioned the Australian Productivity Commission to examine 'the benefits and costs of options for increasing availability of and improving the use of public and private sector data by individuals and organisations.' (Productivity Commission 2017, v). The Productivity Commission's report states:

> With the mass digitisation of data, the capacity to collect data through everyday Internet activity and transactions, and through technologies such as sensors, cameras and mobile devices, means that what is 'data', and who can or should have a say in how it is collected, stored, transformed and used is no longer so simple [...] Data now includes material (raw or processed) on: the characteristics, status, appearance or performance of an individual, product or service, or object (including infrastructure and environmental assets); and expressed or inferred opinions and preferences. The potential value of data is tremendous; as is the scope for Australia to forgo much of this value under the misconception that denial of access minimises risks. (Productivity Commission 2017, 3-4).

The language of the inquiry is illuminating: the Commission speaks of 'options of increasing availability' to public and private data (2017, v), identifying 'legislation or other impediments' (2017, v) to access, especially where credit reporting is concerned, and encourages the availability of 'aggregate consumer data', especially data which enable consumers to make purchasing decisions.

The terms of reference present these changes as having potential benefits for an interesting array of agents: public and private sector organizations, the research industry, academics, and the community (2017, iv–vi). Academics are included specifically as a *class* rather than through reference to the tertiary education sector, but beyond this people are framed within these terms solely as consumer-subjects (2017, v). The inquiry led to the report *Data Availability and Use* (Productivity Commission 2017), which set the terms for increased debate over the nature of data and its mechanisms of access in Australia. The discourse that emerged from this report focuses on twin principles of access and sharing; the idea of sharing is built into policy emerging from these discussions: 'Data Sharing and Release', and a 'Consumer Data Right' among other matters which include the appointment of a 'National Data Commissioner'. This language matters. The Australian Government's response to the Productivity Commission's inquiry stated that its proposed reforms would aim to 'address existing barriers, such as lack of standardized and transparent approaches to data sharing and release, and unnecessarily complex data access processes' (Department of Prime Minister and Cabinet 2018, 5).

Indeed, removing 'barriers to access' has become a key focus in Australian data policy at numerous levels of government, and across industries from health to advertising to housing to education to policing and beyond. The emphasis here is not the legislation itself. This is dealt with adeptly by others (see Bennett Moses et al. 2019a; Meese, Jagasia, and Arvanitakis 2019). Instead, we focused on how this new language describing transactions in data (also noted by Bennett Moses et al. 2019b) signals a change in framing and intention around the regulation of data use by the Australian Government. This new language needs new tools to address data ethics, in terms of handling, reception, and dissemination. We argue that the shift to increased access and sharing of data requires a specifically political language and methodology around *provenance* that allows us to trace the origins and handling of data. For instance, in a discussion paper issued by the federal Australian Government in September 2019 on the legislative reforms for Data Sharing and Release, the liberal party Minister for Government Services, Stuart Robert, suggests that an appropriate data reform agenda is one that facilitates services that are 'seamless, easy and fast' and 'keep pace with the private sector' but with 'enhanced safeguards, privacy and security protections'. In response to this celebratory language, we make a contribution to the *critical* language.

With increased access to and distribution of data, we need to develop a critical lexicon for discussing data handling that is governed in a new way. The governance model in the Australian legislation incorporates sharing data only for appropriate and authorized purposes, involving authorized users in secure environments and ensuring the public outputs of data sharing projects do not identify the people and organizations in the data. This model of governance is based on the notion of building trust between parties engaged in data sharing agreements and 'with the Australian community about the government's use of data' (Prime Minister and Cabinet 2018, 7). Here, safety means the widely adopted 'five safes framework' which sees good governance as safe: projects, people, settings, data and outputs. The framework encourages data custodians to ask: (1) Is the use of this data appropriate?; (2) Can users be trusted to use it in an appropriate manner?; (3) Does the access mechanism limit unauthorized use?; (4) Is there a disclosure risk in the data itself? and (5) Are outputs non-disclosive? (Fivesafes.org)

What is the data represented to be?

Carol Bacchi has developed a rigorous system for understanding the gap between language and actuality as a rich and insightful analytical frame (2000; 2009). Bacchi's 'problem representation' approach involves many factors, but primary amongst them is an interrogation of how a system *claims* to work, which can then be contrasted with how it works *in practice* (2009). The gap can then be analysed to understand how authority and power is distributed within a system, and how the system constructs its problems. While Bacchi's work emerges in a policy analysis context, this same frame can be used to analyse the multiple cases of governance and rhetoric that surround data.

The issue with 'sharing', 'access', 'openness' and 'safety' is the terms have shifted their meanings within the context of digital platforms. We argue that the terms have developed a polysemic looseness – what John (2017) calls a 'fuzzy object' – where the social terrain of sharing has been abandoned in favour of an empty instrumental process. That is, an organization must share, a person must be open, research subjects must provide access. It is not enough, however, to note that this has happened. In part there is still a role for these terms in critically important contexts, such as open government, transparency processes, and to describe sharing practices all of which have really important cultural and political dimensions. However, the language of data transactions conceals their own processes. We cannot take these terms at face value, but the disconnect between the language used to describe a transaction and how data is actually used–such as users 'sharing' their data with a commercial platform–allows us to make the first step in developing our critical data provenance, in terms of what-provenance, as seen in Table 1 below.

Table 1. Critical data provenance.

Approach	Framing concept	Inquiry context
What-provenance	'What are the rhetorics that surround these data?'	Inquiry into the social justification used to explain why data should be shared. Inquiry into the social, legal, and discursive parameters that mobilize the sharing process. Inquiring into the power relationship between actors involved in data capture.
Where-provenance	'Where did the data come from?'	Inquiry into how the structure of a database management system shapes how data are outputted from a database.
Why-provenance	'Why did this particular data arrive?'	Inquiry into how the data that is stored in a database shape what data was outputted from the database.

This mode of analysis borrows from Bacchi (2000; 2009) to suggest that there is a significant political and discursive role in the way that a data transaction is described. To unpack individual cases of data transactions we must treat these rhetorics as approaches that illuminate the political cover under which data transactions occur. Where-provenance and why-provenance question the construction and output of data; what-provenance maps these together to question the justifications of data-gathering in line with the decisions and discourse that emerge from these moments.

Language that conceals data instrumentality

The liberalized yet precautionary language of data sharing does not mean that benefits and risks of access are shared equally. This is especially the case if the government is to keep pace with the private sector where ethical principles are often reframed as ethical 'tolerances' normed against practices that skate the line between legal and ethical, strategically leveraging the definitional ambiguity of the lexicon around data-motile processes. The liberalized language of data helps occlude expressly political questions, in part because the term shifts from implying a community practice (equitably distributing resources) to one that is purely instrumental (brute transactions of data between servers). The language of *sharing*, *openness* and *access* has been transformed significantly over the last two decades, as these terms have become central to explaining how people give and receive information, without qualifying why they have it or what they might do with it.

The language of access is complicated by its uptake outside of data contexts. While sharing and openness have a newness to them that links directly to changes in the digital, access is also linked to developments in discussions of poverty and empowerment, especially when it comes to the provision of healthcare (Sakellariou and Rotarou 2017). Jeremy Rifkin's work, *The Age of Access* (2000) lays out what access brings, and what it replaces. 'Access' has a role in replacing 'ownership' as a paradigm. Access is also indelibly tied to purchase. For Rifkin this leads to a relentless shift towards a relationship of renter to rentier, lessee to leaser, and he attributes this shift as being a product of the increasing expense to purchase and maintain high-tech devices (2000, 74). To be able to access healthcare is not the same as being able to afford it. Equally, being able to access data is not the same as being able to do something with it, or to act with it in an ethical manner. The digital divide can be overcome on an infrastructural level, providing people with literal access to databases and ergo to data, but this does not mean that people have requisite digital literacy to examine and investigate data either.

The language of sharing invokes a degree of reciprocity, or perhaps community, whereby different parties hold relationships with each-other and treasured or necessary things are given to each other in an exchange that is as much about mutual support as it is about the development of a type of kinship or care. Scholars such as Yochai Benkler (2004) and Schor (2016) have noted the importance of sharing as an economic function that predates capitalist markets. Other scholarship on sharing has already addressed the potential emptiness of the language of sharing when invoked to suggest harmonious or natural functions in economic exchange, or further complications in the language. We can watch children engaged in the practice of sharing to understand some of the problems with the idea. Children can demand that others 'share' a toy or treats to gain access to resources that they otherwise do not have, under the rubric of moral injunction in the other, that they are somehow selfish to not allow access to their personal things.

Jenny Kennedy (2013, 2016) and Nicholas John (2013, 2017) study the rhetorics and discourses around sharing and argue that there are ambiguities in these terms that leave a great deal of room for interpretation. As John (2017) notes, the idea of sharing is not just a prescriptive concept for categorizing existing behaviours. It is also a question of what is already described as sharing. The nature of the term is such that it expands to cover behaviours that do not fit literally within the history of the dictionary definition. The term is used strategically by digital platforms to generate an 'association' (Kennedy 2013, 129) with activities that describe a completely different domain of human interaction. For instance, in situations such as the *New Australian Government Data Sharing and Release Legislation* (Department of the Prime Minister and Cabinet 2018; see also the relevant legislation currently under review *Data Availability and Transparency Bill 2020* which shares similar linguistic properties) the term gets embedded even in the name of policies that shape what access behaviour is permitted and which is not. The arguments that these scholars make about sharing is relevant to our other terms too, inasmuch as these terms also get embedded into layers of interfaces, discourses, policies, and methods.

The language of openness around data has centralized around the idea of bringing greater degrees of visibility to government operations. The recent iteration of these ideas has its origins in the open government movement which is in itself a borne out of two larger interlocking narratives stemming from community expectations of voluntary transparency (Heemsbergen 2021) and participation in decision-making through legislation and policy such as Freedom of Information (FOI) and Right to Know. Taken together these form the ideological and legal basis for the management and regulation of open data portals (such as data.gov.au and their state and local government equivalents). The open government movement builds on philosophical arguments in favour of providing greater access and less bureaucracy. In published best practice guidelines, the Office of the National Data Commissioner (Australia) advise that data sharing be guided by the open declaration of the purpose of data sharing (relative to the original purpose of collection), the level of detail in the data, the environment in which the data will be used (assuming this includes access by third parties), the people who are accessing the data and the nature of any published outputs of the sharing agreement. What's missing in this framework, which mirrors the Five Safes data sharing principles, is guidance around documenting the work done to 'prepare', 'clean', 'enrich', 'transform', 'link' data so that it can be used for these stated and declared purposes. This becomes particularly important when these processes might need to be reverse engineered such as in the instances of breach, harm or malpractice.

Openness, too, has a complicated history. Tkacz (2012) traces a history from Popper to the Open Knowledge foundation, but notes that this history of openness aligns perfectly well with models of thought that have helped dismantle democratic engagement with the state, fostering an idea of engagement with platforms and services that increasingly shift the role of the state towards the datafication of its citizens as the only form of knowledge available. As Tkacz notes, the open society, and its commensurate Open Government is put through progressive stages of opening that seems contradictory. The opening is conducted in service to an idea of anti-tyranny, but also dismantles and reduces the function of the state. The state tends to be open but also powerless. This is worth considering in the context of the formation of the principles that have preceded contemporary forms of openness, such as the identification of free flows of information as a human right by the UN during its formative years. Indeed, even before the Universal Declaration of Human Rights was completed (United Nations General Assembly 1948), the UN had voted in favour of principles of free flows of information (United Nations General Assembly 1946). Their development became a major sticking point for disputes within UNESCO, with the US in particular using the principle of openness to require that other nations open themselves to US media content being sold in their markets. UNESCO would later produce the MacBride report to investigate this situation, finding that the free flow of information was severely detrimental to local media production (MacBride et al. 1980; Nordenstreng 2011).

Conclusion

These terms reframe how we understand data transactions. Ethical analysis of the role, purpose, and sourcing of data will continue to struggle as long as it continues to accept these terms on their face value. Trading data about private citizens between commercial entities is framed as beneficent rather than extractive, as community-spirited rather than private. Sharing operates in a wide variety of discourses, including those that emphasize file-sharing in online piracy contexts, but also as an imperative for individuals to disclose personal information on social media (see John 2013). The specifically political language that implies forms of lateral organization and power has disappeared from this language. Instead, insidious undercurrents have taken hold within this discourse, making innocuous phrases like 'safe' and 'data sharing' sound like communitarian concepts while potentially being restricted to transactions in user data between private organizations or when the data being shared is classified or restricted. HASS disciplines can make further informed contributions to data ethics by interrogating how these terms are used to conceal behaviour that would otherwise go unnoticed.

Notes

1. 'Application Programming Interface'. Effectively a means of providing external users and software controlled access to data on a database through a series of predefined and coded 'hardpoints'. Access to APIs may be paid, available upon signup, or, more rarely, freely available.
2. The authors have chosen not to link to these sites due to their objectionable content, however they are readily discoverable.
3. eXtensible Markup Language.

Disclosure statement

No potential conflict of interest was reported by the author(s).

ORCID

Robbie Fordyce ⓘ http://orcid.org/0000-0003-0244-8151
Suneel Jethani ⓘ http://orcid.org/0000-0003-2134-0904

References

Bacchi, C. 2000. "Policy as Discourse: What Does It Mean? Where Does It Get Us?" *Discourse: Studies in the Cultural Politics of Education* 21 (1): 45–57. doi:10.1080/01596300050005493.

Bacchi, C. 2009. *Analysing Policy: What's the Problem Represented to Be?* Pearson: Sydney.

Benkler, Y. 2004. "Sharing Nicely: On Shareable Goods and the Emergence of Sharing as a Modality of Economic Production." *The Yale Law Journal* 114 (2): 273–358. doi:10.2307/4135731.

Bennett Moses, L., G. Churches, E. Watson, and M. Zalnieriute. 2019b. "Submission to the Data Sharing and Release Legislative Reforms Discussion Paper." *UNSW Law Research Paper No. 19-79*, https://ssrn.com/abstract=3467385

Bennett Moses, L., R. P. Buckley, F. E. Johns, G. Greenleaf, K. Kemp, M. De Leeuw, K. Manwaring, A. Maurushat, and M. Zalnieriute. 2019a. "Response to Issues Paper on Data Sharing and Release". *UNSW Law Research Paper No. 19-13*, https://ssrn.com/abstract=3348816

Bishop, L., and D. Gray. 2017. "Ethical Challenges of Publishing and Sharing Social Media Research Data." In *The Ethics of Online Research Vol II*, edited by K. Woodfield, Emerald Publishing Limited: 159–187.

Boyd, D., and K. Crawford. 2012. Critical questions for big data: Provocations for a cultural, technological, and scholarly phenomenon. *Information, communication & society*, 15(5): 662–679.

Buneman, P., S. Khanna, and W. Tan. 2000 "Data Provenance: Some Basic Issues." *International Conference on Foundations of Software Technology and Theoretical Computer Science*, pp. 87–93. Springer, Berlin, Heidelberg.

Buneman, P., S. Khanna, and W. Tan 2001. "Why and Where: A Characterization of Data Provenance." In *International conference on database theory* (pp. 316–330). Springer, Berlin, Heidelberg.

Dai, C., D. Lin, E. Bertino, and M. Kantarcioglu. 2008. "An Approach to Evaluate Data Trustworthiness Based on Data Provenance." In *Workshop on Secure Data Management*, edited by Willem Jonker and Milan Petković, 82–98. Berlin, Heidelberg: Springer.

Dalton, C. M., L. Taylor, and J. Thatcher. 2016. "Critical Data Studies: A Dialog on Data and Space." *Big Data & Society* 3 (1): 205395171664834. doi:10.1177/2053951716648346.

Data Availability and Transparency Bill. 2020. *Australian House of Representatives*. https://www.aph.gov.au/Parliamentary_Business/Bills_Legislation/Bills_Search_Results/Result?bId=r6649

Department of Prime Minister and Cabinet. 2018. "The Australian Government's Response to the Productivity Commision Data Availability and Use Inquiry." https://dataavailability.pmc.gov.au/

Department of the Prime Minister and Cabinet.2018. *New Australian Government Data Sharing and Release Legislation*. https://www.pmc.gov.au/sites/default/files/publications/australian-government-data-sharing-release-legislation_issues-paper.pdf

Eubanks, V. 2018. *Automating Inequality: How High-tech Tools Profile, Police, and Punish the Poor*. New York: St. Martin's Press.

Ford, H., and M. Graham. 2016. "Provenance, Power and Place: Linked Data and Opaque Digital Geographies." *Environment and Planning D: Society and Space* 34 (6): 957–970. doi:10.1177/0263775816668857.

Glavic, B. 2012. "Big Data Provenance: Challenges and Implications for Benchmarking." In *Specifying Big Data Benchmarks. Revised Selected Papers*, T. Rabl, M. Poess, C. Baru, and H. A. Jacobsen edited by, Vol. 8163, 72–80. 2013. Berlin, Heidelberg: Springer.

Guardian News 2018. "Cambridge Analytica Whistleblower Christopher Wylie Testifies before Congress - Watch Live" *Youtube.com*. https://www.youtube.com/watch?v=PCpDi57x4uc

Heemsbergen, L. 2021. *Radical Transparency and Digital Democracy: Wikileaks and Beyond*. Bingley: Emerald Publishing.

Humby, C. 2006. "Data Is the New Oil" ANA Senior Marketer's Summit, Kellogg School."

Iliadis, A., and F. Russo. 2016. "Critical Data Studies: An Introduction." *Big Data & Society* 3 (2): 2. doi:10.1177/2053951716674238.

Jethani, S., and R. Fordyce. 2021. "Darkness, Datafication, and Provenance as an Illuminating Methodology." *M/C Journal* 24 (2). doi:10.5204/mcj.2758.

John, N. A. 2013. "Sharing and Web 2.0: The Emergence of a Keyword." *New Media & Society* 15 (2): 167–182. doi:10.1177/1461444812450684.

John, N. A. 2017. *The Age of Sharing*. Malden, MA: John Wiley & Sons.

Kennedy, J. 2013. "Rhetorics of Sharing: Data, Imagination and Desire." In *Unlike Us Reader*, edited by G. Lovink and M. Rasch, 127–136. Amsterdam: Institute of Network Cultures.

Kennedy, J. 2016. "Conceptual Boundaries of Sharing." *Information, Communication & Society* 19 (4): 461–474. doi:10.1080/1369118X.2015.1046894.

Kitchin, R., and T. P. Lauriault. 2014. "Towards Critical Data Studies: Charting and Unpacking Data Assemblages and Their Work." (SSRN Scholarly Paper No. ID 2474112). Rochester, NY: Social Science Research Network.

MacBride, S. the International Commission for the Study of Communication Problems. 1980. *Many Voices, One World: Towards a New More Just and More Efficient World Information and Communication Order*. Paris: UNESCO.

MacLean, D. 2011. "The Evolution of GMCP Institutions." In *The Handbook of Global Media and Communication Policy*, edited by Mansell and Raboy, 40–58. Malden: Blackwell Publishing.

Martínez, A. G. 2019. "No, Data Is Not the New Oil." Wired.com. Accessed 26 February 2019. https://www.wired.com/story/no-data-is-not-the-new-oil/

Meese, J., P. Jagasia, and J. Arvanitakis. 2019. "Citizen or Consumer? Contrasting Australia and Europe's Data Protection Policies." *Internet Policy Review* 8 (2): 1–16. doi:10.14763/2019.2.1409.

Meyer, R., and A. C. Madrigal. 2021. "Why the Pandemic Experts Failed." *The Atlantic*. https://www.theatlantic.com/science/archive/2021/03/americas-coronavirus-catastrophe-began-with-data/618287/

Michael, M., and D. Lupton. 2016. "Toward a Manifesto for the 'Public Understanding of Big Data'." *Public Understanding of Science* 25 (1): 104–116. doi:10.1177/0963662515609005.

Nordenstreng, K. 2011. "Free Flow Doctrine in Global Media Policy." In *The Handbook of Global Media and Communication Policy*, edited by R. Mansell and M. Raboy, 79-94. Oxford: Blackwell Publishing.

Pool, I. 2016. "Colonialism's and Postcolonialism's Fellow Traveller: The Collection, Use and Misuse of Data on Indigenous People." In *Indigenous Data Sovereignty: Towards an Agenda*, edited by T. Kukutai and J. Taylor, 57–78. Canberra: ANU Press.

Productivity Commission 2017. "Inquiry into Data Availability and Use." https://www.pc.gov.au/inquiries/completed/data-access/report/data-access.pdf

Rifkin, J. 2000. *The Age of Access*. New York: Jeremy P Tarcher/Penguin.

Sadowski, J. 2019. "When Data Is Capital: Datafication, Accumulation, and Extraction/" *Big Data and Society*. Advance Online Publication. 1–12

Sakellariou, D., and E. S. Rotarou. 2017. "The Effects of Neoliberal Policies on Access to Healthcare for People with Disabilities." *International Journal for Equity in Health* 16 (1): 1–8. doi:10.1186/s12939-017-0699-3.

Schor, J. 2016. "Debating the Sharing Economy." *Journal of Self-Governance and Management Economics* 4 (3): 7–22.

Statt, N. 2019 "Hundreds of Active and Former Police Officers are Part of Extremist Facebook Groups." *The Verge*. https://www.theverge.com/2019/6/14/18679598/facebook-hate-groups-law-enforcement-police-officers-racism-islamaphobia

Tkacz, N. 2012. "From Open Source to Open Government: A Critique of Open Politics." *Ephemera: Theory and Politics in Organization* 12 (4): 386–405.

United Nations General Assembly. 1946. "International Conference on Freedom of Information." *UN General Assembly*, Resolution 59. https://undocs.org/en/A/RES/59(I)

United Nations General Assembly. 1948. "Universal Declaration of Human Rights." *UN General Assembly*, Resolution 217 https://undocs.org/en/A/RES/217(III)

Woodruff, A., and M. Stonebraker 1997. "Supporting Fine-grained Data Lineage in a Database Visualization Environment". *Proceedings 13th International Conference on Data Engineering*: 91–102. Birmingham, UK.

Writing the Feminist Internet: A Chthonian Feminist Internet Theory for the Twenty First Century

Nancy Mauro-Flude

ABSTRACT
This paper analytically responds to the collaborative performance work Writing the Feminist Internet as a motif of fourth wave feminism. It probes at the edge of Internet dark spaces that are often occupied by those who point to complacency in engagement with networking systems, by drawing auxiliary attention to the apparatus. Further examination sheds light on the valences and anarchy of technopolitics that transpired and reflects on the call for 'hybrid of feminist activist efforts' noted by Emma A. Jane. Positing towards 'a recalibrated approach to collectivism' (2015, 285) Jane continues to give rise to a vast communal realm for the expression of alternative behaviours. In building upon the feminist 'wave' metaphor there is acknowledgement that the undercurrents of nautical lineages come to endure through 'debt, or inheritance' more often than a confluence of flows. The findings reveal that the potency of a chthonic feminist internet theory lies in its indeterminate stance. In conclusion, it is proposed that ambivalence and prominence in obscurity in such expansive 'dark social spaces' is where new meanings and enunciations can brew and be read as a source of critical and aesthetic ambiguity, amongst the highly revered principles of disarray, pandemonium and incompleteness.

Introduction

To swell the readers imagination of what a feminist internet is, and what it could become, this article refers to feminist webserver communities as chthonic 'dark social spaces' (Heemsbergen et al. 2021, n.p.) to pose broader questions about the convergence of theory, art practice and feminist waves to 'do whatever we know how to order it to perform' (Lovelace cited in Menabrea 1842, n.d.).

The aim of this article is to advance a chthonic feminist critical internet theory, first and foremost kindled by the edicts of science fiction writer Ursula LeGuin who instructs, 'Don't look straight at the sun. Go into a dark bar for a bit and have a beer with Dionysius, every now and then' (Le Guin 1976, xvii). The chthonian is a locus that refers to 'that which is beneath the surface, the underworld and its state of darkness' (Fontelieu 2020, n.p.). It can also be acknowledged as analogous to feminist computer subcultures, those whose activities frequently occur under the radar of sanctioned culture. A key tactic for proposing the term chthonic is to reorient enquiry towards the murkier side of feminist webserver peer production, in order to counterpose such tendencies of how the 'adjective "dark" may bring to mind illegal or immoral activity' (Gehl and McKelvey 2019, 223). Darkness is routinely deemed as the symbol of using power for personal gain or 'evil' nevertheless a chthonic deity, 'the carrier of the projection of human nature's instinctive drives and dark, rejected propensities ... is also a fertile and divine source of abundance (Fontelieu 2020, n.p.).' In this way, the Internet is envisioned as a 'dark social space' (Heemsbergen et al. 2021, n.p.) as place, where culture and speculative realism, fiction and imagining invoke a potent understanding of the complexities of these ontologies in the conception of a chthonic feminist critical theory.

Over the past three decades, computer culture has generated numerous discourses, most conspicuously in the context of copyright licencing, opensource software, and deterministic automation. Expanding upon the 'dark social' to be chthonic can be considered both a critique of the usual instrumental perception of computation, and a metaphor to elucidate the abundant convergence of exchange as a stirring prolific space, oriented towards profusion. This vast idea of modern computation was first articulated almost two centuries ago by Ada Lovelace, whose depiction of computing capabilities contained transcendental and symbolic 'Notes' (cited in Menabrea [1842] n.d.). This proposition contends that below layers of obfuscation her revelations endure in the emergences of bio-technical-cultural transformations of the twenty-first century. One example is the interpretation of Lovelace's visions in line with computer programmer Ted Nelson who coined 'hypertext' and speaks of programming as a 'weaving of plans of events (and where they are to take place) – the choreography of happenings' (Nelson 1987 [1974], 40). This intertwining of people converging amidst temporalities and hemispheres enabled through a composition of computational networks and webserver software has become a common daily ritual for many of us.[1]

Informed by the epistemologies of fourth wave feminism (Clarke Mane 2012; Jane 2016), the article examines a motley crew of threads, perspectives and behaviours that manifested during the online performances of *Writing the Feminist Internet* (WtFI) 2020. To2012 depict the embodied, situated, inexorable, cherished, and radical ways in which the performance enabled participants to conduct provocative frolics on the front lines of text. *Writing the Feminist Internet* (WtFI) 2020 is based on extensive fieldwork within computer subcultures, consisting of ethnographic participation and observation, informed by feminist genealogies that are spectral and manifold, illuminating the plurality agendas that constitute computer mediated interaction.

Amongst this description where obscure symbolic elements, wayward strategies, indeterminate offerings transmit elsewhere, the cauldron of the Internet is an anchor point for the chthonic feminist theory, holding a vast array of materials and brews of transgenerational and transdisciplinary feminist processes. Harbouring what, how and when we contest common understandings of unusual Internet practices, they become:

> highly wrought and so covered over with accretions of alien matter ... hubble-bubble, swarm and chaos. We are peering over the edge of a cauldron in which fragments of all shapes and savours seem to simmer; now and again some vast form heaves itself up and seems about to haul itself out of chaos (Woolf. 1926, n.p.).

Notwithstanding the obvious connection of cauldrons and spellcasting to sorceresses, the current adverse associations and stigma, could be said to be residual effect of 'the medieval war on witches' (Dulchinos 2011, 76), alluding to the continual battle for women online to be considered in unbiased ways, in local and global contexts.

The source of contemporary computation rests firmly in the lap of Ada Lovelace, a site of chthonian expurgation (Stein 1984). Lovelace affirmed in 1842: 'The Analytical Engine has no pretensions whatever to originate anything. It can do whatever we know how to order it to perform' (Lovelace cited in Menabrea 1842, n.d.). Comparable to the obscurity of Lovelace, the Queen of Computing (Harrison 1900, 112), is Persephone, Queen of the stygian Netherworld, the chthonic deity of spring, flowers, death, life, vegetation and destruction. Described as a 'wilful creature' (Dillon 2001, 104) works of art frequently depict Persephone holding a box (or vessel) of which is said to diminish her prominence (Harrison 1900, 103) see Figure 1. The contents of Persephone's mysterious container filled with 'Stygian sleep' percolates obliteration. Among other conceivable readings where for example, 'no such gesture of thanks has come from the Australian authorities to those numerous souls' (Wright 2017, n.p.), such oblivion offers yet another eerie reminder of the women 'computers' operating in the shadows of anonymity.

Figure 1. Chthonic stygian deityIsis-Persephone holding a sistrum in the left and the right hand clasping a box. 'Archaeological Museum in Herakleion. Statue of Isis-Persephone holding a sistrum. Temple of the Egyptian gods, Gortyn. Roman period (180-190 A.C.)'. Image: Wolfgang Sauber (4 April 2009), Creative Commons Attribution-Share

A chthonic feminist critical Internet theory can provide some accoutrements for the reader to appreciate the nuances present in these complex relationships and genealogies. In line with expanded communication milieus and cultures of materialist informatics, infrastructure can be understood to be made up of cyber physical systems. This performance work of WtFI (2020) highlights its neomaterialist spirit that 'a political project that calls upon us to combat the modern colonial tendency to presume that one framework can be marshalled to account for all the others (Van Der Tuin and Nocek 2015, 820)'. Users – known collectively here as participants – divulge the potency of chthonic feminist internet theory, one that rests in the undefined informants and intermediaries witnessed through and within the practice of xenoglossia. A mystical ritual where the speech arrives through a body from an undetermined informant (Patai 1983). In conclusion it is proposed that the autonomous ambivalent expanse of chthonic feminist spaces are where new meanings can ferment in vessels that brew on the principles of engaged autonomy, disorder, pandemonium and incompleteness.

Reimagining internet sovereignty as Feminist Laissez-Faire

WtFI (2020) was a tryptic of two-hour experimental writing sessions that invited the public to engage in editing and expanding upon a draft set of '10 working points' (Mauro-Flude 2018, n.p.). In collaboration with three festivals and symposiums each iteration of subsequent sessions intended to enfold all the 'feminist waves *waves* \0\ \0/ /0/' (Mauro-Flude 2018, n.p.). The working points were then provided as a springboard for participants to erase, contest, remap, reconfigure in the performative writing act of ontological positioning in relation to one another. Collaborators irreverently augmented the numeric stability of the 10 principles. For instance, in Figure 2 we can see additions of '-1' and '0 zero'. The principles were adapted from a pamphlet '10 working points for artists in the new divisions of labour' by Schneider (2010), in turn, yet another derivative – a zealous translation of Petty's (1899) manuscript on the consignment of labour.

Notably, one of main proponents of this *laissez-faire* theory of economy was Charles Babbage, the engineer who, assisted by Ada Lovelace, conceived an early version of a mechanical computer known as the Difference and Analytical Engine. An indication of Babbage obliviousness to the enormous density of this machine, Lovelace's note's observe, 'just as the Jacquard-loom weaves flowers and leaves. Here, it seems to us, resides much more of originality than the Difference Engine can be fairly entitled to claim' (cited in Menabrea 1842, n.d.). Erasure in the realm of writing and technopolitics is not apolitical, nor ahistorical. Elaborating upon the spurious nature of property, ownership and proprietary software, feminist historian Hanna Musial bears witness to:

> The forgotten female laborers, whose removal from that history is paralleled by the erasure of the work of ethnic or indigenous ... coders ... technology itself becomes a medium of critical theory ... not only as a tool of "social dreaming" ... but also as a vehicle for a radical critical ... practice ... often as a remedy to legal and political disempowerment (Musial 2018, 166–7).

Concentrating on gendered racial and socio-cultural inequalities, Bailey and Trudy 'reflect how misogynoir functions in social and institutional settings' (2018, 766). They discuss racial injustice through lack of citational practice (and hence eradication), particularly in social media platforms such as Twitter by popular culture figures. In this spirit, a chthonic feminist internet theory is posed as a means of taking back, salvaging and recovering previously appropriated antidotes, anecdotes and other undetermined offerings by women that have been erroneously diminished.

Contributors of WtFI (2020) were invited to initially meet on Jitsu (an open-source video conferencing platform) which served as antechamber before 'opting in' to the performance. There was acknowledgement of those present via a speech with accompanying cue cards, 'to the guests, hosts and ghosts – ancestors past, present and emerging. The space the feminist server sits on, and the spaces we are all occupying which are in themselves colonised, written, programmed and ruled by dominant other' (Mauro-Flude 2018, n.p.). Subsequently the hosts ushered the participants from the antechamber through to main stage, by the instruction to copy the Uniform Resource Locator (URL) that had been placed the chat element of the Jitsi, in their own browser address bar.[2] To arrive at the location of the main event a purposely configured Ether pad, an open-source text editor for real time multiple authoring (see Figure 2).

Here a technical 'How To' preamble, and a code of conduct was delivered by the host, typewriting the information in real time for the participants to read. The transition from communicating via audio/visual streaming, to reading and writing in a collaborative network space, enabled participants to make a perceptual shift, to tacitly engage with writing and reading even as they read.

Furthermore, the 'How To' presentation highlighted the ways that individuals could represent themselves within the collective online writing environment. The advice suggested participants enter an author name, and to designate a colour of which both could be shifted and modified, at any time during the 2-hour event. The name/colour identification allocations appeared in two places – in a horizontal list below the URL address bar in the easy-to-use collaborative word editing environment (see Figure 2), and to the right in a vertical pop out list (see Figures 3-5). Participants who opted out of name allocation appeared as 'unnamed' (see Figures 2-3). A glimpse of how different participant authors choose how to identify themselves: first name, unnamed, art duo brand, declaration of gender pronoun markers and so on, can be seen at the top of Figure 2, or the view the right of the image in Figures 3-5.

To facilitate the exploration of a cacophony of voices and decentring authorship through cross-over writing methods alongside the development of overlapping individual pieces (revealed by Figures 2–5 and related screen capture videos).[3] Further clarification was made 'when more users start to edit in the document there may be many colours according to who is writing into the text' Mauro- Flude (2020, n.p.), a process that enables the individual subject to be seen as part of the broader collective. Comments such as: 'I just adjusted by colour to differentiate myself ... weird ... Unnecessary?', 'its so quiet but also frenetic', 'I got kicked off mid-sentence and can't find where I was writing lol', substantiate how contributors were reflexive of their experience, as they simultaneously engaged with the ephemeral practise of reading and writing in communion (see Figure 3 , '-1' lime green, dark green, orange and purple); substantiating how beliefs are embedded in acts of writing and how language is implicated in behaviour.[4]

On some occasions, participants deliberately sought to concentrate on the visuality of typography, forming new compositional properties of words or liberating words from the anecdotal limitations of syntax, in a wayward manner arranging the space beyond lexical

Figure 2. Screenshot Session 2 Writing the Feminist Internet – working points for the 21 Century v.1 30 May 2020, 1400–1600 AEST Image: Nancy Mauro-Flude.

norms (see Figure 3). The default text background colour was chosen by the most recent participants configuration. Observing this participants who had self-allocated a colour then began to change their initial colour palate, causing the majority of individual statements to transmogrify into a collective transcription. Dislocated from its source, the text became awash with a chaotic bricolage of tints as a result of the performative encounter of writing – acts of editing, elaborating, correcting, challenging, echoing, repeating, expanding, clarifying, summarising, distilling, nuancing – all of which produced different hues that were anarchically braided around letters or lines of text (see Figure 4).

Additionally, contributors who by default (or by choice) selected the same author colour as another could resemble a form of Xenoglossia, which is analogous to the more commonly known form of ventriloquy, for example, an intertextual weaving of thinking in relation to the infrastructures in and of colonisation (see Figure 3). These examples contain a panoply of characteristics of dark social spaces (Gehl 2018; Heemsbergen et al. 2021) by way of identity theft (ventriloquy), and also the misappropriation of working points as a kind of phishing act (imitation of institutions). Wilful acts of improvisation altering the working points, scrambling verity, authorship became molten, kaleidoscopic, deranged, abundant and chthonian, these are the attributes of a stygian feminist.

The performance events attracted an array of participants – writers of fiction and non-fiction, artists, poets, critics, curators, and transdisciplinary researchers who predominantly identified as womxn – from varied racial-socio-cultural backgrounds and different skill sets.[5]

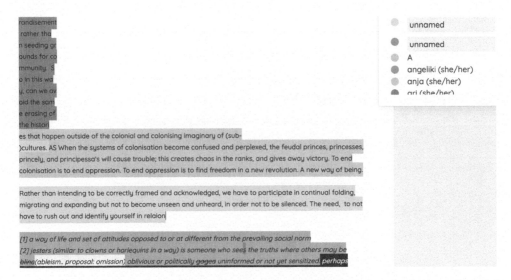

Figure 3. Detail: Screenshot Session 1 WtFI where colour play highlights represent the mélange of individual and collective participation. v.1 30 May 2020, 1400–1600 AEST. Image: Nancy Mauro-Flude.

Individual details relating to the event were entwined with notions of feminist solidarity. Some partakers embraced a 'peripatetic stance' (Mauro-Flude 2020, 91) and others noted the profoundness of play within the limits a given system:

> … [child name redacted] started typing into the etherpad hahaha and i only added like 2 sentences as i just couldnt quite figure out what i wanted to say (also the original manifesto read rly well to me), but listened to the relaxing typing noises! (WtFI participant).[6]

> … it's a beautiful thing to create dynamic/organic flow within fairly rigid technological constraint (document formatting tech etc.). Lots of familiar faces (names) in there! (WtFI participant).[7]

From this comment it was notable to some of the cohort, that the performance gathered, among other participants, different generations of cyberfeminists. The inception of the movement is described by Dement:

> coagulated and sparked in the reject-outsider mutiny, trauma-jouissance and fast hard beat of queer punk. It found visible existence and a manifesto, through VNS Matrix in the (typical) Adelaide heat wave of 1991 … Cyberfeminism, as blurred edge range, entangles carnality with code; machines, blood and bad language; poetry and disdain; executables, theft and creative fabrication. It incites and follows lines of flight powered by contradiction, relatedness, transgression, and misbehaviour. It simultaneously embraces logic and unreason, giving the finger to binaries as it ravishes them Ibid.).

Abandoning *apriori* assumptions of neutrality raging against the complete neglect of specificity, sentiments like these move beyond the putative constraints of discursive, structural norms, corroded by stakeholder commerce.

The provocative unruly punk tactics of cyberfeminism serve as a productive entry point into the analyses of contested terrains and provenance of computers and promiscuous computing such as chthonian social spaces. The act of writing as an entombed annotation, contrasted with the act of performing bound to an ephemeral shape is described by poet laureate and punk rocker Patti Smith:

> I love writing because there are acoustic typewriters and electric ones. It's a physical act but the word is still trapped on the page ... performing ... keeps the act of creation alive. I love the process of creation, although the end product is in itself a necessary evil. Still, I'm glad it's there, otherwise I wouldn't have ... records, ... Burroughs or Rimbaud books to enjoy (1995, 282).

It is striking how Smith's mid-nineties reference to published artefacts of the poets from the beat and libertine generations (notably predominantly male) as the end product as 'a necessary evil' (Smith, Cited in Shapiro 1995, 282) is portrayed in the same light or stigma frequently afforded to the dark web (Gehl 2018).

Perhaps more significant and salient is the ability to capture the paratactic dance of writing in the transfiguration of words.[8] That is enabled by synchronous multiple authoring tools in a networked environment, that opens a cornucopia of potentials for unforeseen sites, repositories and tools for further consideration. The *EtherPad* software archived *WtFI* (2020) performance in real time, recording tacit exchanges of the keystrokes in a choreography of writerly transmutation.

Indicating the tension between being an individual as a part of a collaboration, the following participant account not only addresses the ability to capture 'the process as it unfurled', but aids as a testament to the ways in which a chthonic feminist context enables collaborators to gain a visceral grasp on the actions of their collaborators, who are present within the network, yet physically remote:

> peeped at the femnet link ... how cool you screencapped the process as it unfurled, perfect and yes, it's interesting the editing that we can do ... we identity_runnerz ... one reserves the right to be the word-boss ... im sometimes conflicted about the rightness of that.but sheesh, u wanna be happy with the ballet in the poems/manifestos in the end.and that means some harsh cutting and sensitive line spacing
>
> and i felt your rearranging today! think that's enough housework for the day! (WtFI participant [my italics]).[9]

Drawing upon imbroglios and intermediaries, conferring to the subterranean 'cut-and-paste' nonlinear plots of Virginia Woolf, postmodern literary critic N. Katherine Hayles (2005) considers the inter/intrasubjective inscriptions from the typewriter to the computer, appealing for a counter narrative approach to remedy to techno-determinism:

> amid the uncertainties, potentialities and dangers created by the Regime of Computation, simulations, computational and narrative- can serve as potent resources with which to explore and understand the entanglement of language with code ... the potential to inspire another kind of narrative in which humans are not seen as subjects manipulating objects in the world (2005, 242).

In a bid to decenter the human from the locus of action reveals an acute need to conceive computing practices as dynamic forms and processes, and also to acknowledge the elements that form the assemblage of networks and systems that perform around and act through us.

In this way a chthonic feminist theory envisions the Internet as a 'cauldron' of happenings, a host for inexplicable asemic brews (see Figures 2–3). Because asemic writing is often illegible, vivid and/or open ended, it has no fixed meaning (evidenced in concrete poetry), and where the reader as writer, as conjuror, is faced to think not of communication but rather performances with materialities and related knowledge production in collaboration with the paraphernalia of writerly technologies.

Chthonian feminist processes like these can not only delegitimate authorial authority but compost knowledge production. An exemplar of this is artistic research with datasets trained from conversational machine learning modelling agents by Linda Dement. Contributing in WtFi (2020) she generated a text that responded to the prompts 'A Feminist Internet ... '.[10] In Figure 3 we see how other participants (denoted by colour and syntax) began to riff upon the output from 'The Feminist Internet is ... ' above and below. Transfigure pluralities of 'Feminists internets are ... '; 'Feminists internets' which 'refuses, excels, connects, disseminates, is a bitch mutant, refuses, rejects, WILL EAT YOU' and so on. The bedlam in the browser was in line with the errant, formidable and fecund characteristics of chthonic Stygian deities (Dillon 2001).

The complicit nature of discursive systems established by orthodox concords, writing is a phenomenon often obscured by the conventions of capital be it cultural or financial or otherwise (Bourdieu 1977). Suspending this notion in WtFI (2020) the text became a medium, a conjuring tool for the transmission and transfiguration of thought, rather than the fulcrum of thoughts necessary condition. The term 'Feminist Internet' thus emerges as ornery, capricious, unfixed, and unfinished, always underway, and open to interpretation. It alludes to a trajectory that is forking and diversified, a collective quixotic oddity, where many arms work as one, purposely writing in synchronicity and then in the occasional unpredictable asynchronous deviation (see Figure 3).

Typically, the definition of 'Feminist Internet' is motivated by the confluence of activism and artistic research in a bid to offer digital literacy and to spread awareness of alternative computation methods. One initial version of the 'Feminist Internet' manifested on 18 December 2017, during a residency 'Doing Feminism/Sharing the World' hosted by the*Favour Economy (2017)*and facilitated by this author. In a bid to acquaint a broader artistic community with feminist traditions of technical knowledge production, the starting point for the workshop was to discuss the 'The Feminist Principles of the Internet (2014)', an evolving document that was developed by the Association for Progressive Communications a global Non-Government Organization (NGO) largely active in South East Asia, Africa and South America. Proceeding this a draught 'Feminist Internet Lore Manifesto: 10 working points for the twenty-first century' (Mauro-Flude 2018, n.p.) was published on -empire-.[11] Likewise, a Feminist Internet Manifesto was distributed 19 March 2018 by Feminist Internet, an arts activist collective who conduct public outreach and advocacy to foreground gender inequalities and programmed bias in digital environments mainly operating in the United Kingdom.

Stygian feminists restoring transgressive conceptualism to subvert the conventions surrounding feminist internet or feminist server collectives. Likewise, artist and theorist Rosa Menkman (2014, n.p.) asks 'But what happens when instead of choosing "best practices„ as a point of reference, we chose an unreasonable benchmark? What can we expect from these deranged logics at work?'. Entwining the threads to rewrite computational sovereignty out of its current totalitarian emergence where 'the more incentives for figuring out how to hack it will proliferate' (Ahmed 2016, 156). Beyond the adoption of a solution, *WtFI* (2020) was a ruse to consecrate Feminist Internet futures,a great marsh saturated at the stygian crossroads of theoretical interrogation, art practice and feminist webserver technology (see Figure 4).

The undercurrents of fourth wave feminism

The subjects of feminist politics informed by the confluence of feminist grassroots activists, feminist theorists, feminist artists have actuated in various ways and means throughout generational waves (Van Der Tuin 2015). Given the social and institutional obstacles that stymie feminist ambitions from: the suffragette movement schlepping on the shackles and cables of unforgiving infrastructures; second wave consciousness raising of the broader public to the inconspicuousness of class war, domestic labour, and gender inequality; to the self-determination and autonomy of third wave feminists who have a 'tolerance for contradiction (Clark Mane 2012, 86)'. Through an active resistance of conventions, searching not only for a new milieu but also new forms and processes that steer away from racial and gender asymmetry, and other (techno) essentialist mandates towards other kinds of experiences, outside the yoke of imperialist regimes.

The relationship between the pacts surrounding equivalence and well-defined intentions in feminist internet communities, and the contemporary occulture of chthonic commons latent in many fourth wave feminists embrace of spirited and unruly structures of chaotic entanglements of artistic genre, language, codes, and signals, often staged in Internet subculture through 'the tensions between dark and connected, opting in and opting out, and exposure and retreat' (Heemsbergen et al. 2021, n.p.). Opting in, the participants of *WtFI* (2020) placed themselves with in amidst to computational systems, developing discursive and/or aesthetic positions which at time exceeded these procedures. Freed from the strictures of conventional academic style and with support of contemporaries, revealing the ways in which processes with text can be used together to illuminate and describe unseen realms.

Channelling one another through textual conduits, the ripples accumulated at times were at odds with of some expectations of preconceived feminist imaginaries. A distinct individual 'Growly Gerkin/ccl' in black and white text, commandeering an authorial role, inserting themselves firming in the centre of the act, asking questions '>which feminism is this text referring to?'; >who is the *we* that this text refers to?' (Figure 5). By exhibiting a need for unwavering meaning and the compulsion to be correct, it can be suggested from this example how procedures of acceptability are persistently reasserted by some and rewritten and rendered as mutable by others. These 'received wisdoms' (Ahmed. 2016) are inherited from conformist agendas that can be understood as intolerant of undoing established assumptions in public.

Pondering 'affective temporality' Prudence Chamberlain examines how the fundamental shifts from principles of equality to the beliefs and actions of autonomy have dismayed some (2016, 462). Yet, stygian chthonic deities, capable of anything, except perhaps, are summoned to the clarion call of Jane (2016) to 'forge hybrid activist strategies which involve temporary allegiances between various theories, tactics and feminist generations' (2016, 292). Expanding the aperture and valences of technopolitics through a candid realm of antediluvian parables, possibilities and experiences figures make WtFI (2020) both resonant and contestable for its current moment – asking its own questions, re-examining its own past and envisaging other futures.

Shining a light on how a processual understanding of feminist computing methodologies is able to be more bountiful and wide-ranging, Rök Jóns (2013) enquires 'is the 4th wave of feminism digital?'. Jóns further surmises that if it faithfully is to be so it 'would have to be in part discursive and would require a restructuring of legal, institutional, educational, economic, social, religious, geographical, corporeal and cultural barriers ... ' (2013, n.p.). WtFI (2020) was activated by low bandwidth, user friendly software from 'The augmented homes of shared laboratories, of communal media and technical facilities' (Laboria Cuboniks 2015, n.p.). Founding member of the collaborative group Laboria Cuboniks (2015) and feminist writer Helen Hester (2018) contribute to the fourth wave through a manifesto entitled Xenofeminism. Thus, Xenofeminist's describe themselves as ' ... a labour of bricolage, synthesizing cyberfeminism, posthumanism, accelerationism, neorationalism, materialist feminism and so on, in an attempt to forge a project suited to contemporary political conditions ... a project for which the future remains open as a site

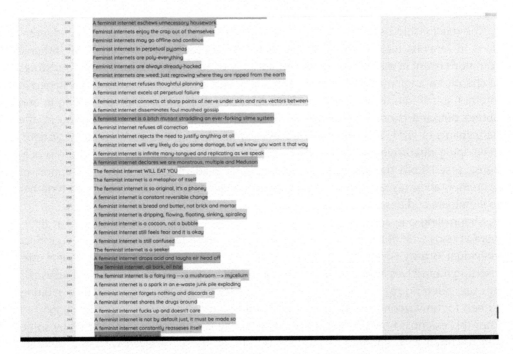

Figure 4. Screenshot Session 2 WTFI v.1 30 May 2020, 1400–1600 AEST Image: Nancy Mauro-Flude.

of radical recomposition (2018, 1)'. Untangling the constructions of supremacy, gender, race, class, opinions' that logically flatten the veracities of aesthetic properties where 'fog-shrouded literary minefields ... full of barbed wire and stumps of dead' (Le Guin 1989, 104). Intense debates propel the motivation for engaging in discourse that is consistently rendered to be equivocal. The energies of these feminist waves must 'move forward with the kind of generosity and commitment to ambiguity ... remembering the utopian thought and solidarity politics that allowed feminists of the past to think beyond gender, to a world of possibility' (Nicholas 2021, 18). Navigating over (and across) notional feminist waves and 'e-bile' (Jane 2016, 289), audaciously the cyberfeminist (as defined by VNS Matrix 1991; Dement 2017) floats over these commonplace issues, to retrieve what Lovelace (cited in Menabrea 1842) envisioned for her engine – the infinite ability to weave new configurations – to remain adrift, so as not to become ensnared in the undercurrents.

Internet of covens and xenoglossia

Affirming the burden of seeking out other procedures for communication as outlined by Irigaray (1980):

> If we continue to speak this sameness, if we speak to each other as men have spoken for centuries, as they have taught us to speak, we will fail each other. Again ... words will pass through our bodies, above our heads, disappear, make us disappear (1980, 69).

To evade banishment and erasure our words must now emerge from the unfamiliar. To unspeak talking for other kinds of exchange may be observed in asemic brews of Xenoglossia, to evade banishment and erasure our words must now emerge from the unfamiliar. Underscoring a chthonic feminist Internet is a twenty first-century form of xenoglossia, dark social spaces that render writing incapable to be claimed with authority because the texts emerge from everywhere other than an original source. These other possible modes of being, evidenced by the assorted desires of WtFi (2020) participants façades through the use of pseudonyms, 'identity_runnerz' altering name handles, chameleon switching hues, annihilating and abandon self completely (see figures 2-3-4). To modify the familiarity of qualities of writing, being for the most part known for many, collaborative transmogrification transports contributors into a wild terrain of online space converge at the centre of a great stygian marsh where dimensions and constraints may vacillate.

The image Witches Going to their Sabbath (1878) depicts a coven engaged in a consensual hallucination (see Figure 6) and was shared by a participant proceeding WtFI (2020). It was accompanied by the following note:

> Thank you dear, I loved this. Want more, more more! adding a little something that popped up while writing ... [12]

These findings entail, how, even if evanescently or fleetingly stygian Internet covens can summon up a semblance of oblivion and xenoglossia. Each actant arrives to the stygian stream with their own flora to contribute, however trivial or substantial, imparting an apophänie, an omen, for further deciphering. Ascertaining the Internet as a vessel of infinite veracity, a cauldron that holds inexplicable asemic brews.

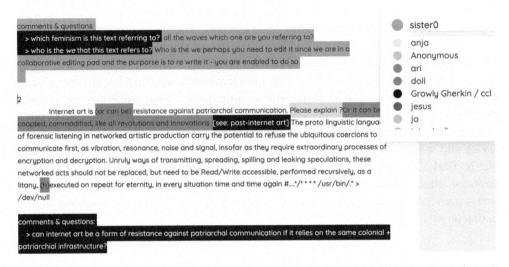

comments & questions:
> which feminism is this text referring to? all the waves which one are you referring to?
> who is the we that this text refers to? Who is the we perhaps you need to edit it since we are in a collaborative editing pad and the purpose is to re write it - you are enabled to do so.

2
Internet art is (or can be) resistance against patriarchal communication. Please explain ? Or it can be coopted, commodified, like all revolutions and innovations. [see: post-internet art] The proto linguistic language of forensic listening in networked artistic production carry the potential to refuse the ubiquitous coercions to communicate first, as vibration, resonance, noise and signal, insofar as they require extraordinary processes of encryption and decryption. Unruly ways of transmitting, spreading, spilling and leaking speculations, these networked acts should not be replaced, but need to be Read/Write accessible, performed recursively, as a litany, (h)executed on repeat for eternity, in every situation time and time again #....*/**** /usr/bin/.* > /dev/null

comments & questions:
> can internet art be a form of resistance against patriarchal communication if it relies on the same colonial + patriarchial infrastructure?

Figure 5. Witches Going to their Sabbath (1878) by Luis Ricardo Falero. Image public domain https://www.wikiart.org/en/luis-ricardo-falero/the-witches-sabbath. Accessed 20 March 2021.

Conclusion

A stygian critical feminist internet theory is an epistemology that ruminates on how knowledge is produced, circulates and is transformed. A dance of obfuscated symbolic elements, in the weaves and weft envisages acts of computing as a form of conjuring that don't reproduce ontological separations between the knowledge that is generated. A proliferation of influences, this theory is multidirectional and full of cracks, bringing about different kinds of remedies, where there is never one correct interpretation nor modus. Relative and situated, knowledge, method and elucidations are rendered according to the appropriateness of a given context and situation which have effects that are palpable but equivocal.

The scavenging and fermenting process-based performance art examined in WtFI (2020) a computational word-based dance that hovers at the crossroads of performance, concrete poetry and conceptual art. Durational sit-ins of textual foraging are rituals of incanting, assembling, seeking and carving out online space away from procedures that inflict erasure. The shapeshifting tactics of elusiveness and ambiguousness depicted are temporal interactions by machinic percipients and assemblages of living entities and matter, following Barad (2012, 2007) (among others). A coven of artists communicating processes by spontaneously combining 'texts' reports perceived from the other side of the performance space are corroborated through acts of alterity.

In the absence of profound infrastructural change, attentive improvised procedures, miscellaneous perspectives together with perplexity and elation, are able to traverse beyond systemic problems associated with the dark spaces of feminism. Terpsichorean innovations surface from the confluence of theories and art practices conducted by transgenerational feminist writers. Guided by the wayward and indeterminant ravines of stygian Internets.

Figure 6. Witches Going to their Sabbath (1878) by Luis Ricardo Falero. Image public domain https://www.wikiart.org/en/luis-ricardo-falero/the-witches-sabbath. Accessed 20 March 2021.

The numinous sense of what is not there, of the ineffable permeating the effable in this flourishing space of possibility language is a provisional and acquiescent system that emphasizes process over comprehension, and which may be experienced without recourse to the usual semiotic correlation between words and the world.

Notes

1. It should be noted that the WtFI (2020) was hosted on an autonomous feminist server run server (not third party software). Although an alternative space, it was not the 'dark web' where the site was only accessible if 'routed through special routing software packages' (Gehl 2018, 5). The Internet Provider IP was publicly accessible through standard Internet Browser, defined as the 'clear web' by Gehl which includes 'websites built with standard web technologies (HTML, CSS, server-side scripting languages, hosting software' (Gehl 2018, 5). 'A feminist server aims to provide a safe space for experimentation with internet protocols community who are considered "prosumers," instead of "clients" who have limited webserver access and permissions antithetical to archetypes of supremacy' (Mauro-Flude 2020, 84-85).
2. One example of a URL provide is here https://miss-hack.org/ether/p/r.0fb164af9342e9ff93429f425974ab8e. Accessed 10 March 2021.
3. Writing the Feminist Internet – working points for the 21 Century 2020 Collaborate Performance Event:
   'Next Wave Festival' Version 1, 30 May 2020, 1400-1600 AEST, https://miss-hack.org/ether/

p/r.0fb164af9342e9ff93429f425974ab8e. Accessed 21 October 2020; 'Hackers and Designers Amsterdam Summer School Academy' Version 2. 25 July 2020, 18:00-20:00 AEST. https://www.miss-hack.org/ether/p/r.83e1e7dbab9c9d44ee00f9e94c0831f7. Accessed 21 October 2020; 'Digital Intimacies 6 Connection in Crisis Symposium' Version 3, 27 November 2020, 1600-1800 AEST. http://www.vvvvvvvvvvvv.net/share/p/r.d00ab7adf70327e2a2681db4df3600b4. Accessed 21 December 2020.
4. In line with Jane (2016), I also will not be writing 'sic' after 'grammatical, spelling and syntax errors in cited electronic communications and online material in recognition of the informality and colloquialism commonly found in such contexts'(2016, 293).
5. 'By participating in the spelling of "womxn" feminists acknowledge the diverse identities of women that are not defined in relation to men' (Oxfam, 2016, n.p.)
6. Email correspondence, 6 June 2020, AEST 23:39:01.
7. Email correspondence, 2 June 2020, AEST 10:35:10.
8. A counter argument could be made for the polyvalency of language written in traditional print, but it is beyond the bounds of this essay. The 'dance of writing' in a networked space is further elaborated upon by Nancy Mauro-Flude and Jo Pollitt in 'I am _your_ Pyrate Dancer', Indeterminacy After AI Leonardo Journal, MIT Press. 2022 (in press).
9. Email correspondence, 27 November 2020 AEST 18:05.
10. See Linda Dement http://lindadement.com/art-peasants.htm. Accessed 10 March 2021. GPT-2 AI developed by Open AI. https://openai.com/blog/better-language-models/ Accessed 10 March 2021.
11. A community who participates in monthly thematic discussions via an email list active since 2002 (founded by Melinda Rackham an Australian cyberfeminist artist, curator, and writer) with the objective to trace 'the emergence of new media theory, practice, and networked culture. https://empyre.library.cornell.edu/. Accessed 10 March 2021.
12. Email correspondence, 25 July 2020 AEST 20:02.

Disclosure statement

The analysis is based on extensive field work and anthropological modes within computer subcultures, consisting of ethnocratic participation and observation. The author would like to especially thank the editors Toija Cinque, Alexia Maddox and Robert W. Gehl and from the Blind Peer Reviewers for their perceptive commentary and constructive critique.

ORCID

Nancy Mauro-Flude http://orcid.org/0000-0003-1340-8067

References

-empyre-: *soft-skinned space*. 2007–. Collective online artist community, e-mail listserv, https://empyre.library.cornell.edu/
Ahmed., S. 2016. *Living a Feminist Life*. Durham: Duke University Press.

APC. 2014. "The Feminist Principles of the Internet." *Association for Progressive Communities (APC)*. https://www.apc.org/en/pubs/feminist-principles-internet-version-20

Bailey, M; Trudy. 2018. "On Misogynoir: Citation, Erasure, and Plagiarism." *Feminist Media Studies* 18 (4): 762–768. doi:10.1080/14680777.2018.1447395.

Barad, K. 2007. *Meeting the Universe Halfway: Quantum Physics and the Entanglement of Matter and Meaning*. Durham; London: Duke University Press.

Barad, K. 2012. "On Touching—The Inhuman That Therefore I Am." *differences* 23 (3): 206–223. doi:10.1215/10407391-1892943.

Bourdieu, P. 1977. *Outline of a Theory of Practice*. Cambridge; New York: Cambridge University Press.

Bratton, B. H. 2015. *The Stack: On Software and Sovereignty*. Cambridge, MA: MIT Press.

Chamberlain, P. 2016. "Affective Temporality: Towards a Fourth Wave." *Gender and Education* 28 (3): 458–464. doi:10.1080/09540253.2016.1169249.

Clark Mane, R. L. 2012. "Transmuting Grammars of Whiteness in Third-Wave Feminism: Interrogating Postrace Histories, Postmodern Abstraction, and the Proliferation of Difference in Third-Wave Texts." *Signs: Journal of Women in Culture and Society* 38 (1): 71–98. doi:10.1086/665810.

Cuboniks, L. 2015. *Xenofeminism: A Politics for Alienation, Laboria Cuboniks*, Accessed 21 October 2020. https://laboriacuboniks.net/manifesto/xenofeminism-a-politics-for-alienation/

Dement, L. 2017. "Cyberfeminist Bedsheet." *Artlink* 37 (4). 1 December https://www.artlink.com.au/articles/4647/cyberfeminist-bedsheet/

Dillon, M. 2001. *Girls and Women in Classical Greek Religion*. London: Routledge.

Dulchinos, D. 2011. *Forbidden Sacraments: The Survival of Shamanism in Western Civilization*. New York: Autonomedia.

Favour Economy. 2018. "Doing Feminism/Sharing the World." Accessed 21 October 2020 https://doingfeminism-sharingtheworld.tumblr.com/FEres

Favour Economy, feminist collective website, Accessed 21 October 2020 https://www.favoureconomy.com

Feminist Internet. 2021. Accessed 21 October 2020 https://www.feministinternet.com/

Feminist Internet Manifesto, 19 March 2018. "UAL Futures." Accessed 21 October 2020. http://web.archive.org/web/20180319084648/feministinternet.com/manifesto

Fontelieu, Sukey. 2020. "Chthonic Deities." In *Encyclopedia of Psychology and Religion*, 445–446. Cham: Springer International Publishing.

Gehl, R.W. 2014. *Reverse Engineering Social Media*. Philadelphia: Temple Press.

Gehl, R. W. 2016. "Power/Freedom on the Dark Web: A Digital Ethnography of the Dark Web Social Network." *New Media & Society* 18 (7): 1219–1235. doi:10.1177/1461444814554900.

Gehl, R. W. 2018. *Weaving the Dark Web: Legitimacy on Freenet, Tor, and I2P*. Cambridge, MA: MIT Press.

Gehl, R. W., and F. McKelvey. 2019. "Bugging Out: Darknets as Parasites of Large-Scale Media Objects." *Media, Culture & Society* 41 (2): 219–235. doi:10.1177/0163443718818379.

Harrison, J. 1900. "Pandora's Box." *The Journal of Hellenic Studies* 20: 99–114. doi:10.2307/623745.

Hayles, K. N. 2005. *My Mother Was a Computer: Digital Subjects and Literary Texts*. London; Chicago: University of Chicago Press.

Heemsbergen, L. J., A. Maddox, T. Cinque, A. Johns, and R. Gehl. 2021. "Dark." *M/C Journal* 24 (2). doi:10.5204/mcj.2791.

Hester, H. 2018. *Xenofeminism*. Cambridge: Polity Press.

Irigaray, L. 1980. "When Our Two Lips Speak Together." *Signs* 6 (1): 69–79. doi:10.1086/493777.

Jane, E. A. 2016. "Online Misogyny and Feminist Digilantism." *Continuum* 30 (3): 284–297. doi:10.1080/10304312.2016.1166560.

Le Guin, U. 1976. *Left Hand of Darkness*. New York: Ace Books.

Le Guin, U. 1989. *Dancing at the Edge of the World: Thoughts on Words, Women, Places*. New York: Grove Press.

Mauro-Flude, N. 2018. "Feminist Internet Lore Manifesto: 10 Working Points for the 21 Century." *Rehearsal of a network –empyre-*, 5 June, http://lists.artdesign.unsw.edu.au/pipermail/empyre/2018-June/date.html

Mauro-Flude, N. 2020a. "Performing with the Aether: An Aesthetics of Tactical Feminist Practice." In *Routledge Companion to Mobile Media Art*, edited by Larissa Hjorth, Adriana de Souza e Silva, and Klare Lanson, 95–81. New York; London: Routledge.

Mauro-Flude, N. 2020b. "Working Points for Writing the Feminist Internet." https://www.miss-hack.org/?Writing_the-feminist_interent

Mauro-Flude, N., and K. Geck. 2020. Taxonomy for the Contiguous Spectrum: Corporeal Computing futures and the Performance of Signal Transmission *WHY SENTIENCE?* Montreal: *ISEA2020.(2020)*: 275–282. Accessed 17 May 2021 https://isea2020.isea-international.org/wp-content/uploads/2020/10/PROCEEDING_271020.pdf?mc_cid=c716641caf&mc_eid=30328f3362

Menabrea, L. F. [1842] n.d. "Sketch of the Analytical Engine Invented by Charles Babbage." In *Bibliothèque Universelle de Genève*, Vol. 82, edited by Ada Augusta, Countess of Lovelace, located at *The Analytical Engine emulator* developed by Stephan Adams (MIT), www.fourmilab.ch/babbage/sketch.html

Menkman, R. 2014. "Benchmarking the Deranged." *Network Art Forms Tactical Magick Faerie Circuits*. Accessed 17 May 2021. https://www.tacticalmagick.net/?rosamenkman. https://beyondresolution.info

Musial, H. 2018. "Metaphors of Decryption: Designs, Poetics, Collaborations." In *Decrypting Power, the Global Critical Caribbean Thought Series*, edited by Ricardo Sanín-Restrepo. London: Rowman & Littlefield.

Nelson, T. 1987 [1974]. *Computer Lib/dream Machines*. Revised edition. Redmond: Tempus Books; Microsoft Press.

Nicholas, L. 2021. "Remembering Simone De Beauvoir's "Ethics of Ambiguity" to Challenge Contemporary Divides: Feminism beyond Both Sex and Gender." *Feminist Theory* 22 (2): 226–247. doi:10.1177/1464700120988641.

Oxfam. "A Gathering of Womxn Activists 69 Years of What", Oxfam.org.za. 2016. Accessed 17 May 2021. http://www.oxfam.org.za/downloads/reports/A-Gathering-of-Womxn-Activists-60-Years-of-What-Report.pdf.

Patai, R. 1983 *Jewish folklore*. Detroit, Michigan. Wayne State University Press. Accessed 10 May 2020. https://digital.library.wayne.edu/item/wayne:WayneStateUniversityPress4426/file/HTML_FULL

Petty, W. 1899. "The Economic Writings of Sir William Petty." In *Bibliography of the Printed Writings of Sir William Petty*, edited by Hull, 633–652. London: Nabu Press. Accessed 17 May 2021 https://en.wikisource.org/wiki/The_Economic_Writings_of_Sir_William_Petty

Rök Jóns, R. 2013. "Is the 4th Wave of Feminism Digital?" *Blue Stocking Magazine*. August 19, Accessed 21 October 2020. http://bluestockingsmag.com/2013/08/19/is-the-4th-wave-of-feminism-digital/

Schneider, F. 2010. "Immaterial Labour in Performance." *Journal Des Laboratoires and TkH Journal for Performing Arts Theory* 17. Accessed 21 October 2020. http://fls.kein.org/view/33

Shapiro, S. 1995. "Patti Smith: Somewhere, over the Rimbaud." In *Rock She Wrote*, edited by Evelyn McDonnell and Ann Powers. New York: Dell Publishing.

Stein, D. K. 1984. "Lady Lovelace's Notes: Technical Text and Cultural Context." *Victorian Studies* 28 (1): 33–67.

Van Der Tuin, I. 2015. *Generational Feminism: New Materialist Introduction to a Generative Approach*. London: Lexington Books.

Van Der Tuin, I., and A.J. Nocek 2015. *Philosophy Today* 63, 4 (Fall 2019).

VNS Matrix. Artist Collective website. Accessed 21 October 2020. https://vnsmatrix.net/

Woolf., V. 1926. *The Movies and Reality* August 4, Accessed 21 October 2020. https://newrepublic.com/article/120389/movies-reality

Wright, T. 2017. "The Modest Spy and Monterey, Australia's Bletchley Park." *Sydney Morning Herald*. 6 July 2017, https://www.smh.com.au/opinion/tony-wright-column-the-modest-spy-and-monterey-australias-bletchley-park-20170706-gx5mxu.html

Writing The Feminist Internet (WtFI) 2020. "Next Wave Festival Version 1 | Hackers and Designers Amsterdam Summer School Academy Version 2 | Digital Intimacies 6." www.miss-hack.org. Accessed 21 December 2020. https://www.miss-hack.org/?Writing_the-feminist_interent/. Accessed 21 December 2020.

Afterword: Troubling the Dark Social

Melinda Hinkson, Roland Kapferer and P. David Marshall

Melinda Hinkson [MH]: The Global Digital Publics Network (GDPN) was formed at Deakin University in mid-2017 to bring together people who were broadly working on digital mediation. As its founding conveners, you will recall David that you and I found it quite an experiment to work out how and in what ways we would talk to each other across our diverse interests, methods, and working assumptions. Our group included scholars in communication, creative practice, criminology, cultural studies, anthropology – some with very empirical interests and ways of working, others who were more conceptually and creatively oriented. We spent a year or so sharing work in progress with an emphasis on 'demystifying technological systems'. It was in that context that Toija Cinque and Alexia Maddox made a terrific presentation on the Dark Web. That presentation opened out to a really energized discussion on the theme of the 'dark social'. We could see a lot of potential in the idea as one that we could tease out from a variety of disciplinary and interdisciplinary angles. As an anthropologist I was aware of a body of 'dark' work that had emerged from a decade of writing on structural violence and new workings of power, as social scientists and humanities scholars were grappling with emergent forms of securitized governance. Technologization and techno-capitalism were at the heart of these developments. As anthropologists, Roland and I would be likely to start our investigations of digital life via the concept of the social. But the first thing that strikes me about the papers brought together in this collection is that their starting assumption is *social media*.

David Marshall [DM]: Yes, Melinda, those assumptions have allowed the group to explore this dark web and uncover its complex structures. But, in a manner similar to the inhabitants of the dark social that is beyond the apparently different corporate world of social media, the articles work with assumptions about the social across an array of disciplines. The very concept of anonymity of users was fundamental to Sherry Turkle's reading of the early era of the Internet (Turkle 1995), where users strategically worked out their various presentations of identity in this online social environment. It may be valuable to step away from 'the social' and use the word 'collective' to capture the array of cultural-to-economic-to-anxiety connections that the Dark Web cultivates. The social is filled with deep-structural meanings and perhaps the collective conception provides a particularized way of dealing with groups, individuality and non-collective aspirations. To get us further into this space – and this is from our own collective work in

GDPN – the dark social articles here help us understand that we are dealing with both a public *and* private space, what I have called a 'privlic' space (Marshall, Moore, and Barbour 2020).

Roland Kapferer [RK]: I think it's important to identify the context of a research group like the GDPN and indeed research institutes in general. This is quite obviously the corporate-state university or the emerging corporate university – what the British Marxist EP Thompson had only a bare inkling of when he wrote a swinging critique of Warwick University called the Business University. That's the elephant in the GDPN room. *Dark Academia* (Fleming 2021) is the context of these essays about the Dark Social. What is more, the very idea of a network in the name of the group demonstrates the close connection between a certain technicity or technology of thought and what is now called 'research.' In view of this connection, David's focus on epistemology and knowledge-work is essential. In only the course of one century we have moved from the cloistered Scholar with monographs of old universities in nation-state conditions to the connected Researcher with research projects in corporate-state conditions – from cloistered to connected in a few decades! But the 'researcher' and the 'research network' are creatures of the emergent techno-capitalist corporate order and, in some senses, a function of the very technological machine that the essays in this volume address. Here, I'm with Heidegger who argued that the very idea of research is itself intimately caught up with cybernetics and communications networks. Research and notions of 'collaborative' clusters, hybrid groups or 'teams' (all the language of contemporary business management software companies like Atlassian) is itself a complicit-defensive reaction in the crisis of metaphysics at the 'End of the Enlightenment'. It is impossible to overemphasize how much knowledge practices today, particularly those of the social sciences, are caught up with the 'technological revaluation of all values' this set of papers addresses. In this context, the social or sociality is being transformed into what I call a digi-sociality or the social understood technologically, the techno-social. This point needs to be taken further. What I argue is that we are in the midst of a technological event, a fundamentally exotic moment in human history which challenges our most cherished beliefs and enables us to re-think – an anthropological revolution as Jean Baudrillard has named it.

The emergence of 'digital publics' throws into relief something about the very nature of social science and social thinking in general as it was practised and is still being practised today. To be a little provocative, perhaps notions of sociality have always-already been determined in a cybernetic imaginary or what Bernard Stiegler following Derrida called an 'originary technicity'? And this is what we are only now beginning to see? As we move from the sociological to the datological (Clough 2018) and into the arena of Big Data, the algorithmic-social and the post-probablistic, key fundamentals of social science methodology and its ontological assumptions are being radically challenged and overturned. In relation to this, and the corporatization of universities, many academics or 'researchers' hold on desperately to theoretical ideas about Society, Culture, Reason, Meaning, Communication, Language and, yes, The Public, that are themselves part of the problem. If this is the era of 'cruel optimism', as Lauren Berlant has noted, then cruel optimism for academics must be the attachment to certain theoretical concepts like The

Social in the compromised condition of their possibility. These essays on the 'dark social' help to illuminate an attachment to problematic objects and subjects in advance of their loss.

DM: You have captured, Roland, an absolute mother lode of ways to imagine what has transformed in our digital reconstructed world and, also, what has allowed the dark social to emerge. What I have also noticed in our discussion so far, we are using the word '**we**': whenever we use the word, **we**, it is absolutely filled with contradictions of what it embodies. So, as these scholars map the dark social, they are charting an online locale, broadly defined, where people have left a visible construct of sociality. Admittedly that notion of sociality that forms our Internet and digital culture is not necessarily what emerged in sociology and anthropology over the past 150 years. The sociality that pervades our digital/internet culture is wedded to an economic corporate system that has prevailed in its 30 to 40-year development and is embodied by a particular neoliberal notion of freedom. The Internet provided an aspirational pathway essentially freeing up the individual to a social that was believed to be independent and a related form of new autonomy that was self – and collectively – generated.

However – and Shoshana Zuboff's book, *The Age of Surveillance Capitalism* (2019), crops up in some of these essays – they deal directly and indirectly with an Internet 'culture' in need of transformation. The dark social space, as Robert Gehl identifies, is filled with an odd anarchic promotional economic culture. In other words, the corporate Internet structure is everywhere – a continuously invasive patterning of our digital lives. The move into darkness, what is identified as the dark web – which at minimum makes one think that it is metaphorically aligned to the *dark ages* and its different negative relationship to awareness, the future enlightenment and knowledge – itself implies that somehow you can escape this pervasive online dimension that forms our knowledge and information, our forms of connection, and our formations of public and publicity. The reality regularly imbricated in these papers is that the corporate world is everywhere: no matter how much you construct a different social environment, a form of unstable capital inhabits the movements that are part of this different dimension of online culture.

The now ubiquitous pancultural, highly visible dimensions of social media help explain why an individual would move into a dark social world: the Dark Web in all its configurations and intersections appears to answer a widespread desire for a different form of intermediation. Those different mediations are actually quite a challenge to political, social, cultural conventions that are in our world right now.

MH: That's right, the idea of dark social being worked with here assumes that the technologized environment is one from which there is no escape. We don't have papers that invoke the Luddite movement, we don't have politics invoked as transformation. Darkness is embraced here, in many of the papers and most explicitly in Alexia Maddox and Luke Heemsbergen's paper, as technologically connected but decentralized, computerized yet distanced from what they refer to as the 'computational gaze'. Darkness is envisaged as a space of creative social experimentation, one where *relationships* rather than communicative regimes can be pursued as Toija Cinque's paper points to. Just as these papers assume there is no escape from computerized interconnectedness, they recognize that securing trust in human relations has become a fragile and highly contingent pursuit, just as uncertainty now pervades life. The shadow that hovers across these concerns with the possibilities and constraints on contemporary politics is of course the Anthropocene.

DM: Maybe it's best to describe the phenomenon being grappled with as the dark techno-social. It is something that is appropriating the notion of what we imagine as interpersonal connections or collective connections that are fundamentally different and produce potentially different collectives. Maybe the dark social is at least exemplifying the different constitutions of how humans congregate and how we all work through the technology that surrounds us. We don't have to think of the entire formation of connection as simply electronic. We all work through the complex environments that surround us as well. And, as Melinda says, in a clearly Anthropocene way, we may have overdone, overtaken and overwhelmed what defines the world. Nonetheless, we are trying to constantly work out our relationship of ourselves to other humans. The technology of online culture has become this interesting intermediary that is perhaps leading people to feel as if they have the *agency* to produce something different.

RK: Indeed, David, this is the case, and this perfectly captures the tensions and the sense of the dialectics of the Enlightenment that dominates the discussion of digital technologies. Here again it's Heidegger's great remark that must be underlined – 'everywhere we remain unfree and chained to technology whether we passionately affirm it or deny it and we are delivered over to it in the worst possible way when we see it as something neutral.' (Heidegger 1977, 4) There is so much in this claim that needs to be thought through. But for me one key aspect of our technological condition is that it brings into full ascendancy the Euro-American ideology of individualism. This has everything to do with the emergence of the new corporate-state or economic ideology as the apotheosis of individualism and it is fascinating to watch how corporations are embracing digital technologies as fundamental to their profits. The best thing that ever happened to corporate capital is the computer! But I think I'm picking up on a fundamental concern here. Melinda, if I understand you, you seek something else or something outside the increasingly suffocating networks of what you very usefully call 'communication regimes'. You seek the Outside or at least many potential outsides. Taking up Maddox and Heemsbergen, you celebrate the dark social as a site of experimentation and creation but also worry that such creation is still set up within the frameworks or parameters of the computational. I love your reference to Luddism or the rejection of the machine here.

I think Melinda's point is crucial. Even under the conditions of the technological event humans seek relatedness. I might add that this idea of relationality and 'human relations' is possibly still caught up in an individualism, but reserve that for another time. So what about escape? Melinda's question resonates very strongly with me. Here, I am reminded of what Nietzsche famously called *'the great separation'* in his preface to *Human All Too Human*. And so, I think there is a concern that such escape may still be an aspect of the incomplete nihilism that pervades the era of the dark social and compromises the idea of escape in the first place? David, you seem relatively happy with negotiation and keeping a distance whereas you, Melinda, seem to doubt the possibility of even this? Such important and difficult questions here! For my part, I am starting to wonder if the dark social is dark enough? There is a necessity of recognizing the urgency of the moment and acknowledging the liminal situation of human being and plunging deeper into the darkness of the techno-exotic. Maybe this is the only way out?

DM: This technological environment – whether we're looking at each other via a Zoom session or whether we're holding a phone and checking social media feeds or whether we're walking down a road with little earbuds listening to a podcast – it is naturalized and normalized across cultures and across billions of people. Possibly, the dark social is trying to take back the idea of how much of what I have is shared with others. Regardless of what is happening in this different social space, do I at least have the sense of a little bit of control of what I share, a little greater sense of my own movement between the self and the world itself?

RK: There is a point made by Slavoj Zizek that perhaps resonates with what you are saying David – it's not a case of our privacy being invaded but that there is now nothing but privacy. It's privacy all the way down. The public space is now fully privatized, in both the individual and corporate sense. Life on the Internet, our most intimate moments, are always already 'shared' – also a point made more systematically by Wendy Hui-Kyong Chun when she analyses the essentially 'leaky' nature of computerized systems. The Internet is an entirely privatized and corporate space – what you do on Facebook or WeChat is owned by various corporations. The essays in the dark social are about separating from this or at least getting some distance from it. And, I agree, a great guide for thinking through the complexities of the techno-social. But is it possible to establish distance in a situation that is perhaps fundamentally *distanceless*? In his brilliantly prescient paper on the society of control Deleuze called this situation a contact-lens. I guess my difference with what you are saying David is that I think the idea of sociality that is being currently produced in the Age of Machines is individualistic in an ontological sense. This is not caused by machines – machines don't explain anything as Deleuze said – the devices we use are an aspect of this but it's the techno-sociological condition that needs urgent investigation. And yet all the concepts and categories we have at our disposal are undergoing major upheaval. It's a fundamentally dangerous situation. Can we find the new practices of thought that are adequate to the titanic occasion that is upon us?

So, what is so dark about all this is still the social. The social is rendered dark in the ascendancy of the techno-logic and darkness is sometimes imagined as a means of escape, or at least a means of negotiation. But are the 'means' we have at hand enough? The need for thinking deeper into the very nature of sociality is required by the human-becoming-machine and the machine-becoming-human. And we attempt to do this when the very means for doing this are being colonized and rendered useless. This event puts into question even the language that we use. We stand right now at a 'gateway moment' and we have reached a critical turning point in human history (which is perhaps why there are so many 'turns' going on in the academic landscape – 'turning and turning in the widening gyre.'). And maybe this turning point will be the end of all turning points – the end of a simply 'human' history? A new beginning.

DM: You are also searching whether the light of the Enlightenment is necessarily good. Is there a notion of a kind of ethics (which definitionally means 'character') that would explain why people would go and play in the dark social? There are versions defined as other forms of 'the social' on social media that help explain what they are trying to get around, explore, escape, and generate. In some cases, a sense this dark social activity produces a sensation of individual power. The power may or may not be individual; but that's the feeling that is connected to the dark social. I think it is vitally important to get that sense of what the dark social embodies individually and collectively through its users, players and pirate-like entrepreneurs that inhabit – and lurk – in that space. What do we expose through technology and what do we gain from it; and has it really been thought through completely and what do we lose through the technology? As you have said very well, Roland, in terms of the corporate structures of that overarching online technology, what do we lose and what do we gain through those processes?

MH: I'm glad you've come to this question David, because I think we lose a lot. One of my touchstones is the arc of transformation people in the Central Desert have passed through over the last three decades, as they have had their relative autonomy as distinctively place-based people substantially diminished. These questions of techno-connection, transformation, and loss require a great deal more space and consideration than we can give them here, but I would simply say that for every move towards embracing interconnected modes of relatedness there are implications for distinctively place-based ways of being in the world and relating to others. We don't need to go to the Central Desert to pose these questions of loss. Roland, you landed us with 'nature' just a moment ago, and also the idea that 'relationality' might simply be a conduit for more individualism. I am completely with you on this. Frederic Neyrat argues that the only way out of the related crises gripping the planet and humanity is to pursue what he calls an 'ecology of separation' (2019). The pandemic, lockdowns, and the mind-numbing experience of having so much of our lives transferred onto zoom, have magnified what is at stake in distinguishing qualitatively distinct forms of relatedness – endless 'relationality' would be one such distinct species of relatedness. The ceaseless expansion and intensification of computerized interconnection does not render such questions irrelevant. On the contrary, it makes them more urgent and ramps up the stakes of such work.

RK: We are in the midst of a total breakdown and reengineering of our most cherished institutions – our homes, our bodies, our brains, our schools and universities, our hospitals, our workplaces, our environment. And this transmutation is *technological in essence*. I don't mean the computers, gene-editing tools, the gadgets, the phones or whatever – these are not technological, they are only the symptoms of an emergent techno-human condition. What can be called the technological event is already transforming the basic understanding of what it is to be human. For me, the essays in the dark social put this fundamentally exotic event in the foreground.

Disclosure statement

No potential conflict of interest was reported by the author(s).

References

Clough, P. T. 2018. *The User Unconscious: On Affect, Media and Measure*. Minneapolis: University of Minnesota Press.
Fleming, P. 2021. *Dark Academia: How Universities Die*. London: Pluto Press.
Heidegger, M. 1977. *The Question Concerning Technology and Other Essays*. New York: Harper Perennial.
Marshall, P. D., C. Moore, and K. Barbour. 2020. *Persona Studies: An Introduction*. Hoboken, NJ: Wiley Blackwell.
Neyrat, F. 2019. *The Unconstructable Earth: An Ecology of Separation*. New York: Fordham University Press.
Turkle, S. 1995. *Life on the Screen: Identity in the Age of the Internet*. New York: Simon & Schuster.
Zuboff, S. 2019. *The Age of Surveillance Capitalism: The Fight for a Human Future at the New Frontier of Power*. New York: Public Affairs - Hachette Book Group.

Index

accountability 54, 92, 93, 102, 105, 111
advertising 2–5, 8–11, 14, 16, 66, 102, 104, 110, 111; platforms 103; social role of 102–103
Agur, C. 75, 80
Aldridge, J. 33, 39
Anderson, C. 35
anonymity 8, 12, 16, 17, 23, 26, 38, 41, 63, 64, 68
artificial intelligence (AI) 87–96
automated decision-making technologies 87–96
automated technologies 89, 95, 96

Bacchi, C. 116, 121
bad actors 3, 46, 49, 50, 53
Bailey, M. 131
Barratt, M. J. 33, 39
Bateman, M. 92
Beschorner, N. 93
Boyd, D. 49
brackish space 67, 68
brackish web 4, 59, 60, 62, 63
Braidotti, R. 28
Breland, A. 50
Bruckman, A. 53
Buneman, P. 117, 118

Carman, M. 47
Carrigan, M. 53
censor 48–49, 73
Chandrasekharan, E. 52
chthonian feminist internet theory 6, 128–141
clear web 2–4, 8, 12–14, 16, 17, 59–61, 63, 64, 68; platforms 59, 61, 62, 67, 68
closed architecture 73–75, 81, 83
computational age 3, 32–43
conspiracy 4, 74, 76, 80–82, 84
conspiratorial publics 4, 72–84
Cornwall, A. 94
corporate social media 8, 13, 16, 17
Costanza-Chock, S. 52
Couldry, Nick 103
covens 139, 140
Craig, D. 92

cryptomarkets 3, 38–40
Cuboniks, L. 138
culture 21, 23, 33, 61, 63, 64, 129, 131, 146, 147, 149

Dai, C. 117
Danaher, J. 34
dark, navigating 11–12
dark ads 5, 101–104, 106, 111, 112; accountability 105–106
dark magic 14, 16; associations 11, 12; system 2, 3, 7, 8, 11–17
darkness 2, 3, 32, 33, 36, 39, 43, 128, 129, 147, 149
darknets 2, 26, 39, 40
dark social practices 24–26
dark social spaces 20, 38
dark social technologies 73
dark web 2, 3, 8–17, 38–40, 63–65, 67, 145; advertisements 10–11; infrastructures 65, 67; platforms 61, 63–65, 68; search engine 5, 9, 14, 15; technologies 4, 60
dark web advertising 2, 7; dark magic 8–9
data availability 119–120
data ethics 115–124
data instrumentality 122–124
data provenance 5, 115, 117–119
data transactions 115, 116, 118, 121, 122, 124
Datta, Amit 105
Datta, Anupam 105
Deleuze, G. 89
demographic variables 106, 107, 109
De Vries, P. 89, 95
digital comfort zones 75, 79
digital imagination 4, 51–54
digital method 23
digital resignation 52–54
digital technologies 52, 76, 88–94, 148
disinformation 47, 49, 50, 74
Doctorow, C. 20
Draper, N. 53
dreams of development 87–96
Duvendack, M. 92

INDEX

8Kun 3, 19–29, 59
electrified social 33–36
end-to-end encryption 33, 38, 41, 73, 76, 77, 79, 83, 84

Faizan, M. 22
fake news 74, 80, 81, 84
fakery 80–82
false consciousness 52
feminist Internet 6, 128, 129, 136
Ferguson, J. 89
Ferguson, R. 12
Fernández-Caramés, T. M. 20
financial technology (FinTech) 91, 92
fourth wave feminism 129, 137–139
freedom of speech 64–66

Galaxy3 3, 19–29
Gehl, R.W. 39, 65
gender 12, 21, 34, 42, 94, 95, 104, 105, 108, 139
Gilbert, E. 53
Gillespie, T. 60
Glavic, B. 117
Global North 88, 90, 95, 96
Global South 5, 87–90, 94–96
good governance 4, 88, 92, 94, 95, 120
Guattari, F. 89
Gulson, K. 92

Hanckel, B. 75
Hayles, K. N. 135
Henman, P. 34, 92, 93
Hester, H. 138
hierarchies 41, 61–64, 68; resistance to 64–66
Horst, H. 91

individualism 148, 150
information freedom 116
insularity 75, 80, 83, 84
international development 88, 95
Internet sovereignty 131–137
Internet technologies 87, 90, 92
intimate machines 3, 19, 21

Jack, C. 74
Jane, E. A. 138
Jhaver, S. 53
John, N. A. 121, 123

Kennedy, J. 123
Khan, R. A. 22
Khanna, S. 117, 118
Kozinets, R.V. 23

language 24, 27, 115–117, 119, 121–124, 132, 135, 137, 146, 149
Lee, A.Y. L. 75

Lim, G. 74
Lingel, J. 41
Loubere, N. 92
Lovink, G. 52

Maddox, A. 33, 39, 40
magic system 7, 8, 10, 16, 17
Malaysian Communication and Multimedia Commission (MCMC) 73, 78
Martin, J. 40
Mastodon 3, 19–29
Mauro-Flude, N. 132
McDuie-Ra, D. 92
McKelvey, F. 39, 40
microfinance 91, 92, 95
Monahan, T. 60
moral reckoning 20
Murakami Wood, D. 60

Nanditha, N. 95
Neyrat, F. 150
Nithyanand, R. 50

Ohanian, A. 61
openness 13, 40, 63, 115–117, 121–124
operational security (OPSEC) politics 11–13
Ossewaarde, M. 52

personal information 11–14, 21, 48, 64, 124
Petty, W. 131
platforms 4, 39, 48, 49, 53, 54, 59–64, 66–68, 76, 80, 84, 105; literacy 47, 51, 53; surveillance 61, 63, 68, 73
popularity 25, 27, 50, 54, 75, 78
Porter, D. 92
post-quantum IoT systems 20
poverty 4, 88, 89, 91, 94, 122
precursor technologies 88, 90, 94
privacy 13, 39, 63, 67, 79, 96, 106, 120, 149
ProPublica tool 104–107
prosumers 61, 62, 68
pseudonymity 4, 60, 63, 64, 68

Rancière, J. 33, 35, 36
rationality 61–64, 67, 68
Reddit 4, 46–54, 59–68
Reijers, W. 52
Rifkin, J. 122
Rök Jóns, R. 138
Rossiter, N. 52
rumours 4, 74, 76, 79–81, 84

Sabbath 139
safe spaces 72–84
Schech, S. 94
Schivelbusch, W. 33, 34
Schneider, F. 131

search engines 9, 10, 12, 14–17
Smith, N. 39
Snowden, Edward 16
social capital 87, 92
social graph 3, 33, 36–37, 41, 42
social inclusion 4, 88, 94, 95
social media 5, 8, 9, 13, 22, 26, 75, 77–79, 145, 149, 150; platforms 25, 61, 79, 84, 92, 94, 111, 131
social networks 13, 20, 24, 36, 65, 92, 106
social relations 17, 38, 96, 111
spies 79, 80
Spinoza, B. 21
sub-Reddits 47–48
supralevel surveillance 21
surveillance capitalism 3, 11, 13, 14, 17, 20, 26, 61, 147

Tan, W. 117, 118
Tapsell, Ross 74
Taylor, E. 91
technological rationality 4, 59–62, 64, 66–68
technologization 89, 90, 145
Ting, K.W. 75
Tkacz, N. 123
torch search engine 14
tor search engines 9–10

toxic conviviality 47–48
transparency system 107–110
Treré, E. 75, 94
Trudy 131
trust 4, 27, 41, 42, 47, 75, 79, 83
trustless infrastructures 38, 41–42
Tschantz, Michael Carl 105
Turner, G. 52
Turow, J. 53, 103

Vas Dev, S. 94
Vinuesa, R. 95
VPNs 21, 41, 42

Walters, P. 39
Webber, Richard 103
WhatsApp 4, 72–80, 82–84; affective pressures of 72–84; safety of 77
Whyte, C. 76
Williams, R. 10
World Bank 88–95
Writing the Feminist Internet (WtFI) 128–141

xenoglossia 131, 133, 139

Zuboff, S. 28, 35, 61, 147

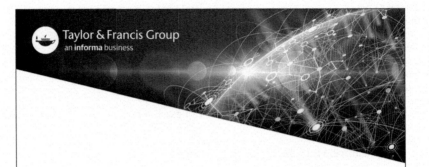